MAN IN AFRICA

Other Anchor books of interest

COLIN M. TURNBULL was born in London and now lives in Lancaster County, Virginia. He was educated at Westminster School and at Magdalen College, Oxford, where he studied philosophy and politics. He then spent several years studying religion and philosophy in India, including two years' work on a research grant at Banaras Hindu University, before returning to Oxford to study anthropology, specializing in Africa.

Mr. Turnbull was formerly Associate Curator of African Ethnology at The American Museum of Natural History in New York City. He is currently professor of sociology and anthropology at Virginia Commonwealth University.

COLIN M. TURNBULL

MAN IN AFRICA

DRAWINGS BY JOHN MORRIS

ANCHOR BOOKS
ANCHOR PRESS/DOUBLEDAY
GARDEN CITY, NEW YORK
1977

Man in Africa *was originally published by*
Anchor Press/Doubleday & Company, Inc., in 1976.

The illustrations in this book were drawn
from the displays in the Man in Africa Hall
at The American Museum of Natural History,
New York, N.Y.

Library of Congress Cataloging in Publication Data
Turnbull, Colin M
  Man in Africa.
  Includes index.

  1. Ethnology—Africa. 2. Africa—Social life
and customs. 3. Africa—History. I. Title.
GN645.T87   960
ISBN 0-385-05674-5

One is born, One dies, The land increases. . . .
(Galla)

CONTENTS

Introduction		xi
1	*The Beginnings of Man in Africa*	1
	Man as a Biological Entity	2
	Man as a Social Entity	5
2	*Grassland*	18
	The Beginnings of Cultivation and the Coming of Iron	18
	A Grassland People: the Pokot Pastoral Cultivators	31
	Women and Land	37
	Age	41
	Government Without Kings	50
	The Uplands of East Africa	53
	West African Mountain Grasslands	58
	The Growth of the State	60
	World View	64
3	*River Valley*	68
	Civilization and Primitive Society	69
	The Nile	71
4	*Forest*	88
	The Beginnings of Forest Cultivation	88
	A Forest People: the Mbuti Hunters	95
	Forest Cultivators	100
	Forest Fishers	105
	Trade and Commerce	109

Science and Belief   112
Sacred Societies   120
Music   127

5   *Desert*   131
Early Life in the Desert   134
A Desert People: the Ait 'Atta   136
The Spread of Islam   138
Water and Politics   144
Savanna Cultivators   152
Desert Hunters   158

6   *Western Woodlands*   167
Trading Kingdoms   170
The Sacred State   171
Totemism   179
Masks and Social Control   180
Craftsmanship and the Divine Presence   182

7   *Slavery*   189
Slavery and Serfdom in Africa   189
The African Tradition in the Americas   195

8   *Africa Today*   203
Africa and Change   204
The Power of Tradition   219

Acknowledgments   231

Index   239

INTRODUCTION

It is a perennial topic for debate as to how far we can generalize about "Africa" or "the Africans" (especially if we are not Africans ourselves) as though there were only one people or culture throughout that vast continent. It is perhaps most frequently done in a political context; when it comes to the social context we usually hear more of diversity than of unity. Yet there *is* a unity, and a powerful one, that runs through all African societies, all African peoples, and all African cultures, and it may well be a unity that links them with the Black Americans in a way that cannot be explained, as some would claim, as a mere political convenience. Oddly enough, this unity is even suggested by the material culture that on the surface seems to support the notion of diversity; but handling a collection of some forty thousand pieces from all over the continent,* while one develops a knack for placing an object with reasonable accuracy because of its appearance, shape, size, and smell in a very specific area with other

* At the time of preparing this manuscript the author was Associate Curator of African Ethnology of The American Museum of National History, New York.

like objects, one gets an unmistakable feel that the vast collection is a whole, and belongs together. For one thing, just about every object is directly functional, even those classified elsewhere as "art" and thus segregated by our own cultural norms into an isolated area of social existence. The African is nothing if not economical; there is no room in his life for useless extravagance, though sometimes extravagance itself may be used. But the kind of unity suggested by the material culture could be extended to other preindustrial areas. It is not specific to Africa, but stands with other so-called "primitive" cultures in distinction from the "civilized cultures," the prime distinction being that every item in the museum's inventory was made by hand, by a single person, to serve a useful if not vital function in the life of his fellows. A similar inventory of our own material culture consists mostly of objects made not even by one machine, let alone one individual, but by several, and only with a highly impersonal purpose in mind—not infrequently a nonsocial or even antisocial one.

The diversity in Africa is plain enough on the surface, but even there it can be misleading. There is a wide and obvious range of physical type, sometimes with extremes such as the difference in height between the adjacent populations of the Tussi, in Rwanda, and the Mbuti hunter/gatherers of the equatorial forest in Zaïre—the tallest and the shortest people in the world living side by side. The Bushmen of the Kalahari have their own special physiological characteristics (such as the epicanthic eyefold and the steatopygial development of the buttocks) that seem to set them apart from all other African peoples. There is a wide and equally obvious variation in skin color, hair form, and other physical characteristics, all of which lend themselves to the facile assertion of diversity. Yet recent work done by leading geneticists shows clearly that there is a strong underlying unity, linking Bushmen to Pygmies as among the oldest populations, and linking both of them to the vast bulk of the Black African population, including both the Bantu- and non-Bantu-speaking peoples of East, West, and Central Africa. The connection with the indigenous Berber of North Africa is still not clear, but this does not justify the regrettably common division of Africa into North and sub-Saharan Africa, as though the one had little to do with the other.

Frequently these outward differences in physical type are accompanied by differences in culture, just as striking and sometimes just as extreme. You have, for instance, Pygmies and Bushmen living as hunter/gatherers with a technology still of the Stone Age, a minimal material culture and little formal social organization, while close by there are sophisticated and powerful traditional African kingdoms and empires, rich in material culture, with an advanced technology and highly complex social systems. But just as there is a genetic unity underlying the outer physiological differences so I believe there is a vital unity underlying the cultural diversity. This unity springs in part from the history of the continent and of the growth and spread of its population, resulting in an over-all diffusion of divers culture traits, and in part from the nature of the physical environment which, together with a minimal level of technology, has everywhere tolerated a perfectly adequate subsistence economy. Often the environment is abundant and the climate moderate; it has never been necessary for a complex industrial technology to develop, but everywhere economic adequacy depends upon a sympathetic, adaptive response from the human population that *must*, under these conditions, function with the totality of fauna and flora as part of a natural world. This has led to the widespread and *conscious* dependence of the African upon his environment. Whereas other cultures, for various reasons, have had to develop an industrial technology and have sought increasingly to dominate the environment and control it, the African throughout the continent sees himself as part of the natural world and adapts himself and his culture, consciously and unconsciously, to its varied demands. This leads to the apparent diversity of cultures with as many cultural types as there are environmental types. The same correlation is highly significant also in any consideration of physical types.

We shall be using this correlation to look at the peoples of Africa, not because it is determinant but because it is prominent, and helps us to perceive the essential fact that the differences are of a totally different order from the similarities and that both exist side by side. We might almost say that the difference is material while the similarity, the underlying unity, is spiritual: for man, in Africa, is at one with nature, and to this extent is at one with himself.

Unfortunately we are still only able to make intelligent guesses at the distant past when man began in Africa. We do not even know for sure where he had his origins, and a new find could always be made tomorrow that would upset all existing theories. However, it is indisputable that man did have an early origin (the earliest known as yet) in Africa, and remains of these early beginnings have been found from the South to the North. There is evidence that the Pygmies and Bushmen are genetically closest to the first Africans, and certainly their culture has changed the least. For unknown thousands of years people like them must have roamed the continent in small bands, gathering and hunting, with little need for conflict, since the population was small and the environment generous. During these early days man almost certainly learned to cultivate certain wild plants, at least to the extent known as "vegeculture" where the plant is not domesticated so much as merely conserved so that it is able to replenish itself and supply a constant source of food for the hunters in their nomadic cycles. Some hunters today even transplant some wild plants, though being nomadic they cannot stay long enough to cultivate them, but place them strategically where, if they survive, they will be of use in some future annual nomadic cycle. Early man may also have learned to domesticate dogs for use in hunting. By sharing common water holes with wild animals it is likely that an almost symbiotic relationship grew up between certain of these animals and the hunting bands, and that pastoralism arose out of this as an alternative way of life. Then there was the dramatic development of true cultivation, partly a development from the earlier form of vegeculture, now domesticating indigenous crops, and partly introduced from the Middle East. Apart from the trend to industrialization, these three major economies—hunting/gathering (and fishing), herding, and cultivation—still form the three major economic classifications today.

This, together with the nonindustrial technology and apparently bizarre (to those who have not bothered to try and understand them) social systems has led some to regard Africans as they have regarded other nonindustrial peoples, as backward or "primitive." The ethnocentric nature of such a judgment does not need comment, but it *is* worth pausing for a moment for each of us to consider how *we* would compare the African, his way of life and thought, with ourselves. For anyone who has not been to Africa and who has been raised in a modern Western culture, it would be difficult not to feel that the African is in some way deprived. It is natural, for instance, to think of material poverty, for we habitually think in terms of material wealth. It is also natural to think of illness and shortness of life, for our ideals include good health and long life. It is natural to think of discomfort and hardship, for we value luxury and anything that makes life "easy." But even so, and even given such deprivations (if they *are* deprivations), are we really any better off?

We are undoubtedly richer in material culture—that is, we have larger and more permanent homes (or better houses, for they are not always homes); infinitely more in the way of personal possessions of much greater complexity; and having a cash economy, we can hoard nonperishable wealth much more easily than say an African farmer who is not living in a cash economy and who can store only a limited amount of perishable grain. But think of the attendant worries we have, and how we are caught up in the vicious circle of this year's luxuries becoming next year's necessities, and in the insidious demand for a constant "improvement" in the standard of living, which merely adds to our problems, and which demands that much more of us. And are we any more comfortable? When we weigh the mental discomfort and insecurity against the excess of material comfort, I would say no. And anyone who has been on a picnic knows how easily material comforts can be shed and the sense of relaxation that comes from this sudden simplification of life. Indeed, it is highly significant that we have institutionalized the picnic and camping holidays to such an extent in our lives.

As to health, in which respect nearly everyone would claim that our progress over the African is indisputable; is it worth living longer if our lives are not correspondingly richer and happier? Is it worth being preserved by modern medical science as a human vegetable, or in order to be thrown into old peoples' homes by children who cannot be bothered to care for us? Or to die of old age in a material poverty such as is never found in any traditional African society where there is always enough because there is never too much? Medical science, moreover, is to a large extent responsible for the disastrous population crisis, destroying the balance between the human population and the rest of the natural world, in a sense making man unnatural and threatening his future existence. The African, in traditional societies, seems to find more purpose to life than to live long in an excess of wealth and comfort, and he finds security in the natural world, including other human beings, rather than in technology.

With these thoughts in mind, let us now look at some specific cultures and peoples and see in what ways they are different from each other and in what ways they are alike. Then we may be in a better position to make a judgment, not only about their way of life, but also about our own. In this book we try to show something of how the great traditional forms of society in Africa operated in relation to the various environments: grasslands, river valley, forest, desert, and woodland. These are not tight, exclusive compartments; there are many overlappings and intermediate zones, and cultures now thriving in one environment may have had their origin in another. The discussion of each environmental area is prefaced by a brief look at the history and prehistory of that area so that the contemporary societies can better be placed in perspective.

African society has always been characterized by a dynamic interaction between man and the world around him, and so it is today with Africa—accomplishing in a few decades what took Europe two thousand years to achieve, transition from a tribal to a national level of organization. The upheaval is enormous and the transition not always smooth, for it strikes at the very roots of traditional life. All aspects of social life are affected, and all are changing. New notions of family and nation are emerging, economic and religious barriers are being lowered, and as horizons grow wider, a new sense of unity, perhaps the greatest need of all, is being born. The leaders of the new nations are their youth, and this youth imparts a vitality and character into the society it is building, blending what is valid of the old with what is worthy in the new. The new "Western" look of modern Africa does not mean a total rejection of the past. This is even more true now that a new generation of leaders is coming into power, those who have not been born and educated within the confines of colonialism, but in freedom. In many ways they are more respectful and mindful of the past than their colonized fathers, and there is more hope that the greatness and goodness of the past will not all be lost.

In this book we deal largely with the traditional past, for this is the source of much of Africa's contemporary greatness and the source of the distinctive character of the new nations. Among the many challenges facing the new nations is how African states, taking their places in the modern world, can still retain those specific traditions that contribute not merely to their own dignity but also to the dignity of the human community. In understanding the past we can better understand the present, both in Africa and elsewhere. Some of the tradition that is being lost in Africa is continued in America by the Afro-American, giving him an individuality and identity of his own. The story of man in Africa is by no means something we can afford to ignore; it is important in understanding our own society and in understanding humanity as a whole.

The relevance goes beyond the simple fact that a large proportion of the American population has an African heritage. By studying small-scale, pre-industrial societies, we can more easily learn how our own vast urban society functions, or malfunctions. With the smaller society we can more easily grasp the whole and perceive the total network of interrelationships that is social organization. We can see it at a group level, in the manner that institutions function and the way different groups of people relate to each other; but we can also see it at the individual level in terms of basic human behavior when shorn of the artifice of civilization. Any one of us, in looking at Africa, can see ourselves portrayed there, at least in part, and what we see may well fill us with a certain envy, for in traditional African societies people relate to each other as human beings, not as mere cogs in some impersonal social machine. They obtain social security not through the manipulation of wealth in the form of cash, but through the creation of a network of effective, interlocking human relationships. In such a society economic wealth becomes relatively insignificant, and perhaps thereby man becomes all the richer. We can also look at traditional African societies as a basis for comparison with our own and explore such issues as the qualitative differences between the individual adrift in the modern urban society and fixed in the prescribed nature of tribal life. While individuality and creativity are present in small-scale societies in many ways—as an art, tool making, hunting skills, and knowledge and use of the environment— the essentials of social, political, and religious life are not a myriad of choices, as is often the case in our own culture, but are defined and prescribed by tradition. This, however, does *not* mean that tribalism (or better, tribality—which does not carry the connotation of intertribal hostility, but rather a carefully defined sense of identity) involves rigid control, the negation of individual freedom. Far from it. And it is perfectly possible that one of the major lessons to be learned from looking at traditional Africa is that by relinquishing certain freedoms, by accepting certain limitations on life style (always with the option of choosing another), a much greater freedom is found, that of true sociality. The Western ideals of freedom and liberty, carried too far, lead to anarchy.

MAN IN AFRICA

CHAPTER 1

THE BEGINNINGS OF
MAN IN AFRICA

DESPITE the vastly improved and sophisticated techniques of archaeological excavation and dating, we still cannot say with certainty how, when, or where man had his first beginnings. Archaeologists and physical anthropologists, while allowing themselves the excitement of discovery, nonetheless temper it with a caution born of the sober knowledge of how fragmentary is the nature of the evidence. It is fragmentary even when it is all placed together; how much more so, then, when it consists of a single bone from a single skeleton, found in one tiny part of one of the world's great continents. But because of the overenthusiastic, and sometimes irresponsible, claims made by the discoverers of such isolated fragments, and their subsequent publicity, the lay public ends up with the impression that much more is known for certain than can even be guessed at. The uncritical use of this flimsy evidence, and even flimsier speculation, by professional writers and dramatists only help to confirm the public impression that we at least have a sound general picture of the origin of mankind. That, alas, is not the truth.

The truth is no less exciting, though certainly it is less spectacular. We simply do not know, and while the evidence now available points in a certain direction, to the beginnings of man in Africa, a single accidental discovery by a construction worker in China might, tomorrow, force us all to reverse our opinions and opt for a beginning in Asia—or anywhere else. While the amount of reliable evidence that has been uncovered is still pitifully small, the wealth of information that lies beneath the surface is incalculable. To be of real value, however, its discovery must be more than accidental. Sometimes years of painstaking preparation and calculation go into the discovery of a significant fossil. It is a costly, lengthy, and tedious business, the course of which must be plotted all the way. The excavation is equally painstaking, and again may take several years, every shovelful of earth being carefully sifted for evidence. If a major find is made, its fullest significance can only be realized under these ideal conditions, where all the associated evidence is clearly known in terms of its geographical and temporal relationships. Thanks to such dedicated and painstaking research we are now in a position to be able to make intelligent guesses, which are very different things from wild speculation.

Man as a Biological Entity

Man had an early beginning in Africa, making his first appearance there during the early Pleistocene.

Both climate and environment have played a central role in Africa, influencing the direction and development of its flora and fauna. Many species of mammal evolved there, including man's nearest relatives, some of the Old World monkeys and apes. Man was similarly influenced: The diversity of human types found there today represents his facility for adaptation to divers environmental conditions. This applies to men as a biological entity and as a social entity. Over a long period there were considerable changes due to gradual desiccation. The countryside became increasingly dry and less wooded, and just as most of the volcanoes died out, so did many animal forms. Certain of the animals known to have existed in the earliest times, however, still exist today, if in slightly modified form. So it may be with man.

Australopithecus is the first of the manlike creatures of the Pleistocene, followed later by a different type known as *Homo erectus*, and finally by *Homo sapiens*. Although we may be fairly certain of the position of these three types on the time scale, the evolutionary connection between them is still conjectural. There are several types of the early, Australopithecine, stage in human evolution. Two of the better known species are *Australopithecus robustus* ("Paranthropus") and *Australopithecus africanus* ("Australopithecus"). Remains of the former were found at Swartkrans and Kromdraii; the later at Taung, Makapansgat, Sterkfontein, and Serkfontein Extension (all in southern Africa). Both forms stood erect, but Paranthropus was taller, heavier, and he was probably a vegetarian. Australopithecus evolved at a time when the climate was drier, and this may have led him to add meat to his diet. Both preferred to live in a park savanna environment, or on the forest fringes.

Two other variants have been found in East Africa, at Olduvai Gorge in Tanzania. *Zinzanthropus boisei* and *Homo habilis* are also Australopithecines, but earlier than their southern counterparts. *Zinzanthropus* may be a type ancestral to later Australopithecines, but *Homo habilis* could well be ancestral to the more advanced hominids.

Stone tools have been found associated with all these forms. In the earlier finds, the tools are rough and natural in form; the later Australopithecines actually manufactured the tools, showing considerable advance in intelligence.

Variants of *Homo erectus* are found in northern, eastern, and southern Africa, and occupy a period that ranges from about five hundred thousand to twenty-one thousand years ago. The variants include several levels of skeletal development leading toward *Homo sapiens*, and demonstrate a continuing increase in brain capacity. Chellean Man is an example of an early type in this stage, and Rhodesian Man of a later type. *Homo erectus* had more varied and much better-made tools than the Australopithecines. Chellean Man used mostly hand axes, cleavers, scrapers, and bolas, while Rhodesian Man developed specialized flake tool industries (the Proto-Stillbay and Fauresmith industries). During this period humans learned to make fire and began to live in caves. They may also have begun to band together and lay the foundations for the development of social organization.

Of course, man is not the only animal to have social organization, and one fascinating question is when, how, and why the social organization of early man differed from that of other primates. By forty thousand years ago man in Africa had developed the biological features of *Homo sapiens*, and the development may well have been accomplished even earlier. There is, however, little skeletal material from this period, and even Florisbad Man may belong to a later date. But wherever the significant biological changes that mark the emergence of man took place, they were probably accompanied by equally significant sociological changes. Man developed his technological skill still further, but with his increased brain power he also developed his ability for abstract thought, learning to grapple with increasingly complex problems, and devising more ingenious ways for dealing with them. He designed stone tools for specific purposes; the tools of this period tell of an increasing economic specialization between hunting and fishing. The smallness of the microliths may mean that larger game had become scarce, for the tiny arrow points seem designed for small game only.

Unfortunately there is no evidence concerning the development of that vital human characteristic, the ability to communicate through a highly complex system of vocal symbols. But with an increasingly complex language the communication of ideas as well as techniques was greatly furthered, and man was at last able to pass on, from one generation to the next, his accumulated store of wisdom, accelerating the development of distinctive human cultures.

We accept that fauna and flora change from one environment to another. Facts such as height above sea level, humid-ity, temperature, and shade or exposure all favor certain forms of life above others. So it is with humans, and as in other continental areas of the world, the peoples of Africa display considerable variation in their physical characteristics. But despite this variation, which in some cases is extreme (Africa has produced the tallest and the shortest peoples in the world), the term "race" is entirely inapplicable, indicating a rigidity of separation that is biologically false. The differences are of form, not kind, and many of the forces that have contributed to this physical differentiation are clearly recognizable. Environmental adaptation is one such force; the arid heat of the savanna, for instance, favored the tall, lanky body characteristic of the Nilotics, while the cool, shady, but excessively humid conditions of the primary rain forest favor the short, squat body of the Pygmy. Not only body proportion but also pigmentation and even facial structure may adapt in this way. Hybridization is another factor contributing to physical differentiation, and this was a major consideration during the great migrations that crisscrossed the entire continent. Isolation equally affects the genetic composition of any population, and mutation also has to be considered.

Man as a Social Entity

In much the same way that the human form adapts itself to specific conditions and undergoes change due to contact, so does human culture adapt and change. The result in Africa is a rich example of the versatility and resilience of man, both as a biological and as a sociological being. There is no question of one form being "superior" to another, for the success of any change or differentiation can only be measured by its survival value. Each basic form, biological and social, tends to be the result of successive and successful adaptations to its particular context, in answer to particular needs. What succeeds and thrives and seems "superior" in one environment may be totally incapable of survival in another. Technological advance has made it possible for man to overcome many of his physiological limitations, enabling him to survive in almost any physical environment. The tragedy is that he has not developed an equal ability, or even the will, to survive in any *social* environment but his own, each group persisting in the illusion that its way of life is superior to all others, not merely adaptively successful. It is worth stopping to look at some of the forces that in Africa have shaped human society into so many different forms, and to do that we have to go back to the time when man really emerged, when he began to make tools for specific purposes rather than merely using any piece of rock, bone, or wood that came to hand for his immediate need of the moment.

Tool making required imagination, intellectual judgment, and a great deal of skill and patience. Africa is important as the earliest known home of stone tools, and in Africa we can follow the development from the earliest pebble tools and fine stonework found in ancient Egypt. This later work demanded a skill and a sense of craftsmanship that could scarcely be rivaled today. The development from pebble tools and early hand axes to the finely pressure-flaked knives and the ground and polished ax heads took over a million years, only to become a lost art wherever man discovered how to work and use metal.

These stone tools are the only surviving possessions of our ancient ancestors that we have, but from them we can learn much about the way of life of early man and his struggle for survival. Comparative studies tell of the geographical dispersion of early man and of his migrations across the breadth and length of the continent. But the evidence is still fragmentary at best, and subject to more than one interpretation. While it informs us in great detail about certain aspects of the growth of human culture, in the more general respects it leaves us only in a position to make educated guesses, and any attempt to trace an evolution of cultural forms at this time is unfruitful. We are on surer ground if we look at some of the contemporary African cultures, and see from what we know of them how much we can learn of the past, in light of what the stone tools and other archaeological evidence suggest.

The first thing that we learn is that life, shorn of its sophisticated trimmings, is an essay in survival, and to survive, man must satisfy a number of basic needs: food, warmth, shelter, and companionship. In companship he finds help in the work of satisfying his other needs, and out of companionship man procreates. In Africa man finds both physical and psychological security, not in individual achievement but in terms of the group, the community. True wealth and true security are not so much a matter of an individual's material possessions as a matter of human relationships, and in studying any contemporary African society we are studying a complex network of interconnecting, crosscutting human relationships. It is toward the maintenance and strengthening of this network that all effort is directed, not toward individual advancement.

Although we cannot say that what we find in traditional organization today represents what might have been found in those distant days when humanity was taking shape, the prevalence and persistence of certain features give us a clue. Early man was more limited in his technology, and consequently more limited by his environment, particularly prior to the introduction of iron. He found different ways of satisfying the basic necessities for survival, each relating to a particular context. The deserts of Africa, the mountains, forests, grasslands, and river valleys, are all reflected in the lives of the people who live there today, for these forces that helped to mold the early forms of society continue to be a powerful influence, and man in Africa still seeks to live in harmony not only with his fellows, but with his *total* environment. While grappling with the problem of how to find adequate supplies of food and satisfy other necessities, early man must also have had to grapple with the problem of how to live together with his fellows in an orderly manner, surviving and allowing others to survive—the alternative being mutual destruction. Traditional societies today show an immense preoccupation with this problem of orderly living, and the varied answers they have found derive from the various situations in which early societies had their beginnings. This process was basically one of trial and error; people did not sit down and draw up a blueprint for living. Organization more likely emerged out of a process aimed at how to get things done in the most efficient and gratifying way possible. The net result is a form of life that, far from being "primitive" in the sense the word generally implies, is full, rich, lacking nothing valued by Western civilization except perhaps in terms of material comfort which, as every field workers knows, is a highly relative matter. Even medical skills, which on the surface might seem crude compared with those of the modern West, are by no means as "backward" as we have thought, and are frequently more in balance with the over-all needs of the society than our own.

Let us now look at three major forms of society found in Africa today that illustrate various stages in social complexity: hunters, herders, and cultivators.

As a form of economic activity, hunting preceded the domestication of animals and crops; the early hunter was not, however, ignorant of other sources of nourishment. Long before the discovery of iron, man in Africa had learned how to live in harmony with his environment, and with his fellows, as a hunter of wild game and gatherer of wild foods. He was a natural conservationist, allowing both game and vegetable life to renew itself. Today, although they do not cultivate the soil, hunters encourage wild plants to survive and procreate, and sometimes even transplant them to supply needs at different places and times in the course of a nomadic cycle. In fact, today's hunters are generally more concerned with vegetable life as a source of food than with game, although hunting may occupy a more prominent place in the ideology of the people.

A Stone Age technology, with stone, bone, and wood as the main materials available for the making of tools and weapons, is what we have with the Bushman and Pygmy hunters of Africa today, for although they sometimes obtain metal from their neighbors, and use it for knife blades, spear and arrow tips, and sometimes in the form of cooking vessels, it is not absolutely necessary to them. Their main weapons and tools remain the bow and arrow and spear, for hunting, and the grubbing stick for gathering. Metal tips are sometimes advantageous in hunting, not always; the Pygmies find that a wooden tip impregnated with poison is more effective than a metal tip, which must strike a vital spot to bring down game before it can escape in the forest. These same tools and weapons were available to the early hunters, who used stone arrow tips and spear blades in place of metal. Even though today's hunters have all but lost the knowledge of stone usage, they still know of other alternatives to metal—for instance, various forms of reed and cane which, when split, provide razor-sharp cutting edges, and there are abrasive leaves that are effective as files and rasps. Fire-resistant leaves can be used for steaming meat, even for warming liquids, in place of metal dishes. Metal is by no means vital to a fully efficient hunting technology.

However, the early hunters, as are those of today, must have been subject to the demand for constant movement, so as not to hunt the game out of any one region, nor destroy the supply of vegetable food. As with all nomads, material possessions will have had to have been kept to a minimum. People lived in small bands, perhaps only three or four families, but if one area was richer than another, or poorer, these bands probably joined together or divided according to the needs of the moment. Some forms of hunting, such as snaring and trapping, could be done by individuals, while others, particularly those involving the "beat," would have called for co-operation among large numbers. The form of hunt itself, while partly determined by the environment, in itself influenced the form that society had to take. The larger the band, the greater the need for complex organization, with clearly demarcated lines of authority to avoid ambivalence and consequent dispute. This does not mean that leadership was an individual matter. Far from it: authority was probably, as with contemporary hunters, divided, so that neither one individual, nor even one group of individuals, had complete control. This creates a real interdependency that in itself lessens the danger of conflict and makes for a stable, harmonious society.

The hunters of today exhibit other characteristics that were very possibly basic to early society. They have a close and intimate relationship with the natural world around them and maintain a flexible social organization so that they can respond immediately to their needs: Communities are fluid in size and composition, authority is dispersed, and role and status are divided throughout the entire group so as to encompass all, regardless of sex or age differentiation, in vital participation. Although frequently individualistic in personality, hunters are essentially egalitarian, and while seeing themselves as different from their fellows, they do not think in terms of superiority or inferiority. They find a great sense of unity, despite the looseness of their organization, through a rich religious life. They do not divorce religion from the rest of life, but see it as the highest sanction of social behavior. Hunters are pragmatic people, living from day to day, and religion is a practical element in their life. They recognize the inherent frailties of human nature, and reason that the order they see in the natural world around them must derive from some other, suprahuman source. In that source they place their trust, and to that source they look for guidance. They equate it with the total world around them, their whole known environment, including their human as well as their animal neighbors—with which they seek to live in harmony. Contrary to what might be expected of a hunting people, the African hunters are gentle and nonaggressive, willing to allow others the same freedom they demand for themselves.

It is often held that hunter/gatherers of today represent social stagnation, a people or a form of society that reached a dead end and never progressed. However, no viable society is static; traditional societies are, in fact, highly dynamic. In Africa they are constantly changing and shifting, usually in subtle ways, but sometimes suddenly and dramatically, and always in an adaptive manner. There is a vast amount of inventiveness in everyday life and, judging from their notable lack of mental disorders, Africans in the traditional societies find a greater contentment with life than many others. We shall be looking at this complexity, which underlies such a seemingly simple exterior, as we go on.

When we turn to the herders of Africa we face a significant change from the hunting ethos, which is one of a total sympathy with the environment, an almost submissive adaptation to the world around, an acceptance of the world as it is given to them. The herders begin to control that world, by the domestication of animals. They are no longer submissive, they no longer accept the natural world as it is, and while they are not directly in conflict with it to the same extent as are the farmers, neither are they completely in sympathy with it like the hunters.

The origins of herding in Africa are obscure. Knowledge and cattle were brought from Asia, but there were also independent beginnings in Africa. There are still, particularly among the hunters, examples of symbiotic relationships between man and beast, just as there are between different species of animals. The best-known example, perhaps, is the "honey guide," a bird that locates honey but cannot extract it, or the grubs that thrive in it, from the hives built in the trees. It flies to the nearest group of Ndorobo hunters (in Kenya, Uganda, and Tanzania, particularly) and circles close over their heads, making a special cry, flying off in the direction of the honey tree and returning to circle again until the hunters follow it. It then waits patiently until the hunters have cut open the hive in the tree and taken what they want, leaving the remains for the bird. Some of the Karimojong herders in northern Uganda and Kenya also make use of the honey guide in this way. There may have been similar early associations between man and other animals, perhaps sharing the same man-made water hole. Certain forms of animal life might have congregated near human settlements for protection against predators, gradually allowing themselves to be milked. The African herders maintain cattle for their milk, even today, rather than as a source of meat. To supplement the diet they often take small quantities of blood from the jugular vein of the cattle, without harming the animals, and either mix this with the milk or cook it separately. Oxen may be killed and eaten on ritual, sacrificial occasions; meat otherwise comes only through sporadic hunting or fishing. Although herders gather wild foods as do the hunters, the herders give prime attention to the cattle, which must be herded in large numbers to provide each family with adequate nourishment.

Whereas the hunter's nomadic movements are determined by the presence of game, wild vegetables, roots, and fruits, the herder's movements are determined by water and pasture. This frequently results in a seasonal movement from dry-season camps to wet-season camps, a movement called transhumance. At certain seasons, when water or grazing may be scarce, the herders either scatter into tiny groups or come together in large numbers, depending on whether the water and pasture are dispersed over a wide area or concentrated in a few centers. This means that social horizons are constantly fluctuating; people who see themselves as being quite distinct and separate at one time of the year may be forced to associate at another time and in another place. This obviously calls for a special form of organization, to avoid the inherent lines of conflict and to establish effective relationships that can be correspondingly elastic. The herders take the basic family structure as their model, for the family is also an elastic concept, expanding proportionately as you trace your ancestry farther back. Herders, like the Fulani, who come together during the wet season in large communal camps, may invoke clan ancestors several generations in depth at that time, and all those who can trace descent from one such ancestor camp together; whereas during the dry season, when they are scattered in tiny groups at the southern end of their transhumant movement, they tend to ignore the clan ancestors and accept only descent from, say, a common grandfather or even a common father, thus effectively limiting the size of the group and providing a recognizable and efficient principle of organization that suits their particular needs at that moment.

The same system provides the basis for the organization of political authority, just as it provides the basis for economic organization, but authority is still far from being centralized, and systems of this kind are called segmentary, reflecting the manner in which a tribe segments into clans, clans into lineages, and lineages into families. However, this vertical division according to ancestry divides as well as it unites, and another principle of organization is called for to unite the herders into groupings that disregard family allegiance, and this is found in the principle of age grouping. The East African herders, with whom age grading is highly developed and formalized, are frequently referred to as warlike, and the system associated with warfare; this is not quite true. They have to be prepared for war, for their large herds need to roam over vast territories, and with the constant expansion and movement of the total population, there is always competition for land. To be prepared for war, however, is a very different thing from being warlike, and while the herders are more aggressive than the hunters, in relation to their environment and in response to their needs, they are still a gentle people. One of the peculiar features we shall see is how raiding and fighting are formalized and institutionalized and effectively prevent the outbreak of even greater conflict.

Other special needs that contribute to the development of a system of age grouping, cutting across the kine groups, are the needs for youth to be mobilized for the protection of the cattle not only against raids, but also far more frequently against the ravages of predators, for the various tasks of milking and bleeding the cattle, and for herding them over long distances in the constant search for water and pasture. Herding often accompanies limited farming, in which case the social organization has to allow certain groups of people to stay and tend the field while others go off, sometimes for months at a time, with the cattle. The organization of the herders into age levels, especially in the form of age sets into which they are initiated at regular intervals, combined with their organization into lineal kin groups, accomplishes for them what the much less formal, more fluid organization of the hunters accomplishes for *them*—an ordered way of living where the potential conflict, both within the group and without, is effectively minimized.

As with the hunters, religious belief plays a vital role in providing the herders with an ultimate and unquestionable authority. In the same way that the forest figures so importantly in the Pygmy system of belief, so the vast, airy stretches of grassland and the open skies play an important part in the belief of the herders. And just as the forest becomes the symbol for the Pygmies of the ultimate authority, so cattle become symbols for the herders and are accorded a special reverence at the same time they are exploited economically. Religion is still, for the herders, a practical part of everyday life, but a different element enters that is markedly absent with the hunters.

It is in keeping with the submissive, adaptive nature of the hunter that he accepts the world as he finds it and does not attempt to control it or dominate it. His religion is a religion of acceptance, and he does not try to use God for his own ends, setting God against nature. There is very little ritual that is designed to work special effects, what is sometimes called magic, and what there is takes the form of "sympathetic magic," in which the performer acts out the desired sequence of events, and hopes that events will fall that way in reality. When a Pygmy hunter throws a piece of damp moss into the air and blows it away, he does not believe that this action will actually cause the rain clouds to move in another direction; it is rather that he is expressing, in a ritualized way, needs over which he recognizes he has no control. His belief is that by correct performance of the ritual the forest will see and do whatever is necessary.

The herder's life is much less predictable than that of the hunter, and the hazards are greater, so it is in keeping with his more aggressive nature and his attempt to control the world around him that he should also attempt to control the spiritual world. Among the herders we get the beginnings of a much more dominating, aggressive form of ritualized action by which supernatural forces are controlled and ordered to the will of man. Instead of being common property, as is the little ritual performance known to the hunters, among the herders we get specialization of ritual action and the growth of a professional priesthood. To try to make sense out of that not always sensible distinction between religion and magic, we might say that we are still in the realm of religion because we are still dealing with the notion of spirit rather than with something abnormal; it may be supernatural, but it is not unnatural. The practitioner, rather than compelling through his acts a specific sequence of events, invokes spiritual aid in a specific form. There is an element of compulsion, and the distinction is a fine one, but we are still not at the point where man feels himself the master of all things.

Even among the traditional cultivating societies in Africa, religious belief is central in their lives just as it is central in their social organization. The character of life, however, is now much more dominating, aggressive, and at times even hostile. The very earth is attacked with a hoe, reshaped and reformed and forced to produce crops determined by man. The knowledge of certain crops, and certain agricultural techniques, came to Africa from outside, but as with herding, there is clear evidence of some indigenous origins and the domestication of indigenous crops. West Africa, Ethiopia, and Egypt are the three early centers of agriculture, each with its own distinctive crops and techniques. Whereas in some cases the knowledge was diffused ready-made, in others it grew naturally out of the earlier gathering activities, which almost certainly included at least a limited form of vegeculture whereby certain plants, though not domesticated, are at least conserved and even tended in their wild state to ensure their productivity.

It may not seem like much of an intellectual step from the tending of wild plants to the collection and sowing of their seed, but the results of taking that step were incalculable. The domestication of crops and their consolidation into small, cultivated areas led to a consolidation of populations. Agriculture imposes a sedentary life on people; they are no longer able to wander about in search of game and wild foods, or even with their herds of cattle in search of pasture and water; they must settle and constantly tend their fields, cultivating them and protecting them against the many hazards of disease, drought, flood, and damage by wildlife. A troop of baboons, a swarm of locusts, a flock of birds, a single elephant—all can destroy a field in a matter of an hour or so unless it is properly tended.

Once again the environment is an important factor, for whereas in some cases it allows for the wide dispersal of fields and thin scatter of population, in others such as river valleys,

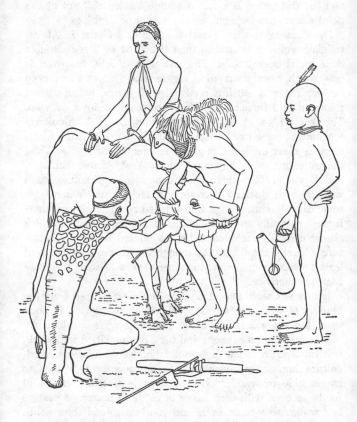

Figure 1. Among the Pokot, as with many grassland peoples, cultivation is as economically important as herding. But herding is closely associated with notions of wealth and prestige, and linked to religious values. A focal point of each day is the painless (and harmless) drawing of a small quantity of blood from the necks of young oxen.

where the fertile land is compressed or limited, there is a much higher density of population, and villages and towns emerge. The organization of labor becomes a major concern, and specialized crafts and occupations develop. The beginnings of ironworking in Africa were inextricably related to the agricultural revolution, and forging and smithing became among the first and most strongly organized specialized crafts. Pottery making also became specialized, as did the working of wood, leather, wool, stone, ivory, and other materials. A much more complex organization was called for, and this created the need for still more specialists such as administrators, chiefs, judges, and doctors. People began to regard each other as different not only because they belonged to different families, villages, or age groups, but also because they belonged to different occupations. Society became stratified into classes and, where specialized occupations became hereditary, sometimes into castes. Complex political systems evolved, leading to the formation of African nations and empires, many of which were flourishing when Europe was still barbarian.

These political developments did not occur at the cost of religion, however; the notions of kingship and divinity went hand in hand in Africa, as in early Europe. Temporal power derived from a spiritual or divine authority. But religion now played another role, sanctioning the use of the power that comes with centralization. Today in the great nations and empires of Africa as with the less spectacular but also centralized tribal farming peoples, religion ensures those values we praise so highly in the Western world: democracy and justice. Its methods may seem peculiar to our materialistic age, but its results often compare more favorably.

In recognition of the influence that environment has on the forms that society assumes then, we shall examine different cultural areas in relation to environment and explore the broad trends, specific linkages, and often subtle interrelationships that exist in Africa between man and the natural world around him.

CHAPTER 2

All your young beauty is to me
Like a place where the new grass sways,
After the blessings of the rain,
Where the sun unveils its light. (Somali)

GRASSLAND

APART FROM the Sahara, the vast part of the African continent is grassland, which covers the southern and eastern part of the land, but also stretches across the northern edge of the equatorial rain forest and up parts of the western coast, where it mingles with forest on the one hand and desert on the other. The grasslands vary from dry scrub to lush verdure, from steamy coastal plains to chilly snow-clad mountains. At times it is difficult to draw the line between arid grassland and desert, or between lush grassland and woodland or forest, so the division we make here is an artificial one. However, there is a certain homogeneity among the grassland cultures, as there is among those of the forests and deserts, though there is also much divergence.

The Beginnings of Cultivation and the Coming of Iron

Formerly occupied by nomadic bands of hunter/gatherers, such groups have now almost completely disappeared, and farmers and herders comprise the bulk of the population.

Even that distinction is a difficult one to make, for many cultivators keep a few cattle, and most herders tend a few fields. The distinction is valid in one vital respect, however, and that is in terms of sentiment, or attitude. Many of the cultivators who keep a few cattle, and most of the herders who tend a few fields, think of themselves as one or the other, and each tends to scorn the primary occupation of the other. The ultimate anthropological importance of the distinction is not so much economic as political.

Whereas cattle herding, which is favored in the more arid areas, free of the tsetse fly, requires a people to wander back and forth over a vast area, changing the size and composition of the social groups according to the needs of the moment, farming settles people more tightly together, in a more permanent fashion, and in relatively fixed locations. As a result, the social organization of the two peoples is quite distinct, and the corresponding difference in their values leads to an even greater sense of opposition and difference. However much variation of organization there might be within one or other of these major groups, each stands united by sentiment at least in opposition to the other. Occasionally, and particularly where there is competition for land, the opposition flares into open conflict. At other times there may be a gradual assimilation. One of the most interesting aspects of these grassland societies is the variety of ways in which these peoples have organized themselves and resolve the inherent problems of opposition and conflict.

Whereas we associate cultivation with the beginning of civilization, this by no means implies that others are uncivilized. On the contrary, among the herders, human relations are honest and direct, filled with mutual respect. Many of them are aware of this, and in full awareness resist the lures of modern society. While they are quick to recognize the material advantages of modern society and have a respect for Western technology, they also see it as bringing a degeneration in man's dealings with man, and to them, in their particular context, human relations are more important and gratifying and offer greater security than material wealth and comfort.

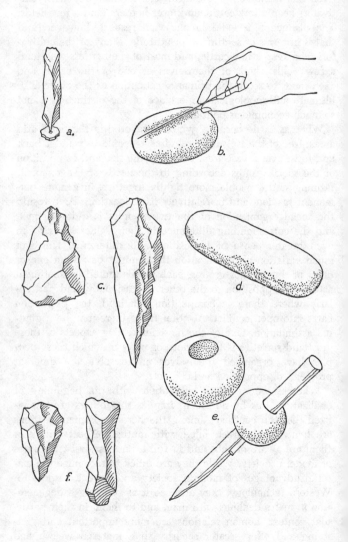

a.

b.

c.

d.

e.

f.

This is not romantic opinion; it is a sober statement of fact, much as stated to me by many a herder in the course of long hours of living and thinking and talking together. And it is this dogged conservatism that has made them the headache of many an administration, colonial and African, that has tried to "civilize" them by forcing them to wear clothes and to go to school and learn how to read and write. I confess it gives me enormous pleasure in the middle of the bush to come across a naked herder who can speak, read, and write fluent English, and who can tell me in my own language just what he thinks of me. For while an increasing number inevitably are getting drawn into the modern national society, there are still many who complete their schooling and, having had a good look at the brave new world, choose to go back to their own.

The African grasslands may be the earliest home of man, whose antiquity there goes back for nearly two million years. He lived by hunting and gathering until some two thousand years ago, using stone, wood, and bone for the manufacture of his necessary tools and implements. The tools show a gradual refinement of purpose, and the usual division of the Stone Age into three periods—Early, Middle, and Late—does not indicate an abrupt change from one to the other. The heavy hand axes and flakes of the Early Stone Age were multipur-

Figure 2a. Vaal River Complex. Among the tools found in this area are those known as "Smithfield tools." They include: a) small borer used for making shell beads; b) grooved stone that probably had several uses, such as straightening arrow shafts, applying poison to arrow tips, and manufacturing bone tools and shell beads; c) thumbnail scrapers hafted with mastic to wooden shafts for use as hand adzes, and in trimming and scraping wood and bone; d) grinding stone for pulverizing collected fruits and seeds; e) borer stones for weighting digging sticks used in grubbing for roots, and as club heads; f) side scrapers and end scrapers that were not hafted but used held in the hand for paring down and shaping bows and arrows, for preparing leather and clothing, and for taking meat off bones.

pose choppers and knives, wooden spears being used for hunting. The Middle Stone Age produced more refined points and flakes used as knives, skin scrapers, and projectile points. The Late Stone Age equipment included arrow heads, arrow barbs, and ultimately weights, used to make the light wooden digging sticks more effective. The Magosian culture of Sawmills, in Rhodesia, clearly shows the changes in tool-making techniques that ushered in the Late Stone Age, the most obvious change being the production of tiny blades used for arrows, as heads and barbs, and as scrapers.

Man began to make pottery toward the end of the Late Stone Age in the southeastern grasslands, and similarities with pottery made today provide us with one ground for speculation about the movement of African populations. The South African Bushmen, one of the few hunting groups living as hunters today, until not long ago fashioned stone tools that resembled those of the Late Stone Age; other evidence indicates that the Late Stone Age peoples in southeastern grasslands were Bushmen. Whether that is where they originated, or whether they originated farther north and migrated southward is still unknown. Most evidence of early migrations indicate Bushmen-like cultures scattered throughout the grassland region. There are still some hunters with physical or linguistic similarities with the present South African Bushmen living in East Africa, and those on the borders of northern Uganda, Kenya, and southern Sudan (the Ik, once known as Teuso) still make and use crude pebble tools—the earliest form of stone implements—although they have also mastered the art of working iron and have recently turned to cultivation.

The illustration showing a cross section of the Vaal River, and a schematic section of the deposits, illustrates something of the techniques used by archaeologists for determining certain sequences, even in the absence of radio carbon and potassium argon dating. The *relative* dates can be determined by the sequence of geological deposits in which tools, or other objects, are found. Nos. 1, 2, and 3 are river terraces, No. 3 being the most recent; Nos. 4 and 5 are wind-blown deposits, with No. 5 being the most recent. Old

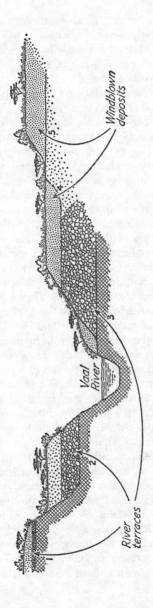

Figure 2b. Cross section of the Vaal River and a schematic section of the deposits. Nos. 1, 2, and 3 are river terraces. No. 3 is the most recent; Nos. 4 and 5 are wind-blown deposits. No. 5 is the most recent.

riverbeds and riverbanks are ideal locations for archaeological research, for early man always needed to camp near
water, which he needed just as did the animals he hunted. As
seen, sequences of successive settlements, showing changes in
the cultures, can sometimes be dramatically and clearly
shown, though the research and task of reconstruction are
lengthy, painstaking, and often tedious.

Enough of the more perishable remains of Late Stone Age
hunters survive, together with numerous rock paintings produced by these people, for us to reconstruct the general pattern of their lives. They hunted with bows and arrows, in
numbers and singly, often using camouflage, disguising themselves as their prey so that they could approach closely. They
also speared fish, a source of food ignored in many parts of
Africa today, and they collected wild honey, which today is
one of the major activities of the remaining hunting groups.
They baked food in stone-lined hollows in the ground, in hot
ashes, and they lived either in caves, rocky overhangs, or in
simple shelters of grass matting. They sewed skins into clothing. On occasion they painted their bodies. They also painted
their dead with red ocher before burying them, giving us evidence of the existence of some kind of ritual life. Their cave
paintings indicate that there might have been ritual in connection with marriage as well as with death, and certainly in
their paintings we get the strong impression of a people who
not only lived in a very real world—fully and actively—but
who also felt positively about that world and who thought
and speculated about its true nature. Although now driven
into the southern deserts, the life of the Bushmen today is
marked by the same kind of vitality and warmth of feeling,
coupled with a high level of speculation and religious belief.

The existence of iron ore and the discovery of iron-making
techniques were to change all this in a dramatic way, for iron
made many things possible that had not been possible before.
The origins of its usage in Africa are uncertain. It is strange
that with all its sophistication, dynastic Egypt did not have
an iron technology, while to the south, a Nubian kingdom
during the first century B.C. developed an industrial center at
Meroë, smelting and forging iron from local ore. It is perhaps

from here that the knowledge of iron spread to the rest of Africa.

From the outset the process was considered secret, and to some extent sacred, and restricted to certain families or castes. Ironworkers throughout the continent have always been regarded with respect—a mixture of fear and honor. Sometimes the attitude swings more to one side or the other, but it would be wrong to make a sharp division, as some do, and say that in some parts of Africa the smiths are despised while in others they are honored. Their art is often associated with supernatural powers; the resultant works can bring both great benefits and great dangers in the form of the tools of peace or the tools of war. It is natural that people should have an ambivalent attitude toward the smiths, needing them but somewhat fearing them. Smiths, then, frequently form separate castes, living apart and marrying among themselves, keeping the techniques secret from outsiders.

Smelting and smithing spread rapidly throughout the whole of the continent, but with ready availability today of scrap metal, smelting has almost died out. The Ciga of southern Uganda, however, not only retain a knowledge of smelting, but also a knowledge of the undocumented art of wire making. They dig ore from ancient sites high up in the mountains of Kigezi, break it into basket-sized lumps, and carry it to a site, often many miles away, where the right kind of clay can be found to build a kiln. Only the highest grade of ore can be used for wire making. The ore has to undergo two smeltings; for this and for the subsequent smithing operations, a great deal of charcoal is needed. Special trees are selected and burned, in shallow pits covered with the moist stems of banana trees, and allowed to smolder until the right kind of coal is produced. For this particular ore it is necessary to have small coals that give an even and intense heat.

Only when the ore is dug and the charcoal ready, is the kiln made, built above a deep pit in which the fire is started. *Tuyeres*, hollow clay pipes used with bellows to create a forced draft, are laid around the pit, and the walls of the kiln are built on top with handfuls of clay, gradually tapering until the kiln is some five feet high and about two feet wide at the top. The fire in the pit helps dry out the clay from the inside, and the sun dries the outside. The last damp spots have barely disappeared when the work begins in earnest. Charcoal is poured into the kiln, then two or three layers of ore, then more charcoal until the kiln is filled up to the top. (This process is actually begun while the kiln is still being built.) Six double bellows are placed around the base, each worked by a smith who pumps up and down on a pair of sticks, forcing air from the bellows, through the tuyere, and into the kiln. In no time all the charcoal is red-hot, and the heat at the base, where the ore lies, is intense.

The smelting is kept up all day without a break. Toward the end of the day the kiln is broken and the hot coals raked aside, revealing great lumps of white-hot ore in between the tuyeres. These are pulled out and beaten to clean them, and when cool they are broken up for resmelting the next day. The whole process is repeated the next day in a new kiln built over the same pit, and only then is the iron considered pure enough to work into wire.

The smiths work at shallow pits filled with charcoal, heated by a single pair of bellows. To make wire they first have to make the tools needed: clamps to pull the wire, and drawplates through which to pull the wire to reduce it in size to the desired gauge.

For anvils, great stone boulders, carefully flattened by chipping, are brought from another mountain some twenty miles away. These boulders contain silica, highly beneficial in the smithing process. The ore has to be hammered into rods roughly the diameter of a pencil and two or three feet long. The hammering has to be done with great care so that there are no impurities introduced, no air pockets, and no poorly hammered folds of metal. Any such weakness will cause the wire to break when it is being pulled through the plates.

The bulbous drawplates are reamed with a hardened spike while they are still red-hot, and after each drawing the aperture is closed and reamed again, cold, to a slightly narrower gauge. To begin with, it takes ten men pulling on ropes attached to the clamp on one end of the rod to force the metal

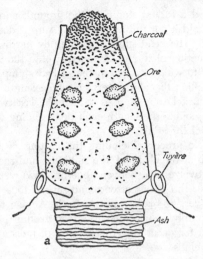

Figure 3. A Ciga Kiln. The kiln, built over a fire lit in a deep pit, is filled with layers of charcoal and ore as it is built.

through. The first time it does little more than scrape the rod's uneven surface into truer and smoother shape, but the next few pulls more than double the length of the rod while thinning it down. In the process of being pulled, the wire and the plate both get hot, and from time to time have to be further strengthened by annealing. After only six or seven successful pulls the wire may be as much as fifty feet long, and the greatest care is needed in handling. If the sun is too hot it will weaken the wire and cause it to break when drawn further; if the weather is too cool or moist, or if the wire, heated by friction, sags and touches the cool grass, the sudden change will also cause the wire to break. Similarly, the slightest unevenness in pulling will break the wire, which by now is the thinness of a sewing needle. The final draws are done by the head smith alone. He anchors one end of the wire around a forked stump in the ground, and the rest of the team hold it out full length, being sure it does not sag to the ground. The head smith has carefully narrowed the hole in the reduction plate and threaded it onto the wire, and he now starts to walk away from the forked stump, slowly and steadily pulling the plate over the whole length of the wire. The wire stretches as he goes so that the last two pulls may more than double the length each time, ending with forty or fifty yards of threadlike wire.

The whole process, including the cutting of the ore, the preparation of the charcoal, the smithing, and the wire-drawing, takes twelve men between one and two weeks and provides two or three coils of wire and several tools such as hoe blades, knives, ax blades, and so forth. Among the Ciga the wire is a purely luxury item used for making bracelets and anklets and for decorating the handles of tools and shafts of spears and clubs.

The scarcity of iron and the laborious techniques for working it make the metal ore one of the foremost symbols of wealth in places. It is also endowed with something of the supernatural quality of the smiths, which adds to its worth. In many areas it acquired a symbolic value far higher than its commercial value. Its utility is also clearly recognized, making it in some senses more valuable than metals like gold, which is so soft as to be useless for anything but decorative purposes. It is frequently made into fanciful shapes, or exaggerated versions or elaborate variants of everyday tools and weapons, not only as a means of storing the metal for future use, but also as a form of currency, either real or symbolic. Sometimes this currency could be exchanged in the marketplace for other goods, but more often these specially wrought pieces of iron, in the form of hoes or knives or whatever, are used as symbols of agreements between people or groups. In particular, iron is used this way to symbolize the exchange of obligations at the time of marriage. Such pieces are sometimes referred to as "marriage money" or "bridewealth," but these terms are misleading. Brides are not "bought"; any wealth that changes hands does not serve as a measure of the bride's value, but rather as a symbol of the exchange of a complex set of obligations, duties, and rights between the two families.

The diffusion of an iron technology had far-reaching consequences in all aspects of social life—domestic, economic, political, and religious. It contributed to the rise of kingdoms and states, for iron increased the efficiency of weapons for defense and offense, just as it increased the efficiency of the tools of the cultivator, enabling him to expand more easily from the grasslands into the forests, where the trees could only be cut down with metal blades.

Although gold, silver, and copper were known in other parts of Africa even before iron, it seems that iron was the first metal known in southern Africa. The earliest people to smelt and use it spread through the area in the first millennium A.D., leaving behind them distinctive forms of pottery known as channeled ware—stamped and dimple-based pottery. They may have been Africans from the center of the continent who mingled with the local Stone Age Bushmen hunters. They raised cattle, and they cultivated the land with iron hoes. Their knowledge of ironworking probably came from Meroë in Kush (Sudan), but it may have been derived from the West African tradition.

In Rhodesia the smiths also worked gold, copper, and tin, which they bartered to Arab traders along the coast, laying the basis for the trade that flourished between the Arabs and the Monomatapa confederacy in the fourteenth and fifteenth centuries, long before the arrival of the first Portuguese merchants. The Monomatapa and later Rwozi confederacies were groups of loosely federated African kingdoms covering a large area south of the Zambezi. They were the builders of the unique stone fortresses and ritual centers that stretch inland from the coast, including Zimbabwe. The Zambezi was used as a trade route from very early times. Ingombe Ilede, on its upper reaches, was inhabited by peoples rich with gold. The peak of these civilizations dates back to the ninth century A.D., but elsewhere local Iron Age cultures developed in a less spectacular fashion throughout the grasslands—such as the early Kalamo farming culture in Zambia.

Khami is a late example of one of the stone ruin sites of

Rhodesia traditionally associated with the Rwozi (who may or may not be connected with the contemporary Lozi or Shona people). The African kingdoms of the Rwozi confederacy broke away from the earlier Monomatapa alliance with which Zimbabwe is associated. The Rwozi traded with the Portuguese and the Dutch along the coast, and even pieces of Chinese pottery have been found at Khami. The site is spectacular, built on a terraced hill overlooking the Khami River gorge. It was probably the residence of a Chief or other notable, judging from the rich polychrome pottery and the ceremonial regalia found in the buildings. The wealth included a hoard of bronze and iron weapons, ivory carvings of lions, ivory divining boards, and beads of gold and glass. The inhabitants used iron hoes in the cultivation of grain, and also raised cattle. And there our knowledge, frustratingly, stops.

Another important site is Bigo, a series of earthworks in Uganda. It is the site of a large later Iron Age encampment on the south side of the Katonga River, near an ancient cattle ford, and is the most extensive of its type in western Uganda. There are outer and inner rings of ditches, seven to fifteen feet deep, cut into solid rock and covering a total length of over six miles.

At the highest point of the hill are three mounds; excavations indicate that occupation was short. The occupants were cattle herders with a material culture much like that of contemporary inhabitants of the area, and guesses have been made that they were the Bito, the sixteenth-century forerunners of the great Nyoro and Ganda peoples. In the oral tradition of those kingdoms, sites such as Bigo are associated with the legendary Cwezi, a short-lived dynasty that predated the present dynasties of the kingdoms. Legend describes the Cwezi as "tall, big men with long noses and of pale color" and says they came from the North. Some have claimed they were Arabs, but this is little more than pure speculation.

There is scattered evidence of Arab settlements throughout eastern and southern Africa, particularly along the coast. Gedi was one of a number of Arab trading cities on the eastern coast that flourished between the tenth and sixteenth centuries, dealing in precious metals, ivory, and slaves. It lies fifty-three miles northeast of Mombasa, and only eight miles south of Malindi, both of which were Arab ports. The presence at Gedi of important Islamic glazed pottery and of Chinese celadonware of the fourteenth and fifteenth centuries indicates this as the peak of Gedi's trade importance. A Chinese source records the visit of a fleet of junks to Malindi and Mombasa between A.D. 1417 and 1419. During the sixteenth century the Portuguese took over the ports, and Gedi began to decline. It was finally abandoned completely in the early seventeenth century.

The picture we get throughout the grasslands is one of a widespread early hunting and gathering people, very likely associated with the present-day Bushmen (now confined to the southern deserts). Then, with the advent of iron technology, came the sudden explosion of another African population of somewhat different physical type who occupied the grasslands in several waves, sometimes assimilating those already there, sometimes driving them still farther on into less hospitable territory. Most of the historic sites indicate mixed farming, grain cultivation, and cattle raising, and this would probably be the case today if it were not for areas of the tsetse fly where cattle simply cannot be kept.

A Grassland People: the Pokot Pastoral Cultivators

Anthropologists often refer to the East African grasslands as the East African cattle area, but that is misleading, since most of those cattle herders do some cultivation as well. Even among those predominantly cultivators, cattle values may emerge, as cattle play a special role among the grasslands people, ritual as well as economic. For this reason, and since we cannot descibe all the variations in a general coverage of this kind, the Pokot people were chosen for special reference. Due to a combination of historical and geographical circumstances, the Pokot today are divided into sections that practice all three of the major grassland economies—some are purely herders, living off their cattle and growing no food; some are purely farmers, living at an altitude where cattle cannot survive; and those literally in between, for they occupy the lower slopes of the mountains above the cattle-herding plains, practice mixed farming.

Driven into their present homeland by more powerful tribes of cattle herders, the Pokot found refuge high up in the mountains just below the western escarpment in the Great Rift Valley in western Kenya. Although they lost their cattle, they survived by taking to irrigation farming, and as times improved and they were able to move back down the mountain slopes, some of them began to return to their old cattle-herding ways, finally leaving the mountain slopes to live entirely by herding in the plains below.

Despite these differences, the Pokot remain one people. While an unyielding sun bakes their lowland plains to concrete hardness, only a few miles away heavy rains encourage lush hardwoods, bamboo, and grass. High, razor-backed mountains plunge abruptly into the plains below. Despite the different life styles that must be followed in these different surroundings, all Pokot regard the mountaintops, particularly the twin peaks of Cheptulel and Mwina, with reverence. This reverence is also extended to the Pokot who choose to live there, in the high, wet, cold *masob*. It is the more adventurous youth who go down to the *keiou*, the plains, spreading out with their vast herds of zebu cattle, sheep, goats, donkeys, and camels. In the midlands, the *kamass*, is the meeting place of the two extremes, and all Pokot either move back and forth or vicariously partake in the life of the other sections through relationships established by kin or simply by trade. For instance, the inhospitable masob, where cattle cannot survive for long, makes an ideal temporary hiding place for cattle stolen in raids on other peoples. And while the strict irrigation farming in the masob provides an adequate subsistence, life is greatly eased, as it is for the frugal herders in the keiou, by trade with the kamass.

The Pokot also offer a good example of how people define their social units in terms of the environment and have a specific and functional relationship with it. The Pokot are at best loosely organized, being rather composed of small social units. The term they have for these small units is *korok*, and that term refers to any rise in the ground between two waterways, any ridge. This is a device used by many peoples, but for the Pokot it has special significance because of their highly developed system of irrigation, which is vital to their survival.

Any group of people living on such a ridge are also referred to as korok, and in the mountains this means that just as a ridge may extend from the high masob down into the kamass, so may a group of people who think of themselves as a distinct social unit occupy both kinds of territory and be able to make use of the different opportunities offered by each. This adds greatly to the sense of interconnection between the three economic activities, and where a korok is not physically linked with another level it will find links through marriage and trade. Economic necessity is translated into social organization to ensure the continuance and perpetuation of these opportunities.

Unlike the plains korok, frequently a small and impermanent, almost imperceptible mound, the masob korok is easily defined by mountains walls or ravines. Its population can rise from one hundred to four hundred people but remains fairly constant throughout the year regardless of seasonal change, which so affects the movement of men and cattle in the keiou. Leadership also is clearly defined, and derives by patrilineal descent from the first men to clear the land in that korok. Environment also affects the social organization that links different members of a hamlet to each other, and links different hamlets within the same korok. Members of the korok see themselves as related to each other not only by kinship, but also by the sharing of a common water supply, which necessitates community labor on the irrigation canals. In places these canals consist of bamboo pipelines led around cliff faces on scaffolding, and in other places of dug ditches following the natural contours of the mountainside for several miles. Sometimes the gradient represents a fall of only a few inches in a hundred feet, accurately judged by eye and constructed with home-made tools. The ditches lead to fields where the water is subdivided into plots, which again clearly represent the social subdivisions within the korok.

While there are a few fields in the high masob, it is too cold and damp for crops to mature well, and eventually the water finds its way down to the irrigated fields of the mid-level kamass. The masob Pokot hunt not only for food, but also for the furry animals that provide them with their clothing, blankets, and slings for carrying babies. They exploit the forests for their wood, vital for the manufacture of bows and arrows and spear shafts, as well as for the irrigation troughs, water carriers, food bowls, mortars, pestles, other kitchen utensils, and household furniture. These are, of course, rare commodities in the kamass and keiou, where hardwood trees are scarce or nonexistent.

The korok located primarily in the kamass is not so clearly defined as that of the masob, either geographically or socially, although the boundaries are clear enough. Any one korok is likely to overlap several kinds of terrain, offering different exploitative possibilities to its inhabitants. The greater ease of living and the more varied activities that are possible give the kamass community a different character altogether when it comes to relationships among the various kamass korok. The high-level korok are sharply separated geographically, and each develops its own character independently of the others; inter-korok relationships are marked either by rivalry or by co-operativeness, hostility or friendliness. This pattern becomes set in time, since the population remains so constant in composition.

The herders of the lowland keiou, some ten thousand feet below the peaks of their kin in the masob, are compelled to be on the move constantly, in search of pasture and water for their cattle. Their korok correspond, territorially, to slight rises or depressions in the land and to the courses of dried-up rivers. The population of any one korok fluctuates, rising to two hundred or so during the wet season. But with the advent of the dry season the units become progressively smaller as grazing and water sources become more scattered and scarce. When they reassemble for the next wet season, once again in larger units, the composition of a korok may be greatly different. Under such circumstances a clearly defined political authority would be an impossibility, for there is little continuity. In the keiou order derives from the principle of age rather than that of kinship; such authority as there is lies with the elders of the various age sets into which the keiou Pokot are divided, rather than with lineage elders.

The economy is much more precarious than in either the kamass or masob. Cattle are the focus of life, and the maximum usage must be made of them. To add to their meager diet, the Pokot, like other herders, tap the blood of their cattle without harming them by pricking the jugular vein (which has been distended by tightening a thong around the animal's neck) with a blocked arrow. After they draw a safe amount of blood, they release the thong, which collapses the vein and closes the puncture. Sometimes they rub the wound with clay to prevent infection and to ensure complete sealing. Ideally, each animal is bled in this way only once every two or so months. Together with the fact that the animals are not killed for meat, except on ritual occasions, this means that each family must maintain several hundred head of cattle to provide adequate milk and blood. In times of drought the cattle weaken and the bleeding and milking further debilitate them, to the point where they sicken more easily and die. The only way to survive then is to replenish the herd through raiding.

During good times raiding is minimal and assumes an almost ritual form, to remind everyone of the rules of the game, one might say. In times of drought the Pokot play the game in earnest, but they still follow the rules; they do it out of necessity, not pleasure. Nor does it necessarily arise from or cause any lasting hostility. The Pokot of the keiou raid their pastoral neighbors and prey on refuge bands of hunters like the Ndorobo. Their neighbors reciprocate with little if any animosity, and the cattle get shared by all. In peacetime there are frequent visits between these same peoples.

As with other pastoral peoples, the men seem to lead the more exciting, dramatic life, and to wield more power. However, beneath an apparent feminine docility and subservience, the mien usually assumed in the presence of foreigners, Pokot women have a vigorous life style and power of their own. From childhood women learn to be competitive, particularly with respect to the attention of men. Even at six years, girls begin to scarify their bodies and decorate themselves with beads and other ornaments, competing with each other for the approving glances of boys and men. After puberty they undergo the operaton of clitoridectomy, publicly performed so that each girl can display her courage. The operation is also the public announcement of her ability and readiness to bear children, and she immediately becomes marriageable.

Prior to marriage each girl has probably had several affairs with different boys, often leading to deeply affectionate relationships. It is the nature of these relationships for the girl to make constant demands on her boyfriend, forcing him to demonstrate his love and loyalty by gifts of increasing value. This forces the boy to turn to his friends and relatives for help and, when he is old enough, to take part in raiding parties to prove his affection. He is also proving his own courage and manhood, and his own suitability as a marriageable youth.

But in societies like this, marriage is more than an agreement between two individuals in love with each other; it is also an agreement between two groups, with strong political and economic overtones. Among the Pokot many a long love relationship is rudely broken up by the necessities of a suitable marriage. These overtones add to the tensions and difficulties the women find in being married to a man they do not know or love, and who may be many years their senior and already have one or more other wives. The competitiveness Pokot women felt as girls now turns to co-operation in competing with the men—in trying to curb their power and assert some measure of control over them. One very effective method of control is through gossip and the threat of scandal, for the men are proud and deeply afraid of being humiliated by their womenfolk.

The old flair for competition returns when a woman's daughters are of marriageable age, and women once again compete with each other in securing the most advantageous marriage for their offspring. Their motives are partly selfish —they are naturally thinking of their own security in their old age and will try to arrange marriages that will guarantee them the maximum protection. But the same motives also work for the social good, and marriage is one of the most vital ways, in many African societies, that the necessary bonds are formed that link divers social groups together in a coherent, cohesive system of interlocking relationships. Wherever possible, society will allow the young to choose their partners, determining for them only the general direction of their choice. Where such freedom is not possible the women find other compensations, and carry on clandestine affairs with their lovers. To say that such affairs are socially tolerated would be putting it too strongly, but they can become an institutionalized way of behavior, regulated by a set of rules that prevent them from harming the social and economic relationships established by the lawful marriage. Indeed, in some cases the existence of such affairs contributes directly to the stability of the official marriage by allowing for an outlet for affection on the one hand, and the performance of duty on the other, and, incidentally, giving the woman a measure of control over her husband through the threat of openly shaming him.

Women and Land

As among the Pokot and others in the East and North, the importance of the role played by women in the southern grasslands is underrated. It is often an unspectacular and rather private role, contrasted with the more dramatic and public role played by men, but the home is the province of women. The myriad domestic chores, from cleaning and cooking to child-bearing and rearing, are extremely time-consuming. Cooking alone, with its laborious methods of food preparation, is a full-time job. From all these activities women get satisfaction, for they are not taken for granted.

Throughout the grasslands women are eagerly courted and

cosseted, and even after marriage, particularly among the southern Bantu, a man must continuously give his wife gifts of clothing and jewelry so that she can make a good showing and maintain his own status. In polygynous societies where each wife has her own household, the husband is often little more than a guest in any wife's house. Central to the role of women, of course, is their power to bear children, and many of the southern grassland peoples recognize this by the institution of matrilineal inheritance, the female line dominating that of the male. In such societies the male may continue to wield power, but he can only do so by virtue of his membership in his sister's lineage, and total authority and power will descend through her children, not his.

Society recognizes the enormous domestic importance of women by the institution of bridewealth, which not only guarantees the husband's good behavior (in default of which his wife may leave him and he forfeits the wealth) but which also places him in a subordinate position, for the payment of wealth carries no absolute rights over the woman but does carry heavy obligations. Above all, the wealth is a symbol of the exchange that has taken place between two groups—not an exchange of a woman for money, but an exchange of reciprocal obligations, duties, and responsibilities. Often there are preferred directions in which a marriage should take place, and while the individual has a free choice in selecting his or her partner, it is free only within specific limits. These marriage systems are designed to perpetuate the kinds of intergroup relationship originally established, and generally answer to very specific political and economic needs. The prescribed or preferred nature of marriage indicates the importance the culture places on the establishment of social bonds between groups. The incest taboo and rules of exogamy accomplish an exchange of women through marriage, between distinct groups, and create unending affinities that facilitate co-operation, economic and otherwise, vital in an otherwise precarious world. What better way to ensure continuous ratification of these bonds than to establish them through the web of marriage, parenthood, and the sentiment that is usually implicit in the concept of kin?

The family, after all, is a natural as well as basic form of organization, and in many African societies it is taken as the model upon which an entire tribal structure is built. Thus several families form a lineage, tracing their common descent from a single known ancestor. Several such lineages believe themselves to be descended from an even earlier ancestor, though they may not be able to trace their ancestry back in an unbroken line; together they form a clan. A number of clans that claim to be descended from a remote, often mythological, founding ancestor, form a tribe.

Sometimes the descent is in the male line, sometimes in the female, but it is always through the person of the woman, and she is honored above all things for her power of fertility. This gives her particular power over economic activities. Even among the grassland herders, where cattle are nominally the province of men, the women have specific rights and on occasion take charge of the cattle themselves. Where the economy is one of crop cultivation, the women have direct control, for the same power of fertility that they have over human life is, or can be, transferred to the land, it is thought, and without her blessing and her touch, the crops will not mature.

Men may do the rough work of clearing the fields, but frequently it is the women who plant and tend and harvest the crops. A woman's granary is considered inviolable, and though her husband may have provided her with the land, even in a patrilineal society she has control over the produce. In some cases men may have gardens of their own but are not allowed to plant certain vital crops, placing them directly in the economic power of the women. Where a surplus can be grown or where there is time for specialization in crafts such as pottery or basketry, women have the additional economic advantage as marketers, and even the cash wealth of the family may in this way lie in their hands.

In the economic realm, as in that of the home, women have importance and power. It is a mistaken judgment, based on values that are narrowly our own, to claim that the African woman is held in low esteem because she is made to do so much hard physical labor. African women for the most part are extremely proud of their physical strength, and for a man to offer to lighten a load could be a deadly insult. Fragility in women, the kind of delicacy we still often associate with femininity, would appear to the healthy African woman as a great weakness, and in Africa would deprive her of her position and power.

While there are some spectacular exceptions, women fade into the background in the political realm. Unless women rule the tribe, as among the Lovedu, it is difficult to see what direct political authority they have, even in matrilineal societies. Most often the apparent ruler is a king; men wield the authority even when it descends in the female line. However, even in the great kingdoms of the southern grasslands where men wield all the outer symbols of authority, the woman is the power behind the throne. The man does not have the power to transmit royal authority; this lies with his sisters, and he relinquishes his authority to their children, not to his own. The royal sisters often have courts of their own and take some share of the burden of ruling, or at least act as counselors. Among the Lozi the royal title means "earth" and is directly associated with women, who control the land and its fertility. The King's sister is "The Earth of the South" and rules over the southern half of the kingdom. The King's capital is called Namuso, "Mother of Government."

Although the Lozi women are theoretically in strict legal tutelage to men, they have explicit means by which to exercise political authority. Women prepare the special beer for all ceremonial or public events; without their co-operation, which they may refuse, the ceremony would be fruitless. In this way women have good bargaining positions by which to attain their goals, and are openly recognized as indispensable to national success and as possessed of a very real power of their own.

It is in the area of spiritual power that we touch most closely on the source of woman's prestige, especially in the southern grasslands. This spiritual power is reflected in all areas of social life: Women are diviners and doctors; they control the fertility of the land; they perform the ritual through which rain can be brought, the land gives birth, and the crops are safely harvested and stored. These rituals do not occur as frequently as those of lesser importance, and even then, with few exceptions, they are not particularly dramatic, but they pervade the life of the people.

Even among the militarily aggressive Zulu the word of the *inkosazana* (Rain Princess) is greater than that of the Chief, and she can exert direct authority over him. Through her libations of beer alone are the sins of the Zulu absolved. Among the Tswana, rain cannot come unless young maidens fill the sacred pots with water and carry them ceremonially throughout the land, sprinkling the ground with the water to bring fertility as well as rain. Women are so powerful spiritually that ordinary objects touched by them can become charged with a power of their own. For example, women sometimes seize musical instruments men use in their rituals, particularly rattles and drums, and thereby convey special power to the instruments and to the ritual, as though the ritual might be impotent without their intervention.

Age

While descent may pass through the female line by the indisputable nature of physiological maternity, the bonds that so intimately unite a child with its mother, and by systematic extension unite entire kin groups, are also divisive. The bonds that unite one group of kinsmen (patrilineal or matrilineal) at the same time divide them from other similarly constituted groups of kinsmen. While theoretically all descend from a common ancestor, kin who can effectively trace their relationship feel more closely bound to each other than to those with whom there is no treaceable relationship. This is particularly true in the larger tribes and nations. For both economic and political purposes some other kind of principle has to be found to cut across these vertical lines of kinship, and the grassland herders in particular have developed the principle of age for this purpose.

Other societies recognize age as an important organizational principle, allocating divers tasks according to age, just as they may be allocated according to sex or family or any other principle. But the *age set system*, so highly developed in East Africa, is more than a convenient device for the division of labor, it also creates through dramatic and periodic rituals of initiation the strongest bonds of sentiment, binding large groups of men (particularly) throughout the land, regardless of kinship, in common cause. It provides a second major and distinct set of loyalties. It provides a means not only for distributing labor, but also for distributing authority. It provides young and old alike with clearly defined roles suited to the general capabilities of their age level, and each person accepts his role without argument as part of the inescapable fact of age itself. It causes young men to act together, if necessary, in defense of their land, their cattle, or their crops. It leaves most of the vital decisions to the elders who may no longer be agile enough to take part in the active life of the youth but who have the advantage of an accumulated store of wisdom. It enlarges social horizons, providing a new dimension in which a man or a woman may move to find friends as dependable as kin in times of need. It creates an almost spiritual community.

Where age becomes a major principle of organization, it is often formalized into age set systems of remarkable diversity, each responding to certain specific needs. There are two basic types—linear and cyclic. The important facet of each is that men (and sometimes women) are initiated jointly into an age set over a given period of time, after which the set is "closed" and no more candidates are taken in. The initiation may have taken place all the way across the land, admitting all boys between certain ages. The whole set is given a name, which becomes as important to the boys as their family names.

The set remains closed for a number of years, during which time the initiates learn their new tasks and fulfill their responsibilities. At the end of the given period, which may vary from five to fifteen or more years, a new set is opened. The ritual by which the new set is opened, initiating a new batch of youths, serves at the same time as a signal for the ritual advancement of each existing age set into the next

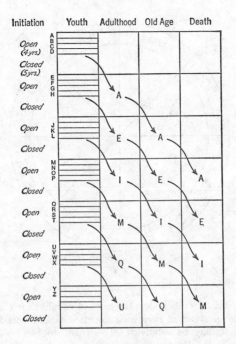

Figure 4. THREE TYPES OF AGE SET SYSTEMS. a) *Linear.*
Here each age set is divided, initially into a number of sub-
sets according to the year in which the boys are initiated.
When the set opens with the first initiation all other sets
move up into the next highest grade, or level. There may be
four years in which the set will be "open," after which it is
closed for the remainder of the life of that period, with no
more initiates being allowed in. Each sub-set preserves its
identity, perhaps each having its own area of activity, only
for that first level. On advancement from youth to adulthood the subdivisions disappear and the set takes on one
single identity (usually that of the senior sub-set) which it
keeps for the remainder of its life. On death of the last
member, the name and the identity disappear for ever.

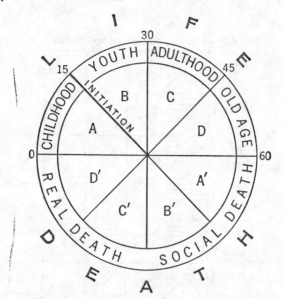

b) *Cyclical.* In this system the concept of rebirth is clear. In the model sketched here each initiation period lasts fifteen years. It may be subdivided (perhaps into two sub-sets) but as in the linear system retains its single identity from advancement onwards. However, old men in senior grade, if they reach the age of sixty, have the satisfaction of seeing children born that will, in their fifteenth year, be initiated into the shadow set bearing the same name as that borne by those passing into death . . . real or social. There is a strong feeling that there is continuity between the sets, each having its own nature and character, which will repeat as the name repeats, every sixty years.

stage or grade. Children become youths, youths become adults, adults become elders, elders become dead (either actually or socially), and the unborn become alive. Whereas you might enter your set as an individual or in the company

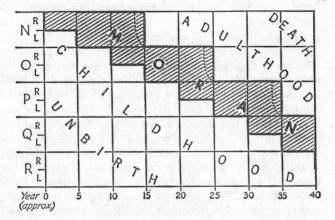

Year 0   5   10   15   20   25   30   35   40
(approx.)

c) *Step*. This system combines something of each of the two major forms, linear and cyclic. The Masai have a system of this kind, and it allows for a special kind of organization by which the sets, instead of always being divided, are linked by brief periods in which they overlap within the same age grade, or level. Each set is subdivided into two halves, those of the right and left hand. As the diagram shows, members of the right hand enter first, and share the grade of *moran* with the previous set for a brief time. That set advances before the left-hand sub-set of their successors is initiated. Then the entire set, right and left hand, shares the moran age level briefly with the incoming set.

In this way members of each right-hand sub-set have for a brief time shared their life with both adjacent sets, senior and junior. Members of each left-hand set have shared with the junior set's right-hand members only.

of a few friends, once the set is closed you are no longer primarily an individual and you no longer go through life as such. From then on the set as a whole does whatever it has to do, and during the periodic rites of passage the set as a whole advances from one grade to the next. Only in rare cases, as among the Masai, does a man leave his set, temporarily, by passing to a senior grade before his fellows, and then it is only because of the inheritance of special duties and responsibilities.

The Masai age set system also differs in allowing for very different periods of occupancy in the major age grades in which young men become *moran*, defenders of their land. But like several other systems, the Masai divide each set into two halves, initiates of the right hand and initiates of the left. Those of the right hand remain longer as moran than do those of the left hand, who are held back by the priest and not allowed to join the set until it is halfway or more through its existence. This gives the priest a chance to distinguish between the strong and less strong boys without opening the less strong to ridicule. To counterbalance their apparent secondary position, the initiates of the left hand are given special duties and responsibilities. In some cases the half effectively forms the administrative part of the set, while the other half forms the executive. Sometimes the division is between secular and sacred; sometimes there is no real division at all. Where there are such divisions, they are forgotten as though an individual constantly widens his social horizons, from the moment he enters the small group of fellow initiates in a sub-set through the time the sub-set begins to perform its common duties as a whole, and until he emerges into a higher grade as a member of a single set without subdivision, finally merging with all foregoing sets in the afterworld of death.

It is the cyclic age set system that seems most concerned with continuity. With the linear system a name is given to a set when it is "born"—that is, with the act of initiation. The name identifies all the set members until the last one dies, when the name passes out of existence. With the cyclic system there are a limited number of names that keep reappearing in sequence, only so many of them being alive at any time, with the others in limbo, waiting to be reborn. The name given under the linear system usually relates to some special event in the year of initiation. It fixes the set and its members in a given point in time and history. A cyclic set inherits its name from an earlier generation and to some extent may think of itself as inheriting the history of that past era as it inherits something of the personality of its members. In some cases the names go in pairs, a name and its shadow or counterpart name, so that as the oldest generation is dying out and their set name with them, they have the satisfaction of seeing their shadow set with their counterpart name at least being born. They may not live to see the initiation that gives the set its formal identity, but they have the assurance that it will come, and as they pass into limbo they know that the turning of the wheel will, in a few generations, bring them back to play their role in the unending history of their people.

The age set system offers a sense of identity different from that conveyed by kinship; it offers a community of spirit; it contributes significantly to the general social order and to the security of the moment; and it offers a very real sense of security for the future, in this life and beyond. It removes the ambivalence that is otherwise inherent in the process of aging by the clear allocation of role according to social age, everyone's social age being determined by a series of periodical public ceremonies. Everyone in such a system has a sense not only of belonging, but also of being a useful and functioning part of the whole. More specifically, the notion of brotherhood based on age enlarges the intricately woven threads that tie men together for co-operative action. The very nature of the organization of work in farming and herding requires joint effort ideally based on an unconditional reciprocity that can most surely and abundantly be obtained through the fraternal sentiment.

Writers frequently mistranslate the term moran, widely used among the Nilotes to designate the age grade of early manhood, as "warrior," just as they describe these East African cattle herders as fierce, warlike people. In fact, they are a gentle people, but the life they lead is far from gentle. One of the main roles of the moran is the protection of the cattle from the constant threat of predatory animals, and occasionally from raiders. The moran also help their kinfolk wherever help is needed, even performing such unwarlike tasks as helping the women draw water. Time spent as

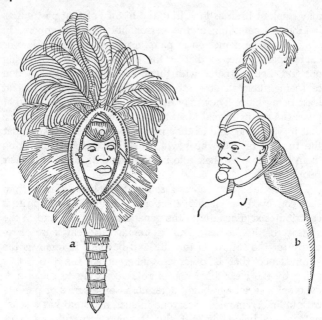

Figure 5. a) Feather headdress with leather frontlet, as worn by a *moran* or "protector of cattle." Masai. b) Headdress of senior "warrior" age grade, with alabaster lip plug. Jie.

moran is time when the high spirits of youth are allowed full rein but are channeled into socially functional directions. Above all, the youth assume responsibility for the whole future of their people, and they meet the responsibility with enthusiasm. It is a time the youngsters look forward to with anticipation and it is a time to which the elders look back with pride, for it is a time of glory and honor, and each set passing through the grade of moran tries to add to the total stock of the greatness that is already theirs.

The system also minimizes the conflict that inevitably arises from growing old. There is a natural reluctance to grow old and an even greater reluctance to die. In many Western societies where people try to cheat the process, the results are neurosis, despair, and suicide. Although such behavior is rare in Africa, there is still reluctance to growing old, even where every incentive is offered—such as allocating vital roles to the aged, removing any ambivalence, and providing a conceptual framework that offers hope for the future in an afterlife. The conflict is frequently manifest in hostility between adjacent generations. When a generation of moran see that the time has come for a younger generation to be initiated, they know that it is the signal for them to pass on into elderhood. Many will still feel young and vigorous and will resent the upcoming generation. With good sense, and rather than pretending otherwise, they accept the feeling and formalize it openly in a ritual battle between the generations in which the younger is expected to prove its superiority, its greater fitness to be the moran, the guardians of the people and their cattle.

The adjacent generation hostility is also alleviated by an active relationship of affection between alternate generations. The youth who expects yet resents discipline from his father can look with assurance to his grandfather for affection. This does not mean that there is no affection between father and son, merely that the resentment each will feel toward the other as the one inevitably forces the other into old age and death is accounted for.

Anxiety concerning death is met not only by systems of belief in afterlife, and by cyclic notions as evidenced in some of the age set systems, but also sometimes by associating death with power. The older one gets, the closer one approaches death, so the more power one acquires. Those closest to death are closest to that unknown beyond, and to the ancestors and the spirit world. Only at birth is one completely free of death, but then one is also devoid of power. Among some of the peoples of the grasslands of northern Nigeria this is explicitly recognized, and everything is done to encourage the individual, from the moment of birth, along the path of power, toward the ultimate power, death. Shortly after birth a boy is given a miniature bow and arrow, and a girl is given a miniature grindstone, symbols of their impending adulthood. As they grow older they wear special clothing to designate their increasing age and, consequently, their increasing power. In a sense they conquer death by possessing it.

Earlier we discussed the ambivalent attitude of people toward ironsmiths, an attitude best described as respect—a mixture of fear and honor blended out of necessity. The same is true of old age. People fear the old because, being so close to the supernatural, they are touched by its power. For instance, it is more often the old who are accused of being witches and sorcerers. But the old are also honored for having lived so long and done so much, and for having begotten children and grandchildren. In the same way that society needs the smiths for their special skills, so it needs the old for their accumulated store of wisdom, for their ability to reach far back into the past—into "the way of the ancestors." Many an old person knows very well that this is his position and takes full advantage of it, encouraging just the right amount of fear, offering just the right amount of advice, and living out his old age in security and in the affection of his family.

Government Without Kings

While family and economic organization contribute greatly to the over-all social order, as do the crosscutting systems that form people into groups according to age, sex, and residence, more is implied when we speak of government. By that we imply conscious direction of public affairs at any level, and in this sense all societies possess government. It may be minimal, as with the hunters and gatherers, or maximal, as with states, nations, and empires. It always involves some degree of representation and some delegation of authority, the bases of democracy. This diffusion of authority and power is all the more important in traditional African societies, since the ruling elite are not backed by the power of physical coercion, but have to rely on persuasion.

Environment has played an important part in the development of government in Africa, as we can see by examining the riverine Nilotics, the peoples of the East African uplands, and a mountain people of western Africa.

The Nuer, Dinka, and Anuak are all Nilotic-speaking peoples who occupy the *sudd,* the vast marshland of the Upper Nile. Their arid environment lacks stones and metals, barely tolerates a limited form of agriculture, and forces the cattle herders to continually drive their cattle back and forth in search of pasture and water. The Nuer and Dinka are almost completely dependent on their livestock, not only for the milk and blood that constitute the major items of their diet and the occasional meat from a ritual slaughtering, but also for most of the everyday materials in their lives—horn, skins, bones, hoofs, and gut. The only other readily available materials are mud and grass, both used in housing, and papyrus for matting. Metal objects, most importantly knives and spears, have to be obtained by trade. Cattle form the content of their social and spiritual life as well. Kinship is reckoned in terms of cattle exchange for women. One can almost trace genealogical connections by ascertaining the movement of cattle from owner to owner. Nuer art, prayer, and folklore reflect their notion of the great gift of cattle—the sustenance of life. The Anuak lost nearly all their cattle to the tsetse fly and so do not have to leave their villages and follow the annual transhumant pattern, but remain close to their villages and their crops. Cattle values are therefore less dominant.

The Nuer form a nation divided into tribes and subdivided into clans and lineages. The effective unit is the lineage, and this operates at four levels: maximal, major, minor, and minimal. The Nuer trace descent through the male line, and the senior descendant of any segment is the head of that segment. Though his authority is restricted, his influence can be considerable. The relationship of this segmentation of the family and the consequent diffusion of authority to the topography are clear. The Nuer build their villages with their cattle barns on top of small hills along the banks of the Nile and its tributaries. These hills and ridges become islands in the rainy season, isolated from each other by the floodwaters. During the rains the Nuer society is broken down into minimal units, corresponding to minimal lineages; authority lies effectively and almost exclusively in the hands of the lineage heads at this minimal level. They make whatever decisions are necessary, and settle disputes within their sublineage. But with the coming of the dry season and the retreat of the floodwaters, the Nuer have to move their cattle out quickly in search of water and pasture. Were it water alone they could remain along the riverbanks, but they have to wander farther and farther inland for good grazing. As they move farther inland, water becomes more scarce, and the minimal segments that were so isolated during the rains now begin to amalgamate and gather around the few common water holes. A dry-season cattle camp, unlike a wet-season village, is a large unit, corresponding to the maximal lineage in the segmentary system. The family is still the basis of social order and the source of authority, but it is now the family at its widest extension. Beyond these maximal units there is little sense of unity, and life is marked by feuding and raiding.

The constant movement, the process of seasonal fission and fusion, together with the thin dispersal of the population, all necessary for survival in that environment, make centralization impossible; the locus of authority shifts with each movement, but to refer to it as "ordered anarchy" is to miss the essential point that the anarchy is only apparent, and relative to our own viewpoint, whereas the order is real. The system is adequate.

So it is with the Dinka, who are neighbors who live on slightly higher land broken more by ridges than hills. This leads to a larger level of socialization. A further significant environmental difference lies in the greater availability of pasture along the riverbank: The change that this necessitates in their seasonal transhumance is best seen in Figure 6. What is significant from the point of view of government is that the maximal unit gains in importance over the minimal, which is the reverse of the Nuer, and consequently authority is that much more centralized though still definitely segmentary. There is also a difference in the importance of the ritual figures found in each of these two societies—the Leopard Skin Priest of the Nuer and the Master of the Fishing Spear of the Dinka. Both of these serve to unite these peoples at a still higher level, and cut across the lineal divisions, serving the same function as the age set systems both peoples possess. The Master of the Fishing Spear does have more political authority than the Leopard Skin Priest, however, perhaps due to the higher level of association.

The Anuak, who have mostly become cultivators, still tend to regard themselves as cattle kin to their Dinka and Nuer neighbors. Anuak land is divided by parallel streams separated by stretches of desert. In the wet season the lower corner of Anuakland is flooded and villages are isolated, but the higher, southeastern corner is not. It is precisely in that southeastern corner that a competitive league has developed, linking the villages in a kind of political federation, with an embryonic King at the head. He is the one who, at any given moment, holds the royal beads that are the goal of the competitors. The holder may relinquish the beads or they may be taken from him, and in this way the beads and the "kingship" move from village to village. Otherwise, each village is under the control of a lineal elder. A village becomes distinguishable from the rest only when its "noble" acquires the beads and it becomes the capital of the competitive league. The holder of the beads has no real authority, though he may serve as an arbitrator and adjudicator, but he is of particular use as a rallying point in times of war, uniting the otherwise independent and sometimes isolated villages, even those beyond the league.

As with the Nuer and Dinka, however, kinship plays a vital role in the business of government at the local level. Groups that either are related or pretend to be, are likely to co-operate with and help each other, while those that are not related or pretend not to be, may be in a permanent state of war. Cattle raiding, for instance, is largely governed by the divisions and bonds created by kinship.

The Uplands of East Africa

The fertile uplands of East Africa offer another example of how environment relates to government, favoring subtle differences among similar peoples.

The uplands are ideal for farming and herding. Different peoples migrated from the North and West, each trying to establish and maintain its own territory against pressure from its neighbors who were pressed by waves of southward migration. Except for the groups living in the particularly favorable region of Lake Victoria, the people of the uplands did not develop kingdoms or elaborate forms of government. However, those who cultivated the land successfully did develop large, permanent settlements and a richer culture than the people of the Nile marshlands. The size and permanence of the settlements required a more centralized form of government than the Nilotic division of people into family units; in the uplands families could not survive alone, and the interdependence within and between each settlement led to the creation of various systems of chieftainship. Once again we can see how minor variations in topography led to corresponding variations in the degree of centralization.

Peoples living in an undulating territory such as the Kavirondo overlapped each other, and the ease of communication led to a wider sense of identity than among the peoples living in hilly areas who were divided from each other by gorges and ravines. In both cases the people organized themselves by clans and lineages, in which they believed they were grouped by birth. Such groupings have the advantage of being relatively indisputable, thus minimizing conflict that arises from more voluntary or arbitrary forms of association. Clans and lineages set the pattern for inheritance of property and establish the boundaries of marriage. Feud and warfare are not so important among these people as among the Nilotic herders, and the greatly improved level of communication led to the amalgamation of the large lineal units into tribes, recognizing the authority of tribal leaders. These leaders were usually hereditary, but did not have the power that goes with kingship. Priests and prophets played a vital role in uniting the people at a different level, and prophets here, as in the Nile marshlands, were crucial to the massive resistance with which these peoples faced the European colonialists, uniting the people as they had never been united before and as the traditional chiefs and elders alone could never have united them.

The Kavirondo and Kikuyu, both of Kenya, live on land that is rolling and hilly, respectively. (See figure 6-d.) The Kavirondo land is less easily defended, which contributes to their need for greater centralization. The fact that the village settlements flow and overlap across the rolling countryside, rather than being concentrated on hilltops or ridges, also encourages political solidarity. The ease of communication that this brings facilitates disputes that range far beyond the familial level, where they could be settled amicably by the lineal elder. Lineage is still a prime political device, but now there is need to go beyond it for reasons of internal order and external defense.

The Kikuyu, on the other hand, traditionally had no chiefs at all until the British colonial government appointed them for administrative convenience. The Kikuyu live in high hilly country, on ridges separated by ravines with steep sides that are impassable during the rains because they are slippery. (See figure 6-c.) Each ridge is surmounted by a familial homestead; these are almost independent in themselves, and are defensible units. Yet these people communicate throughout the year as much as the Kavirondo despite the unfavorable geography of their land. Groups of neighboring ridges, divided by ravines and streams connecting in a more important stream or small river, associate in a manner both familial and political. Traditionally each segment came under the authority and influence of an elder, and groups of elders met to decide matters pertaining to regions rather than ridges. Ideally, the Kikuyu as a whole could be represented by such a council of elders, but normally co-operation was at a much lower level—between the elders of neighboring ridges.

In both cases the hills and ridges were occupied by what were primarily familial units—males of the founding lineage, their wives and children. This is common among both herders and cultivators, but with the cultivators, where lineal authority begins to be overlaid with a more centralized political authority, and villages are more settled and life more sedentary, it was not uncommon for members of foreign lineages to settle in a village. Sometimes these foreign lineages became numerically superior, in which case they acquired political authority, with the founding lineage retaining ritual authority. The Pokot are an example of a herding people where this happened, but it happened primarily in the high-

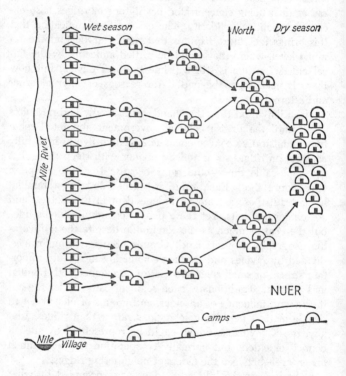

Figure 6. Transhumance Systems a) NUER: The Nuer abandon their riverine villages in the dry season, during which time they drive their herds farther inland. Neighboring villages isolated during the rains gradually come together at this time and then split up again as they return home at the approach of the next rains.

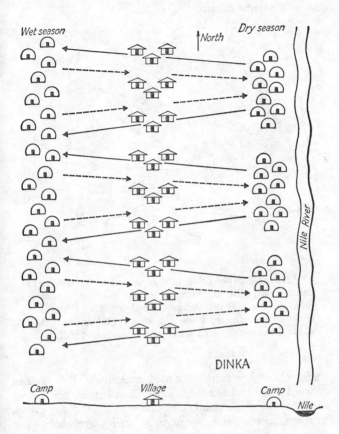

DINKA

b) DINKA: Villages are higher than those of the Nuer, and
so are less isolated. The Dinka herd their cattle near the
Nile in large dry-season camps, then drive them to small inland wet-season camps. As the next dry season approaches,
they drive the herds back to graze stubble left in the fields
after the intervening harvest.

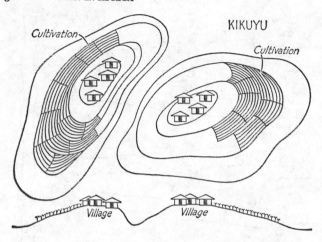

c) KIKUYU: Sharply rising hills separated by ravines make defense easy. Hilltop villages are compact and isolated; fields do not meet or overlap. Several adjoining ridges may comprise an extended lineage or clan regarding themselves as kin, but basically each ridge is an independent unit.

lands, where they cultivate almost exclusively. This division between ritual and secular authority is not rigid, but it is an effective way of distributing authority so that no one group, let alone any one person, acquires so much power that he can abuse it. Sometimes it seems that strangers are invited to settle in a village just to bring about this kind of diffusion. It is yet another mechanism in the list of institutions in African political systems that help to ensure democratic government in the interests of all the people.

West African Mountain Grasslands

In northern Nigeria, lofty mountains and plateaus rise from inland forests and woodlands. Peoples in the lower grassland areas, where communication is much easier, organize them-

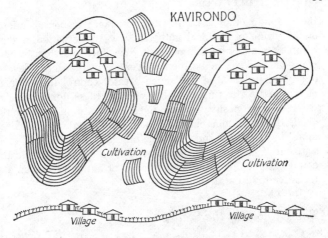

KAVIRONDO

Cultivation

Cultivation

Village

Village

d) KAVIRONDO: Gently rolling hillsides lead to spreading settlements, continuous cultivation, and boundaries not always clearly marked. Need for combining for defense encourages wider political solidarity and more centralized leadership.

selves loosely. Each group has its own identity, but all feel a wider bond uniting them, at least in sentiment. They also see themselves as united because they belong to the lowlands, as distinct from the peoples who inhabit the uplands. It is common for geographical factors to correspond to unities in this way, just as people practicing one form of economy see themselves as united despite tribal differences, in common opposition to those practicing another economy (as with herders and cultivators).

Although there is a similar feeling of over-all unity in the mountain areas, it is dissipated because geographical features help to make political boundaries more rigid and more secure. Tribal areas are more isolated from each other and government becomes more centralized, with tribes sometimes developing into small principalities, with hereditary Kings at the head. In other areas there is resistance to consolidation and freezing of political authority, yet the situation is too complex to allow for the more informal lineage system to operate unchecked. In northern Nigeria, chieftainships developed with rulers who had much greater control than chiefs of the East African uplands, but whereas these upland chiefs derived their positions from lineal seniority and so were fixed, the mountain chiefs in northern Nigeria held office more by election, and the chieftainship moved from one segment of the group to another so that no one lineage or clan could become dominant. This rotation of authority was an alternative to dispersal of authority.

The Growth of the State

A number of factors contributed to the growth of the African states. Population increased, leading to migration and warfare, and social organization became more complex. As people turned to agriculture they became more sedentary. They still respected the lineal divisions that organized them in family groups up to the clan, which they conceived of as the family "writ large"; but to survive they needed an even wider sense of unity and a more powerful central authority. They achieved this by extending the family concept still further, uniting clans in the belief of common descent from a remote ancestor. Tribes even united into nations in the same way, creating the myth of a common ancestry. At first the King was held to be the direct descendant of the original ancestor, and ruled by virtue of his descent. In case he should abuse his position, however, provision was made for his replacement by a more desirable candidate of the same line. Even when the position was taken by force, the usurper frequently pretended to some connection or formed one by intermarriage. As far as the people were concerned, the King was not divine in himself, nor did they owe allegiance to him as a person. It was the office that was divine and to the office that they owed allegiance. All respect and authority stemmed from the original ancestor.

The King of the Shilluk, northern neighbors of the Nuer on

the Nile, is a classic "Divine King" whose power is minimal in a direct political sense, but through whose divine authority and ritual performance the nation is believed to prosper. Most of his duties as King are ritual, the correct performance of which is essential to the well-being of his people. If the nation fails to prosper, the people blame the King. They believe he has either fallen into impurity, been negligent in his ritual duties, or become senile. His body has become unfit as the receptacle of the ancestor, Nyikang, and is disposed of by suffocation.* The ritual of coronation of the successor shows clearly how this kingship came into being.

The Shilluk, unlike their neighbors, live on a long ridge well above the floodwaters in a hundred or so settlements strung in a line. These settlements are never isolated from each other, as are those of the Nuer and Dinka, and the consequently greater sense of unity led to the emergence of the Reth, or King. At first the kingship moved from settlement to settlement, rather like the Anuak royal beads, avoiding the dangers of abuse that come with consolidation and localization of power and authority. The kingship moved from one part of the nation to another, from North to South. The settlements, strung in a line, fall naturally into North and South divisions, and ultimately the kingship settled at Fashoda, directly in the center. Alternation was now secured by choosing the King first from the North half of the kingdom, next from the South. His coronation is an act of possession in which his body is captured and inhabited by the spirit of Nyikang, whose image is kept at the extreme northern end of the kingdom. Prior to the coronation the settlements of the North mobilize themselves and bring the image of Nyikang to Fashoda, while the settlements of the South similarly mobilize and send an opposing army. There is a mock battle between the two halves of the kingdom, symbolizing the latent danger of hostility, and the King-elect has to fight against possession by Nyikang. Once possessed, however, he becomes Nyikang, and the empty image is returned to the North until Nyikang tires of his new body and returns.

* There is no evidence this ever happened, however.

The division of the kingdom into two halves is ritualized, each having certain specific functions with regard to the King and the kingship. The Reth is the living symbol of their unity. Effective political authority remains in the hands of elected settlement chiefs, however, though appeal can be made over these chiefs directly to the royal court at Fashoda if there is any question of abuse.

To the south in the East African grasslands, there are similar divine kingdoms, especially in Uganda. The Kabaka of the BaGanda is the living representative of the original founding ancestor and heads a powerful nation. Once again, the kingship is made to rotate, this time using yet another device. Instead of forming a royal clan, each Kabaka takes, on his accession, a number of wives, one from each of the Ganda clans. His male children by any of these wives are all potential heirs to the throne, and although he may express his preference for the succession, he cannot determine it. That is left to a council that acts in the best interests of the nation, seeing to it that a kingship does not rest in any one clan and that a Prince is chosen for his qualities of leadership rather than for his being the oldest son of an oldest son. Unlike the Shilluk, these upland Kings acquire great secular power and have united their countries not only in ritual, but also as military units for defense and offense. Their authority still derives from their divine ancestry, however, and still the King as a person is not considered infallible. With the Ganda, for instance, there are the royal drums to which a subject can appeal, even against the King; recognition that divinity, in contrast to its human agents, *is* infallible and always just.

Sometimes kingships that were divine in origin acquire such great secular power as to appear entirely secular, but everywhere a trace of divinity remains, and always the ruler is more than just that—he is the fountainhead from whom sprang order, cohesion, and prosperity. Rarely, as among the Venda of South Africa perhaps, he is deified and worshiped as a god. The more usual pattern is for him to be recognized merely as a vehicle for divinity. This is so even in the trading states of the West African grasslands ranging from tiny principalities in the Cameroun mountains, such as the Mum, to the elaborate feudal empires of the Fulani, the Mossi, and the Hausa, and to the smaller but more complex societies of the Nupe and the forest states of the Yoruba. The Mossi and Hausa states came down from the great West African empires of the Middle Ages such as Ghana, Mali, Songhai, and Bornu. These were built on trans-Saharan gold and slave trade with the Arab peoples. The American slave trade drained much of their prosperity, as this new trade was based on the coast rather than the inland region, and today their ancient splendor has waned. Most of these states were Muslim, ruled by emirs whose ancestors subjugated the pagan peoples in a series of *jehads*, or holy wars. Ritual and belief played a vital part in the maintenance of these kingships, despite their basically economic origin.

The great migrations originating in West Africa and along the Nile finally reached into the far South, but not until relatively recently. It was a time of turmoil, for not only were the Bantu-speaking peoples trying to establish themselves, but they also had to contend with European settlers expanding inland from the coast. In the nineteenth century a series of states were established by conquest, and the power of the Kings was based almost entirely upon force and military prowess, the army and its regiments playing a central part in the organization of government. Despite this, the notion of divine power persisted, and Kings were held in check by factors such as the vital rituals that were delegated to other officials, frequently to women. Kingship in these conquest states offered an easy road to despotism, but despots were usually short-lived. The founder of the Zulu state, Chaka, came to power in 1818 by his conquest of the neighboring Nguni tribes; he was assassinated in 1828 for his despotic behavior. It was still the office and not the individual that was respected as sacred; religious beliefs still permeated the system of government, and justice was one of the main qualities by which a ruler was judged. The jural systems of the traditional southern African states were renowned for their respect for basic human rights, as indeed were those of the ancient West African empires.

World View

The practical role that religion plays in African society can be seen in almost every sphere of life, and it does not necessarily have to be manifest in such a dramatic way as in divine kingship. The East African grasslands are home to divers peoples, some of whom, although neighbors, hold directly opposite views and beliefs about the world, its nature, and how man should live in it. Yet while opposed to each other, they live together in relative peace. When warfare occurred in the past it was usually due to large-scale movements of population, which caused severe competition for land. This movement included the southward thrust of Nilotic and Cushitic cattle herders, and there arose a basic opposition between these migrants and the farmers they found already established in the grasslands. Various ways were found for settling the land question; some peoples moved elsewhere, some accepted foreign domination, some became assimilated. But the opposition of values has always remained.

It has been an opposition largely without hostility or animosity, however. Typifying this inner conflict are the Masai herders and their neighbors the Kikuyu farmers. They fought bitterly to establish their rights to the same land, finally dividing it and living side by side in an uneasy peace, completely segregated. Raiding became a major feature of life, for through such raids each side was able to express its latent hostility and so reinforce its own values and sense of superiority without involving the whole tribe in total warfare. Far from being an act of war, the raid acted as a mechanism for the maintenance of peace.

The Masai moran live in *menyatta* or compounds, two of which usually protect some twenty nomadic cattle camps. Placed centrally, the moran can move separately or jointly as occasion demands. The age set occupying the grade of moran protects the people and cattle, mostly against wild animals. The moran, or youth of the Masai, also carry out the raids, and by their deeds of bravery perpetuate the pride the Masai have in their very being. There is no central political leader, though the *laibon*, or priest, is a major unifying force in this continually shifting society. The age set system handles the business of government at the local level, authority being divided between the moran and the elders.

Like many herders, the Masai despise farming. They may eat farm produce, but they prefer a diet of milk and blood. Meat of their cattle is eaten only when there is need for the ritual slaughter of cattle; they may not be killed simply to provide meat. Cattle are the focal point of Masai economy. The whole social organization serves to meet the needs of grazing and watering large herds and protecting them from any predators. In the symbolism of the Masai, grass—that which gives life to cattle and to the Masai—is the symbol of peace. When a man wishes to make a pact with another he offers a handful of grass. When he dies he is not buried in a hole in the ground, a thought that is horrifying to these herders, but he is laid out in the open with a clump of grass in one hand, a pair of sandals and a cattle stick in the other, ready for whatever onward journey there might be. The useless body is disposed of by vultures and jackals, spending its last moments under the stars that, for the Masai, represent celestial herders driving celestial cattle across the sky. If there is a heaven, for the herder this is surely how it must be.

The Kikuyu settle on family ridges and recognize the authority of clan and lineage elders. Streams form boundaries, and each ridge is an independent family unit, or *mbari*. Families occupying several adjacent ridges think of themselves in the wider sense of a clan, a *moherega*, and unite in opposition to other ridges. All clans descend from the original nine daughters of Gikuyu, the founding ancestor. Mobility is minimal, and the Kikuyu farmers fought rigorously with Masai invaders who sought to take their land. In the process of fighting, however, female captives were taken and the two peoples intermarried, leading to much exchange of ideas and the adoption by each of certain elements of the culture of the other. But the basic opposition between their world views remains. The Masai love to roam constantly over the open spaces, frequently sleeping under the night sky, admiring the vast plains of waving grass. The Kikuyu look with more feeling at the rich red soil of their homeland. Whereas the Masai consider it a sacrilege to destroy grass in order to plant, the Kikuyu feel just the opposite. The Kikuyu cultivate their land industriously and say that land left uncultivated is free for anyone who wants to work it. Farming means a way of life that ties the people to one place, physically and spiritually; most important to the Kikuyu are the sacred bonds that hold families to the land first tilled by their ancestors. The Kikuyu ideal is to be born, to live, and to die on the family land; to be always wandering in life and to be left in the open at death is to be utterly homeless in this world and the next. Only burial in the sacred ancestral soil can assure the Kikuyu a happy life in the fields of the afterworld.

Here are two neighboring peoples whose ways of life appear inimical to each other. Each claims right to the land by virtue of the fact that the other abuses and desecrates it. Associated systems of belief and diametrically opposed world views heighten this opposition to the point where hostility seems inevitable. Yet the Kikuyu developed an age set system similar to that of the Masai and so organized themselves to meet any act of aggression. Had the opposition been less complete, the result may have been endless large-scale warfare, but its completeness led rather to a voluntary mutual apartheid, each people preferring to leave the other alone aside from an occasional foray on the part of the youth, which served to maintain both the opposition and the separation.

The depth to which world view may affect the individual, uniting those who share the same view in opposition to those who do not, is perhaps most easily seen among the cattle herders. Cattle are, for them, inextricably bound up with notions of goodness and beauty. This is seen not only in the use of cattle hide, horns, and even bones for dress and ornamentation, but also in the attitudes of the people toward their cattle. The men in particular select certain cattle and beautify them, binding their horns to grow into a variety of distinct styles. They groom these special "name" cattle and sometimes paint their bodies. Every skin color and marking fall into some recognized category, and each man has his favorite. Both men and women love nothing better than to watch their cattle grazing and to admire their shape, the sway of their humps, the fold of their dewlaps, the toss of their heads, and the switch of their tails, finding beauty in the tiniest detail. The people compose poems, songs, and dances in honor of the cattle. All this is more than an acknowledgment of economic dependence, it is also an acknowledgment of something that is beautiful as well as good and useful that has come into their lives, and above all an acknowledgment of the existence of some power greater than man, the God who let the cattle down from the sky and for whom alone the cattle can be sacrificed.

The first game that children learn to play concerns cattle. They build a *boma* or cattle compound just like a real one but in miniature, out of twigs and wood shavings. Among the Karimojong herders it has a separate pen for calves and another for milking. The Karimojong children also look for stones that have markings and colorings corresponding to recognized cattle markings. They then chip these stones to indicate special horn shapes and, as with real cattle, these toy cattle are given names, and the young children compose their first love songs, not to a living thing, but to a small white stone. They grow up and spend their entire lives surrounded by the essence of beauty, goodness, and godliness.

CHAPTER 3

Thou makest the Nile in the Nether World,
Thou Bringest it at thy desire, to preserve the people alive.
O lord of them all, when feebleness is in them,
O lord of every house, who risest for them,
O sun of day, the fear of every distant land,
Thou makest (also) their life.
Thou hast set a Nile in Heaven,
That it may fall for them,
Making floods upon the mountains, like the great sea;
And watering their fields among their towns.

How excellent are thy designs, O lord of eternity!
The Nile in heaven is for strangers,
And for the cattle of every land, that go upon their feet;
But the Nile, it cometh from the Nether World for Egypt.

(Praise of Aton by King Ikhnaton and
Queen Nefernefruaton
from Breasted, James Henry: *A History of Egypt*
Bantam Classic 1964, p. 315)

RIVER VALLEY

TERMS SUCH AS "the birth of civilization" generally go together with others like "the cradle of the Nile," "the Fertile Crescent," "the Indus Valley," and so forth. This juxtaposition, connecting civilization with river valleys, proceeds from a woolly ethnocentricism that measures "progress" by the process that has led to the present form of culture known to the Western world as "Western civilization." The fact that our present "civilization" is on the brink of a cataclysmic disaster, and that these former civilizations, or high cultures, only remain today as crumbling ruins, whereas the lesser cultures of the "noncivilized" world continue to thrive, is seldom dwelled upon. In glorifying these ruins as we do, we are glorifying disaster, and anticipating the day when all that will be left of our own "civilization" will be ruins.

Civilization and Primitive Society

This bears directly on our understanding of what has happened and not happened in Africa. It is often argued that the ancient civilizations, though subject to rot and decay, nonetheless all made great contributions to the world, and that these contributions remain, as tangible as the ruins of their origins. Among the contributions cited are the wheel, writing, mathematics, astronomy, and so forth. The absence of these elements is held to be the mark of a "primitive" society, which is also supposed to lack the finer points of culture as music, poetry, painting, sculpture, and other characteristics reserved to civilization, except in their crudest form. Recently there has been a fashion in "primitive art," but note that it is still kept firmly in its place by calling it "primitive."

Now, there is an element of truth in all this, for river valleys throughout the world have, under certain circumstances, produced similar forms of social development. Some of these riverine cultures independently arrived at the same inventions; in other cases they readily adopted new elements that diffused their way. It is true that our Western civilization, in its present form, rests on such basic inventions as the wheel and writing, and that without them it could never have achieved that form. The converse is also true, namely that "primitive" societies not possessing these inventions can never achieve the same form of civilization until they either invent them for themselves or at least accept and adopt them, which, rather nicely, quite a few steadfastly refuse to do. All that is unquestionable; what is very much in question is whether or not this makes one form superior to another, and as long as we regard African traditional societies as "primitive, therefore inferior," we cannot begin to understand them, let alone learn from them.

To beg the question for a moment, it might be helpful to

look at the matter as one merely of magnification. The mathematical problem of what is the sum of two oranges when added to two other oranges is basically the same as that posed by two million apples added to two million other apples. The application of the results will vary enormously, but the only basic difference is one of magnification. So, when human beings come together to live in association with each other, they face certain basic problems, which remain the same regardless of the form or size of society. If there is to be any regard for order (as for mathematical exactitude), there can be only one answer that is valid. Two and two make four, whether in hundreds or millions, apples or atoms. Human beings in association either survive or perish, and the basic problem is simply one of survival. Even add some of the refinements, such as comfort, leisure, health, and so on, and when all the debits and credits are balanced, "primitive society" seems to compare favorably with Western versions of civilization. And when we consider the vital ingredient (given the necessities of food and shelter) of human relationships, civilization lags disastrously behind.

Africa is so diverse that on that single continent you can find most of the environmental possibilities that the earth allows to man anywhere; yet whether hunter, herder, or farmer, an African has much in common with all those who share the continent as well as with men elsewhere. Nevertheless, the uniqueness of *how* people live is strongly related to *where* they live. This is true not only in terms of their economy, but also equally in patterns of residence, kinship, and age grouping (among others), which did not occur spontaneously but emerged from the interrelationships among people and where they lived.

In looking at the African river valleys we can see different ways in which the inherent challenges offered by that particular kind of environment have been met. The responses of people to the Nile, Niger, Zambezi and Congo point to the significant fact that "civilization" develops only when it is forced to, almost as if with reluctance. When population pressure is exerted within an inadequate environment, the result is either disaster or civilization—which might yet prove to be an even greater disaster. This happened along the Nile; it tended to happen along the Niger; both were areas of population expansion and limited resources. The Congo and Zambezi, though offering the same potential for economic exploitation and political expansion, produced somewhat different results, due to the inequality of other factors that enabled the residents of those valleys to survive without having to accept "civilization." Here we shall look briefly at only one African riverine context—the Nile.

The Nile

The history of Egypt has always been connected with the Nile. Originally this was a swift-flowing river running through a land more humid than the Egypt of today. The land supported wildlife including big game such as elephant and hippopotamus, and from earliest times bands of hunters roamed throughout the region, not confined to the riverbanks, as the population is today.

These hunters were joined by others who practiced some farming, and who began to form more settled communities along the Nile and around nearby lakes, as early as the fifth millennium B.C. The distinctive hunting culture began to give way, and villages like Merimdeh set the pattern for a new way of life. Farming techniques improved, irrigation was introduced, and food surplus became a fact of life. Life was enriched not only in terms of material goods, but also in terms of structure. Political divisions, or *nomes*, were formed, and by the late predynastic era, firm foundations were laid for the great civilization that was to follow.

ANCIENT EGYPT Food surplus was the basis of ancient Egypt, making all sorts of things possible that had not been possible before, but at the same time making certain demands. The irrigation system alone called for a strong central administration, and when this weakened for any reason, the whole economy was in danger of collapsing. After 1000 B.C. Egypt began to disintegrate and succumb to foreign domina-

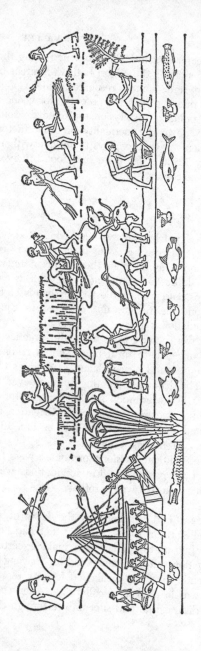

Figure 7. Reconstructed scene from various Egyptian tomb paintings showing the vital importance of riverine agriculture in ancient Egypt.

tion. The Romans in particular were ruthless in their exploitation of the land, and Egypt has never fully recovered from the impoverishment it suffered at Roman hands. Under Turkish rule it became the center of the Islamic world, and enjoyed a new prosperity derived from trade, but all the time the gap between the size of its population and its ability to produce enough food was growing. Today Egypt is faced with a problem just the reverse of that of ancient Egypt: an agricultural economy that is hopelessly inadequate to supply the needs of a rapidly growing population. Great steps have been taken by modernization of the irrigation system, land reclamation, and industrialization, but the population growth outstrips every economic gain that is made.

In the early days the Nile River Valley was much more fertile than it is today, reduced as it now is to a tiny strip frequently less than a mile wide and giving way abruptly to barren desert sand. Both the destiny and distribution of the population, even after farming replaced hunting, were different. Prehistoric settlements such as Merimdeh multiplied, and settled life spread up the valley from the delta, but for a long time people hunted and farmed simultaneously.

Population growth and progress in technology marked the predynastic period. The gradual compression of the population and its increasingly sedentary nature led to the growth in the complexity and nature of the social organization. There was a gradual shift from the uncentralized and fluid tribal form of life to elaborate chieftainships resting on a variety of local religious beliefs and social customs. It was in this kind of setting, still essentially African, that pharaonic Egypt arose. The fertile Nile River Valley, hemmed in by desert, gave birth to an African civilization.

Even the religious elaboration that so characterizes pharaonic Egypt had its beginnings in predynastic times. From the graves of that period we can see development from the earlier, prehistoric burials where a few material possessions were placed in the grave, to the typical predynastic burial where the many funerary objects placed with the dead suggest elaboration of a religious belief in future life. In late predynastic times we can tell from different graves that there had also been considerable growth in a social hierarchy, for certain classes of people were then buried with more wealth and in more formal tombs than others. This is far more sophisticated than the burials of the early Merimdeh farmers, where the dead were buried between the dwellings, in the old flexed position, unaccompanied by any wealth or possessions. Such forms of burial, however, suggest by their emphasis on the proximity of the dead to the living that there might have been a notion of ancestral spirits.

Important to the unification of Egypt was the navigability of the Nile and the happy circumstance that while the current flows from south to north, the winds blow from north to south. In predynastic times, as we can see from the painted pottery, reed boats were already common. Trade flourished and spread up and down the Nile, over the desert to the Red Sea and Sinai and to the western Sudan. Egyptians imported copper, lead, silver, malachite, lapis lazuli, ivory, flint, and fine stone. They augmented cereal cultivation, which they may have imported from Asia, with horticulture; their flax growing flourished. Towns arose and became the traditional centers of local districts. Representations painted on pottery vessels of boats with animal or other symbols indicate local beliefs and traditions, including totemic clans indigenous to the districts. Conflicts between allied districts, especially those of the delta (Lower Egypt)and the valley proper (Upper Egypt) mark the end of the predynastic period. The unification brought by the victory of Upper Egypt over Lower Egypt heralds the beginning of dynastic, or pharaonic, Egypt. Like other civilizations, it arose out of war.

The agricultural surplus on which dynastic Egypt rested supported a great number of specialized nonfarming groups, such as the priesthood, administration, and various classes of skilled and unskilled laborers. Craftsmen working in fine stone, precious metals, ivory, and other materials made Egypt famous not only for its monuments but also as a center of manufacture. As the natural resources in metal and wood were depleted, Egyptians exploited international sources and developed trade with the Mediterranean. As a result, for many centuries dynastic Egypt was the paramount power along the Nile, the Red Sea, and the eastern Mediterranean basin. The Egyptians of that day recognized the source of their prosperity and thought of the Nile as the center of the world. They addressed the God Hapy, sacred to the Nile, as:

"Father of the Gods . . . who nourishes, feeds and finds provender for the whole of Egypt . . ."

The great river so vital in their everyday life was becoming equally central in their religious belief.

During the summer months the Nile flooded over the valley floor and deposited silt brought from the South. In this way it refertilized and moistened the soil each year. The winter months were the busiest for Egyptian farmers; they plowed with the help of oxen, sowed seed, and covered it with a wooden hoe, all lengthy and tedious tasks. As the crops grew, water was needed, so they raised it by hand from the low river; this lasted until the spring harvest. Later on, the *shaduf* was introduced and facilitated the raising of water no matter how low the river level. The shaduf continues to be a major factor in contemporary Egypt. The farmers bred cattle and fowl; they geared their vineyards, orchards, and truck gardens to the same annual cycle. The vital timing of this cycle was emphasized by an accompanying cycle of ritual. Fishing with a weighted line or hook was both a source of subsistence and a leisure pastime.

Today we focus on the magnificence of ancient Egypt and overlook the fact that the splendor derived from the skill of a professional class of artisans, who formed privileged groups and lived apart, especially those employed in preparing the royal tombs. Their skills were frequently handed down from father to son, and the classes became hereditary. The great stone monuments that still stand testify to a skill that is not matched by any of today's craftsmen. Masons and carpenters were so well versed in mathematics that their errors over even the largest distances can be measured in fractions of inches. Others specialized in pottery, weaving, metal working, or as embalmers. The workers were not all slaves, as is sometimes asserted. Those employed in the building of the monuments had rations of food and clothing supplied by the administration, and workers were known to strike when the government was slow in providing these rations.

The bulk of the people lived in villages and paid an annual tax in kind to the government. By far the most important activity of the year was agriculture, but during the annual inundation, when work in the fields was minimal and transport was facilitated through the flooded land, numbers of people were gathered together to work on special projects such as building temples or royal tombs. At other times of the year navigation and irrigation canals had to be cut or maintained, and a class of laborers was always kept for such tasks. Such workers were fed as well as paid a stipend, and conditions of employment were clearly stated. Slavery did not develop until the New Kingdom, and even then it was not as harsh as that later practiced in the Americas.

Specialization and economic surplus made Egypt a byword for luxury in the ancient world. Luxuriousness and wealth characterized the domestic life of the upper classes and, to some extent, the middle or artisan classes. By the end of the Old Kingdom a hereditary nobility had grown up from the system of passing on the office of *nomarch* from father to son, and their estates resembled miniature royal courts. The large estate typified dynastic Egypt. It was self-sufficient economically, and the land owner employed local peasants to whom he supplied seed and draft animals, and who returned a portion of all their produce in the form of taxes. He appointed local headmen to supervise the village organization. The peasantry were to some extent protected against abuse because of the very real need of the nobility for the workers. Tomb paintings give us many details of daily life on these estates, both leisure activities such as singing and dancing and making music, hunting or boating, and everyday activities such as grinding flour, baking bread, pressing wine, brewing beer, spinning cotton, and weaving linen.

Not only the King and nobles owned such estates, the temples also became rich land-owning communities, with stewards to oversee the work, and scribes to keep records. Many estates reached such a state of independence, economically and administratively, that during the course of Egypt's history both priests and nobles were able to challenge the King's power.

In the villages the male lineage elder was the source of authority. Marriage was monogamous (except for the royal family), and while property was inherited from either the father, mother, or both, office was always descended, ideally, from father to son. The Pharaoh was deified, and he and his wife, and to a lesser extent the rest of his family, stood outside the social hierarchy that became a dominant feature of the state. The court, however, consisted of both a landed and an office-holding nobility. The priesthood, though a separate class, had noble status. Below the nobles came the artisans, followed by the bulk of the populace, the commoners. Social mobility was the rule rather than the exception, however, and many commoners rose to key posts during Egypt's long history.

Women in Egypt were respected and often held positions of influence. The wife of a wealthy man was mistress of his estate and as such joined with him in overseeing its many varied economic activities. Several professions were open to women. If well-born, they could belong to a special order of the priesthood, or serve in temples in a minor order as singers and musicians. They were midwives, and professional mourners and dancers at funerals. Women of the peasant class worked in the fields with the men, and skilled women assisted in the manufacture of textiles.

The state that developed in this way required a strong central government to function properly. Power was vested in the monarchy, which controlled the entire governmental hierarchy. Irrigation and the tilling of the land came under undisputed and undisrupted organization, and the farm economy throve. Conversely, the moment the political authority was challenged, the economy suffered. The complexities of the government were such that the King had to delegate much of his authority: There was little opportunity for despotism. By the Old Kingdom, the office of the vizier was particularly important as the chief administrator for secular affairs. His messengers traveled throughout the country, carrying his orders to the local administrators and reporting back. Treasurers, scribes, generals, engineers, and others all held important posts and acted in the King's name. Competence was a virtue and overrode class distinction. In the latter part of the Old Kingdom the increasingly independent economic and political power of the nobles and priests brought about the collapse of the central administration.

After the unification of Upper and Lower Egypt, the country was divided into political districts known by the Greek term *nomes*. Each was based on an earlier traditional grouping and was administered by a governor, or nomarch. Under the nomarch there was a regular bureaucratic system attending to the digging of canals, tax collecting, and other local business. The boundaries of the nomes were redrawn according to the development of irrigation, land reclamation, and agriculture, or to suit the political needs of the moment. In the Old Kingdom there were thirty-eight nomes; later there were forty-two.

During the Old Kingdom there was no large standing army; local governors raised contingents of men from the countryside whenever this was necessary. The few permanent forces were normally used for peaceful missions, public works, and trade. The New Kingdom was an era of professional soldiery, however, engaged in the acquisition of an empire. The soldiers, both local and foreign, were treated well and rewarded with booty and by being excused from taxation. They formed a privileged land-owning class, which became one of the pillars of the New Kingdom. At this time there were two sections to the army, which included many Africans from the South—an infantry and a more privileged group of charioteers, whose officers were given the rank of royal scribes. The infantry consisted largely of Egyptians who had made the army their career, and prisoners who had become mercenaries. At the end of the Eighteenth Dynasty, the already powerful army brought to the throne its own leaders, and from this time on, the Kings, as descendants of soldiers, distrusted both the nobles and their own troops.

The role of the priests is misunderstood. They were not spiritual leaders but "Servants of God." They were temple personnel whose duty it was to maintain the shrines in which the deity was thought to reside, and to perform the daily temple ritual. This ritual was considered a vital and essentially practical matter—essential to the preservation of universal order—and without which all things would return to chaos. The temple was a place of purity that the common people could not enter. But the priests were not separated from the community as a whole. After his nine-month-long tour of duty in the temple, the priest returned to his village to live for three months as an ordinary citizen. His most important obligation was to maintain physical purity by personal cleanliness, so that the rituals would be effective. To this effect he was subject to a number of taboos, differing according to whichever God he served. He was in many ways just another form of specialist, and the temple was merely his place of work; religion was a practical matter. But the ancient texts also contain many passages emphasizing the high moral ideal to which the Servants of God were expected to aspire.

The temple personnel fell into several categories. The administrators were in charge of all the economic organization of the sanctuaries, controlling the estates, collecting the revenues, providing for altars and priests, and negotiating with other temples and with the royal administration. The clergy were divided into two groups, "the Servants of God" who performed the ritual, and the "purifiers" who carried out more menial tasks and were often only chaplains. On the fringe of the hierarchy were the scribes, who copied temple texts and read them at ceremonies, and who were also specialists in such subjects as astronomy, astrology, and medicine. The temples also employed musicians, but they were not members of the priesthood. "The First Prophet" was the most important member of any priesthood and frequently played an active part in politics. At the end of the New Kingdom the "First Prophet of Amun" became Pharaoh and established a dynasty of priest-kings. Priestly offices were often hereditary, but a man could become a priest by co-option, by buying his office, or by royal favor. The King used the latter method to control the often alarming power of the priesthood. In the New Kingdom the priesthood also exerted influence in the selection of the dead King's successor through the medium of oracles.

Closely associated with the priesthood, the scribes were important as a class since they were the men who effectively ran the country. They were trained from early youth to take part in the administration, and military scribes controlled the army. Many government departments and the royal palace had their own schools, which became centers of priestly learning. The scribes' workshops attached to temples were known as "Houses of Light." The scribes formed another powerful and privileged class exempt from taxation. The hieroglyphics in which they wrote evolved from simple picture writing and combined ideographic and syllabic elements to produce their characteristic form.

Ancient Egyptian religion fused many ideas, traditions, and beliefs, some of them contradictory. All, however, were part of the fundamental concept that the universe was filled with the supernatural and the divine, and that man was a part of the universe and had a role to play in it. The land itself was at the heart of the religion, and the role of the local gods was to ensure the fertility of the land and the general well-being of life. These gods were symbolized by familiar animals, such as the hippopotamus, the lion, the vulture, and the ibis, whose peculiar characteristics of size, strength, and aspect embodied features of the divine power. Egypt's chief gods were linked with animals or birds, which in real life deserved care and respect as embodiments of the divine, good or bad. In each town the local god was incarnate in an animal that was protected by taboo, and the slaughtering of such an animal could provoke fighting between one province and another, so vital to unity was the sanctity of the symbol. Sometimes such an animal was enthroned in the temple, as was the Apis bull at Memphis. They were mummified and buried in special cemeteries or tombs, and innumerable statuettes of animals and birds were made for use as votive offerings to the gods. The ibis was Thoth, god of learning; the Apis bull was Ptah and later Osiris, lord of the dead; the ram was Amun of Thebes, who rose to the position of supreme god by the Middle Kingdom; the falcon was Horus, protector of the King.

Despite the multiplicity of cults, however, religion served not only to satisfy man's personal questions about the nature of life, and afford him a sense of security, it also supported the social order and brought a measure of unity at the national level, just as it did through local cults at the local level. Certain beliefs were universal, and vital to the social order was the universal belief, from the Fifth Dynasty onward, that the Pharaoh was a sun god, the source of light and life throughout the land. This belief contributed directly to the power held and exercised by the central government under the Pharaoh, and hence to the stability and prosperity of Egypt.

The concept of kingship in Egypt went through three major changes in emphasis. At the dawn of history, Egypt's Kings were chiefs whose patron deities gave them certain powers that brought success in cultivation and in war. In the Old Kingdom the office of kingship became wholly sacred, and the person of the King was considered as a living incarnation of the sun god Ra. Later, the Kings of the Middle and New Kingdoms, while still retaining divine attributes, were thoroughly secular in much of their daily life, their activities and responsibilities, and to some extent were more like the early warrior chiefs than the divine Kings of the Old Kingdom.

At his most powerful, the King filled both religious and secular roles. He was heir to the gods, to whom he offered filial worship, while at the same time he was their incarnation. He was the chief priest of all the sanctuaries and head of all sections of the administration (chief justice, head of the army, and so forth). The priests and generals and other officials were only royal substitutes. Therefore, the whole nation was concerned about the King's health and equated it with the health of the universe. As a King grew old, after some thirty years of reign, the *heb-sed* festival was held to allow him to renew his vital force and to ensure his return after the death of his aging body. Although chaos threatened the universe with the death of a King, his return in a new, younger, and healthier body gave new life to the original creation and re-established the equilibrium of nature.

The King's divine nature implied that he had to be perfect in every respect: invincible in battle, all-knowing, a just administrator, perfect even in health. Any weakness was taken as a sign that his body was unfit for his divine role and he could be ousted. His divine status did not even protect him completely against witchcraft. We have a record of Seti II calling upon magicians to defend him from a curse. As with other African divine kingships, while the King is invested with seemingly unlimited power by the belief in his divinity, he is also compelled by the same belief to be the most perfect of all possible beings.

Egyptians believed that one was judged by the gods and rewarded according to one's merits. This belief permeated their religion and contributed to an all-pervasive morality, influencing later religions such as Judaism and Christianity. In the Osiris cult the soul wandered on an underworld journey until after its judgment and acquittal, when the dead man occupied a plot on the Osiris estate and resumed his earthly activities of plowing, sowing, harvesting, and hunting. To ensure his safety in these wanderings, and acquittal after judgment, the dead man was provided with magical incantations, spells and hymns that are known to us as the text *The Book of the Dead*.

The elaborate funerary beliefs and practices so characteristic of ancient Egypt were devised originally for the King, and found their theological justification in his divine nature. It was a belief that functioned for the benefit of the peasants also, for without continuity of kingship all would perish, but in the course of time both belief and practice became adopted in a modified manner by even the peasants. The increase in the use of magical and ritual devices that could overcome the hazards of afterlife accompanied this expansion of the original concept and led to a breakdown of the earlier lofty moral ideals.

Only the rich and noble were buried in the sumptuous manner we associate with ancient Egypt. Not only were the initial costs enormous, but also endowments had to be made to ensure the preservation of the tomb and to prevent its violation by robbers. Embalming ensured the preservation of the body for the afterlife, for without a body the soul could not come to rest, and man could not continue to survive in his normal earthly manner beyond the grave. Death was seen as the gate to the hereafter. The dependable yearly cycle of life and the secure feeling born of geographic isolation gave the Egyptians an optimistic view of the world, and we have a dramatic, vital picture of this ancient ideal in the royal tombs.

Embalming took seventy days, when accompanied by the correct ritual, and was the most expansive feature of the funerary rites. When the body was ready for burial professional mourners, usually women, wailed in honor of the dead. The bier was then placed on a sled drawn by oxen or on a boat if proceeding by river, followed by the cortege, until the tomb was reached. For royalty and nobility in the days of Thebes, this meant crossing from the east bank of the river—the land of the living—to the west bank—the land of the dead—for burial in the barren mountain valleys there. When the tomb was reached the body was placed upright, and rites were celebrated such as the "Opening of the Mouth" to restore the soul that had fled at death. After lamentations by the relatives, the mummy was carried into the tomb and placed in its sarcophagus.

Inside, the tomb walls were elaborately painted with scenes of daily life, so that the dead man would feel at home on awaking. The various chambers were filled with objects he had known when living, and with wealth and food to sustain him on his onward journey. Models were used in large numbers and *shawabtis*, or statuettes of "servants." The models and statuettes were animated by magical incantations to serve the deceased after death.

With the decay of morality and an increasing belief in protective magic, the royal and noble tombs, which were effectively vast treasure houses, became the prey of robbers. In later times elaborate precautions had to be taken, for desecration of a tomb meant final death for the occupant. Pits were dug, entrances blocked, false passages built, but in nearly every case to no avail. The wall paintings alone, however, are a treasure in themselves—one of the most dramatic and poignant historical documents known to mankind.

Much of what was ancient Egypt thrives in other parts of Africa today. We can see it in objects of daily use, such as clothing, ornamentation, toys, furniture, and household utensils, as well as in social organization, particularly divine kingship.

CONTEMPORARY VILLAGE EGYPT In contemporary Egypt, much of the similarity to the past in the peasant organization stems from continued dependence on the annual inundations of the Nile prior to the construction of major dams and mechanical irrigation systems. The level of technology has not greatly changed, and many of the agricultural implements in use today resemble those pictured in the tombs of dynastic Egypt. The shaduf remains a prime means of raising water, and though other irrigation techniques have been added, they still call for close co-operation among fellow villagers, leading to some similarity between the political as well as the economic life of modern and ancient Egypt.

The major difference is the tremendous scarcity of arable land in relation to the present population, resulting in a few major urban, industrial centers. But apart from these, the population is still divided into a series of largely autonomous villages strung along the Nile, and each village is held together by the sheer necessity for mutual co-operation. The shaduf, for instance, is about the only irrigation implement of major importance that is individually owned, and even then, when the river is at its lowest, several shaduf may be needed working at different levels to raise the water up to field level. The *tambur*, Archimedes screw, a later but still ancient invention, is rarely owned individually, but is more frequently purchased by two or three villages, for their use as well as for hiring out to others. Its use, however, is limited to work on a smaller scale than the shaduf. Another invention still widely used is the *sakya*, "Persian wheel," of which there are several varieties. All are commonly owned, and there may be only one to a village, since it is capable of handling so much work with so little manpower. A horizontal wheel is drawn continuously by draft animals, water buffalo, or oxen, and through an interlocking gear turns a vertical wheel that scoops up water either in pots or in scoops that form the outer circumference of the wheel and release it into a canal at a higher level, from where it is distributed to all the fields. Deep well water can be similarly continuously circulated with a minimum of human labor by using a trip device on hide buckets raised and lowered by draft animals. When the full bucket reaches the mouth of the well, a trip rope automatically releases its contents into the canal, and the animals feeling the change in weight, if well-trained, retrace their steps up the ramp until the bucket is refilled and once again drawn to the surface. Even with water pumped mechanically from a government pumphouse, the basic organization remains little altered. Irrigation still has to take place on a regular schedule, since the canals are high for only a specified period of time.*

The main cash crop is cotton, and the main subsistence crop is corn, with secondary crops of wheat and clover. In some villages rice is a major crop calling for special irrigation techniques. Vegetable growing is a specialized affair; people do not attempt to grow a few for their own use on their land. Specialization continues to characterize village Egypt just as it did in ancient times. Apart from cash and subsistence crops, which are grown by everyone, almost all else is specialized. Most villages have their own carpenters, masons, and basketry makers, while the more important ones have metalworkers and jewelers, and the most important ones have a potter. Some villages are built on the pottery industry, supplying their wares over long distances up and down the Nile. There is a specialist in almost every area of human need. Even for a simple need such as sewing, the villager goes to a specialized seamstress. Different villages acquire renown for proficiency in certain crafts and the exchange of goods among villages, in markets, has long been a means by which the otherwise limited political horizons of the peasant

* See Chapter 5, "Desert," for illustrations of various water-raising techniques.

people are enlarged. Women do the marketing, which gives them an important role in village economy.

In prerevolution Egypt each village came under the control of a headman, frequently autocratic, who nominally represented his village to a remote central government. There was also a reconciliation committee made up of leading men in the village. In the absence of the headman, or *Omda*, the committee ruled; at other times it advised the Omda and assisted in the fair adjustment of internal disputes. The leaders were wealthy, successful men who had to be dignified and take an interest in the welfare of the community. Ideally, a committee member or an Omda should do his best to prevent a dispute from ever reaching the committee by using his powers of persuasion to effect a reconciliation.

The office of Omda was abolished following the overthrow of the monarchy, but before the revolution the Omda had considerable powers, as did his counterpart in ancient Egypt. He had the right to put villagers to work on roads or other projects of communal importance, and by law everyone was compelled to contribute time in communal labor. People riding donkeys would dismount if they passed the Omda while he was on foot so that they would not be higher than he; when the Omda entered a room, everyone stood until he gave permission for them to sit; and nobody could walk away from the Omda by turning his back, but had to back away while still facing their superior.

Even in recent prerevolutionary times it was useless to complain to the police about any decision of the Omda, for although the police represented the central government, the Omda held the power. As in ancient Egypt, however, that power was subject to a number of checks and restraints that prevented much abuse.

Magicians in the marketplace sold charms and potions that were used to work against the will of the Omda, or to bypass the Omda and committee by securing a favorable end to a dispute before it reached the formal hearing. Magical protection was thus frequently thought to be as effective as political protection, and in many ways the magician served to offset the power of the headman.

Religious authority has also continued to modify the power of village leaders. Today Islam establishes a moral code of behavior, which the leaders are expected to exemplify. A highly religious man, particularly one who has made the pilgrimage to Mecca, is accorded honor equal to that accorded the Omda in many respects. The mosque is a symbol of the central nature of religion in village life, and their religion is one of the major preoccupations of even the simplest villagers. They are faithful to the strict discipline enjoined by the Scriptures, attend the mosque regularly, and adhere to the periodical summonses to prayer that punctuate the day at regular intervals. The children also participate, fasting when their parents fast, feasting when they feast, and spending their evenings in Koranic recitation.

Another feature of religious life in Egypt that reminds one of ancient times is a form of ancestor worship in which shrines are maintained in honor of saintly persons who are buried there. Most villages have such a shrine, and apart from periodic festivals commemorating the saint's life, reminding the villagers of his virtues and powers, devotees may visit the shrine privately to secure his assistance and blessing. The notion of a suprahuman power is still very much alive, counterbalancing the political power of the headman.

But the ultimate power is still in the river itself, and it is only by controlling the river that a central government can control the independent spirited villages. In ancient times that control was sought through ritual practice; today it is still sought, but through technology, and for the people of the land that does not carry the same weight.

CHAPTER 4

> My heart is all happy,
> My heart takes wing in singing,
> Under the trees of the forest,
> The forest our dwelling and our mother. (Pygmy)

FOREST

IRONICALLY many Africans today are ashamed of those who still adhere to the old way of life, particularly those who do not dress in Western style (or who do not dress at all) and who do not take part in modern economic and political life. They have begun to judge their own people by the non-African standards just described, in terms of a purely Western concept of progress. To understand a people or a culture we *must*, if only temporarily, shed that concept.

The Beginnings of Forest Cultivation

In the dense equatorial forest that stretches down the west coast and over halfway across the continent at the equator, traditional ways of life still thrive, and people who live outside the forest regard its inhabitants with a mixture of scorn and respect, as backward and primitive and somehow dangerous. Even within the forest this is so; the most recent inhabitants are farmers who were forced into the forest from the grasslands a few hundred years ago, and they regard the people they found there, the Pygmy hunters, with respect they try to conceal as scorn. In the Ituri Forest of north-eastern Zaïre, the village farmers offer first fruits from their plantations to the very people they pretend to look down upon, and accredit them with supernatural powers. It is the same throughout the world: People who live in forests, or in isolation, or as hermits, are frequently suspect of being in league with the supernatural. And so they are, in a way, for they are living necessarily close to nature, in league with it rather than hostile to it, making do with what it has to offer. This is the source of their power and of the respect with which they are regarded, perhaps arising from envy. For them nature offers all the security they need in terms of food, shelter, and warmth—man's most basic needs. Instead of de-voting additional time and energy to acquiring a surplus, which in their forest they could easily do, the Pygmy hunters of the Ituri make do with a perfectly comfortable and ade-quate minimum and devote the rest of their time to the art of living. This does not mean that they hunt for a few hours and then sing and dance for the rest of the day. To live well, to live at peace with one's neighbor, with one's family, requires time and effort just as much as do the more basic ac-tivities of food getting, building shelters, and making the nec-essary material artifacts. To live well requires that man should not only live with his neighbors but also should know and understand them and share the same *basic* view of life. If there is no time for socialization, if it is all taken up in the effort to amass a larger and larger surplus, then man lives in ignorance of his neighbor, and society becomes a mere con-glomeration of individuals, each seeking his own good. By maintaining economic need at a minimum, the hun-ter/gatherers are free to spend most of each day in sociali-zation. This may take the form of visiting neighboring bands, passing the time at their own family hearths, playing with children, discussing any problems that face them as individ-uals or as a group, telling legends that express their charter for life so that the young learn the moral code while it is being constantly reiterated for the benefit of adults as well. Above all, there is time for discussion and for everyone to participate in it, and in this way not only is the general course of daily activity mapped out, but also the more serious disputes are either avoided or settled peaceably, and major disruption is averted.

This is not to say that life is idyllic, for proper discussion can be as taxing as any physical effort. But there is a sense of wholeness and security that seems idyllic to many who live more fragmented lives, beset with a multiplicity of problems and in less security. There is the security, for the hunters, that comes from living *with* nature instead of trying to control and dominate it, and from the knowledge that given a minimum of effort, the basic needs of life will always be satisfied. And there is considerable security that derives from having the time and opportunity for a form of socialization that enables all problems and disputes to be talked to a peaceful conclusion.

The African learned this lesson early, for as the population expanded and life became more complex and more demanding, as man began to oppose the environment by cultivation and domestication, the people retained a closeness to the environment and preserved a sense of balance, allowing for a social system that was truly social because they had time to socialize and were expected to do so. Traditionally there are no legal codes or strictly penal systems by which a man can be speedily and summarily judged and punished because of a given action. Each action has to be assessed in context, and the co-operation of all those concerned is demanded. The focus is on justice rather than on law, and this demands the co-operation of society as a whole. It is not relegated to a few specialists and a jury of twelve, who probably know nothing of the people involved and who are not in any way personally concerned.

We may have seemed to have wandered rather far from a description of forest life, but that is not so. This is all the essence of life for those essentially forest people, the Pygmy hunters of the Ituri, and it is an essence that has been preserved throughout African life elsewhere, however much the outer form of life may have changed. Those who have migrated into the forest from outside came as farmers, with a farming technology and social organization, and they found the forest a harsh and hostile environment. It has to be attacked and cut down, burned, for them to survive, and having done all this, they still had to work long and hot days to keep the forest from growing back. No wonder they regard the Mbuti hunters with a mixture of fear and respect, watching them live with apparent ease in the cool shade of a forest that seems to protect them just as it seems to oppose the farmers. So the farmers form a ritual association with the hunters and put themselves in accord with nature in this way, using the hunters as a medium. That is, although they are opposing the forest, opposing nature, by cutting it down for their plantations, they still recognize its pre-eminence and submit to it. The forest, its fauna and flora, forms the center of their ideological and conceptual systems, even though their attitude to it is one of hostility rather than one of devotion. Throughout the forest, the farmers have developed elaborate beliefs in witchcraft and sorcery, while the hunters have no such beliefs of their own.

The same environment, then, can offer contrasting possibilities for human occupation. If man submits to it entirely, as do the Pygmies, then there is no need for a complex technology; in fact, a complex technology would destroy the almost perfect balance of nature by making it possible, almost inevitable, for the hunters to overkill and overgather. As it is, the hunters form an integral part of the total ecological picture, and their hunting is part of the mechanism by which nature maintains the balance. The Mbuti are, for instance, the prime mechanism by which the otherwise destructive elephant population is kept in check. They themselves are kept in check by a birth control system that, while quite unconscious, nonetheless rises naturally from their way of life and its demands and from their recognition of the demands of nature. Infantile mortality, sickness, and disease, although relatively slight among the Mbuti hunters, also function for them, as for other African populations, as means of keeping the living population in balance, giving it a better chance of living a healthy and productive life.

The submissive adaptation of the Mbuti hunters means that, for once, the environment really is largely determinant, whereas at a more complex level of technology it is merely influential. At their level of technology the hunters are compelled to live in small hunting bands and to live a nomadic life, never settling in one place for longer than a month. This obviously has profound repercussions in the total social system that is only paralleled where others, like the Bushmen hunters, have made a similarly submissive adaptation although to a totally different, desert environment.

The topography itself bears direct relationships to the political systems to be found in the forest. Where communication is difficult, social organization is small-scale, and the way to political aggrandizement is through federation rather than centralization. Only on the Guinea coast, in the western woodlands, and on the southern fringes of the forest did great kingdoms and empires arise. Even the greatest, however, invariably acknowledged (if only by some small ritual act) the even greater power of the forest, the spirits they believed to inhabit it, and held in curious respect the tiny, shy, and gentle inhabitants who continued to live their old way in its depths.

Man has lived in the forested areas of Central and West Africa for at least fifty thousand years, but until recently little archaeological investigation has taken place to uncover their history. Stone Age man lived by hunting and gathering, and as the Pygmies demonstrate, these activities may be carried on as successfully in a forest as in open grassland. In the Middle Stone Age period, stone tools were developed in the forest whose function may be compared to modern woodworking tools—adzes, gouges, chisels, planes, and scrapers as well as axes, knife blades, and projectile points. This is known as the Lupemban culture. During the Late Stone Age in the Congo, the people of a culture referred to as the *facies neolithique* may have used stone hoes to cultivate indigenous African plants as early as 4000 B.C., and similar stone hoes found in Ghana may represent the westernmost extension of a hoe vegeculture that began at this time in the Congo. In West Africa cultivation also began as early as 4000 B.C., but in the grasslands north of the forest, only spreading into the forest in the early centuries B.C. The spread of cultivation was not a simple question of its being introduced at one point and diffused from there; there were several or even many independent beginnings, at different technological levels and in different forms and with different types of crops, and there was much interchange in all directions. However, it was not until the early centuries A.D. when Asian food plants, well suited to the forest environment, were introduced that a population explosion took place in the forest, causing the migration of Bantu-speaking people into the southern half of the continent. They acquired the knowledge of making iron spears, knives, and hoes, which helped them gain technological ascendancy over stone-using peoples who continued to live relatively undisturbed in the area for many centuries more.

It is not easy to establish continuity between these early inhabitants of the forest and those who live there today. Even the connection between the Pygmies and the early forest hunting cultures cannot be demonstrated, though probably the Pygmies have always lived in the forest and there *is* a connection. Even when we come to peoples of the Iron Age we cannot be sure, though occasionally there is a startling continuity in terms of material culture or art form. One good example was found among a group of burial goods found with a skull in a cave near the Bushimai River, in the area of Bakwanga, in the Kasai district of the Congo. One of the pots found there, made in the form of a woman holding a bowl, is similar in remarkable detail to wooden carvings made by the Luba of Katanga, although this type of pottery is unknown to the Luba of today. The burial may then have been of an early Luba cultivator, living before the founding of the first Luba empire in the early sixteenth century.

The history of the crops grown in the forested areas of Central and West Africa is an interesting one. The cultivation of root crops probably developed naturally out of the gathering activities of Stone Age hunters, and it is therefore difficult to fix a date for its beginnings, since the presence of digging stick weights or hoes in the archaeological record does not necessarily indicate that the people who used them were dependent on cultivation as a way of life; they may have used them for gathering wild plants. Hunters may have always practiced a limited form of vegeculture, since for survival they must have been conservationists; even today, with no more than a digging stick, they can be seen replanting or even transplanting to ensure continued production in a given area. Vegeculture on a more intensive scale may have started in the Congo as early as 4000 B.C. Cereal crop cultivation is a more complicated task whose origins have stimulated much controversy. The early introduction of Asian food plants encouraged the Bantu expansion into Central Africa; and the introduction of American plants, introduced by the Portuguese just before the sixteenth century A.D., profoundly affected the life style of the forest Africans, who today subsist largely on crops that once were foreign to Africa.

The following table shows something of the complexity of the picture:

Staples of the Forest Zone

Indigenous African plants
    Guinea yams (*Dioscorea cayenensis, D. rotundata*)
    Rice (*Oryza blaberrima*)
    Fonio (*Digitaria exilis*)
    Oil palm (*Elaeis gunieensis*)
    Kola palm (*Cola acuminata, C. nitida*)
    Raffia palm (*Raffia ruffia*)

Introduced from Asia
    Between 200 B.C. and A.D. 1500:
    Water yam (*Dioscorea alata*)
    Banana (*Musa sapientum*
    Cocoyam (*Colocasia esculenta*)

    Probably not until the fifteenth century:
    Chinese yam (*Dioscorea esculenta*)
    Rice (*Oryza sativa*)

Introduced from the Americas
    Maize (*Zea mays*)
    Manioc (*Manihot manihot*)

A Forest People: the Mbuti Hunters

The Mbuti Pygmies of the Ituri Forest represent in its purest form the entire Pygmy population of the equatorial forest. Their small stature, reaching a maximum of 4½ feet, and their light skin color help them to move about easily and unobtrusively in the shade of the forest. Their economy requires a minimal technology, still at the Stone Age level, though they no longer use stone tools; they domesticate neither plants nor animals, and they live in intimate sympathy with their forest world rather than by trying to control it. The gathering of mushrooms, roots, fruits, berries, and nuts provides the bulk of the diet, but it is largely the hunt that shapes the form of Mbuti society. No band can grow in size beyond what the local game and vegetable supplies can feed, and to prevent excessive consumption in any one area, the bands must move from camp to camp, never staying more than a month in one place.

For those who hunt primarily with bow and arrow, the size of a band can drop to as few as three families, though during the honey season the archers come together in bands of maximal size for the communal beat hunt, the *begbe*. But for the net hunters, to the west, a minimum of seven families is needed, and preferably at least double that. If a band swells to over thirty, however, it subdivides; there is ample room in the Ituri for the population of some thirty-five thousand Mbuti, and each band claims its own territory, with a large no-man's-land in the center of the forest.

The family is the basic unit, but in a sense the entire band considers itself as a single family. A band does not necessarily consist of families related to each other in one line or another, and in any case the composition changes with every monthly move; but there is great affection and intimacy among all its members. The co-operative nature of their economy accentuates the family feeling. When a net hunt starts out, families may set off together, but they soon divide into informal age groups. There are no rigid age sets as among the cattle herders of the grasslands, but age is none-

Figure 8. The Mbuti Pygmies of the Ituri Forest typify both physical and sociological adaptation. Their small stature (four feet, six inches maximum) and light skin color help them to move about easily and unnoticed. The family starts out together on a hunt, but soon splits into age groups. The men set up the nets and stand guard with their spears. Youths stand farther back to shoot any game that escapes the men with bows and arrows, or catch it with their bare hands.

theless a vital structural principle. The men set up the nets and stand guard with spears; youths stand farther back to shoot any game that escapes the nets with bows and arrows, or else they try to catch it by hand. Women and children form an opposing semicircle at some distance and drive the game into the nets. Then when the game is caught, the women put it in the baskets they carry on their backs, held by tumplines around their foreheads, and often after two such casts of the nets the band has more than enough for the day, and everyone returns to camp. All the time men, women, and children gather as they go, and often by noon every family is cooking a large meal over an open fire in front of its small leaf hut.

Youths and older men may wander off on their own to shoot birds and monkeys with poisoned arrows, or they may stay back in camp when the hunt goes off, to help look after the small children left behind. But even the young children have a role to play, for whether they go on the hunt or not, before it can set off they must light a special fire at the base of a tree so that the smoke will attract the attention of the forest god and bring success to the hunt. Some say it is an act of propitiation for despoiling the forest of its game and vegetation, for the Pygmies have an ambivalent attitude toward hunting. It fills them with excitement and pleasure, and they enjoy meat as a food, but somehow they consider it wrong to take life, since God created the animals of the forest just as he created the people of the forest. At this early age, then, the young children are introduced to this concept of dependence on and trust in their forest world, made to feel a part of it, and given the responsibility of lighting the fire of propitiation, without which the hunt cannot succeed.

The high degree of mobility of the Pygmies leads to a fluid social organization. Since the bands are continuously changing in size and composition, there can be no chiefs or individual leaders, for they would as likely move somewhere else as anyone, leaving the band without a leader; and since the Mbuti have no lineage system, there would be no easy way of dividing the leadership when the bands split up, as they do once every year, into smaller elements. Age again plays a vital role in government, with all but the children having an essential part to play. Even the children play an informal role, for one of the major means of correcting misbehavior (laziness, quarreling, selfishness) is not by any penal system, for the Pygmies have none, but rather by ridicule. At this the young children excel. For them it is a game, but nonetheless they learn the values of adult life in this way, and quickly shame any wrongdoer into better behavior. Youths have a large measure of control over adult life, expressing their pleasure or displeasure with the band as a whole, rather than with individuals, during the religious *molimo* festival. The adults, as hunters, have prime say over economic matters, but that is all. The elders act as arbitrators, and make decisions on major issues facing the band, and the old are highly respected by all.

The intimacy in which the Mbuti Pygmies live with their forest world is seen in the fact that they personalize it and refer to it as their father and mother, for they say it provides them with all they need, with life itself. They adapt to this world instead of trying to control it, and this leads to a profound difference between their attitude to the forest and that of other forest dwellers such as fishers and cultivators. Mbuti technology is simple, and this makes the hunters look poor in the eyes of others who possess more material wealth, but such wealth to the nomadic Mbuti would be cumbersome and disadvantageous, and their technology is more than adequate for their needs. They do not burden themselves unduly with excess of any kind. They make clothing out of bark hammered with a piece of elephant tusk and use skin and vine to make slings in which to carry babies, quivers for arrows, bags, ornaments, and decorations, and twine for use in the manufacture of hunting nets. The Mbuti make houses and furniture within a matter of minutes from saplings and leaves, which they cut with the metal machetes and knives they get from the village peoples around them. Some say they still would be able to use stone axes if they had no metal, but this is doubtful, and the Pygmies are slowly entering the Iron Age.

An example of the bounty of the forest can be seen in one tree, *kasuku,* that provides resin, when taken from the top for cooking, and when taken from the bottom for lighting the houses at night. The Mbuti use the same resin to seal the bark containers they make for carrying and storing honey. A child learns early in life how to exploit the world around him without destroying it, taking only what is needed for the moment. His education consists of imitation of adult life. His toys are miniature replicas of adult possessions, and a boy soon learns to use his miniature bow to shoot slow-moving and small animals, just as a girl wanders off and fills her tiny basket with mushrooms and nuts. At the same time these children are helping in the economy by providing some of their own food, though for them it is still a game.

The sense of dependence and belonging taught from birth unites the Pygmies in common opposition to neighboring tribes of forest farmers, who have a very different attitude to the forest, thinking of it as a hostile place they have to cut down in order to survive. With these farmers the Pygmies trade, not because the hunters need to for economic reasons, but to prevent the farmers from encroaching into their forest world in search of meat and other forest products that the villages always need. The villagers fear the forest people just as they fear the forest itself, and constantly guard themselves against both with medicine and ritual. The only medicine the hunters know is "sympathetic"—charms made of forest vine decorated with tiny pieces of forest woods, or a paste made from the ashes of a forest fire mixed with the fat of some game and put into the horn of an antelope and then smeared on the body for success in the hunt. The thought behind such charms is that by bringing the Mbuti individual into even closer physical contact with the forest, the needs of the Mbtui will automatically be taken care of. The religious rather than "magical" nature of such acts is best seen when a mother wraps her newborn baby in a special piece of bark cloth (even though she herself may now have access to the softer trade cloth) and decorates the infant with amulets of vines and leaves and bits of wood, and bathes it in a special forest water, which it stores itself in certain enormous vines. Through this physical contact she offers the child to the forest and places it under the forest's protection. In times of trouble, the Mbuti say, all they have to do is sing their sacred molimo songs to "awaken the forest" and draw its attention to the plight of its children; then all will be well. It is a rich but simple faith, in stark contrast to the beliefs and practices of their neighbors.

Forest Cultivators

Of all forest cultivators, the Bira have made the least successful adjustment to their environment. They live in perpetual fear of the forest, a hostile world that at every turn thwarts their efforts to survive. They cut it down to plant their crops, but it immediately begins to grow back up. The first year's crop is always poor, for the field has still not been properly cleared nor the soil cultivated. The second year's crop is the best; if they get a third year's harvest, it will be the last from that field, for the soil is then exhausted, and the field looks dry and barren. Yet within weeks of abandoning it, the lush forest vegetation has taken over and sprung up from soil that refused life to the crops of the villagers. Excessive rains and hailstorms and gale winds can destroy a field, and either a troop of baboons or a single elephant can do the same within an hour. The villagers work hard; they plant various crops including plantains, manioc, beans, peanuts, and dry rice, but they never harvest more than a fraction. They blame the hardship of their life on the forest, which to them is the home of the Pygmies and evil forest spirits, both of which are dangerous and both of which need propitiation.

These villagers entered the forest between two hundred and four hundred years ago, fleeing from pressure in the grasslands. The ramifications of the dislocation of these cultivators to an alien environment can be seen in their maladaptation to the forest. They broke up into small independent groups, each allied to a band of Mbuti that helped them as guides in the forest; after much fighting among them they settled down in tiny village enclaves, each autonomous and mutually suspicious of each other. They resorted to ritual protection (including witchcraft and sorcery) for defense against neighbors, forest spirits, and Mbuti alike, and continue today to fight against the world around them, unable to believe that the forest can be good and kind. For the Pygmies the forest is an unalterable fact, recognized and accepted as such; but the Bira, in their effort to possess the soil,

1. The Semliki Valley, running between Lakes Edward and Albert, beneath the Ruwenzori, supports a rich traditional fishing economy. The game that abounds on both banks, however, is now protected from hunting by the existence of national parks.

2. The Shilluk still maintain a divine kingship, where the king is the living symbol of the unity of the people rather than a political power. His homestead, shown here, is more elaborate than that of a commoner, and is carefully separated; yet in both respects it is close enough (in appearance and distance) for him to be recognized as human as well as divine.

3. *Riverine*. This one man, singlehanded, felled and trimmed the tree and with a locally forged adz carved it out into a great fishing canoe. It took the whole village, however, to drag it the mile that lay between it and the river, and in a sense it thus became at least partially village property, and was used for the benefit of the entire community.

4. A corner of an Mbuti hunting camp. A newcomer prepares phrynium leaves for covering the frame of her hut while a friend takes some to prepare a leak in *hers*. Life in such camps is totally communal, members regarding each other and referring to each other as members of a single family; but because of the intimacy tensions build up, and the monthly displacement from one camp site to another is as necessary for political purposes as it is for economic reasons.

5. Mbuti values are maintained, or adapted as necessary, through song and dance, but perhaps most of all through the telling of legends, which can become powerful social comment in the hands of skilled raconteurs, like Cephu.

6. Traditional festivals are highly adaptive, and incorporate elements of colonialism and nationalism, thus publicly supplying a sense of continuity and a sense of the security that so marked the traditional forms of life.

7. The use of masks, such as this "firespitter," is seen by some as having today become secular rather than sacred, but although the function may be different, and may be seen more as a form of entertainment than of instruction, it none the less relates the increasingly secular present to the sacred past.

8. Ik teen-age girls: youth alone, among the Ik, has a good chance of survival. The weak have already died off, and "old age" will not set in until the twenties. Girls such as these have the additional attribute of bodies that can be sold in what we would call prostitution but what for them is merely another survival technique.

9. Ik women have just about the same survival chance as Ik men, but the effort to survive is costly, and old age sets in, as here, about the age of twenty-five.

separate themselves from the forest, and it is this separation that constitutes the organizing principles of fear, conflict, and struggle between the tenacious Bira and the powerful forest.

Another form of adaptation can be seen far to the southwest at the forest's edge, among the Lele. Their villages are mainly in the grassland but on the edge of the forest, and the Lele face the difficulty of having to relate to both worlds. Like the Bira, they fear and respect the forest, and this attitude permeates their segmented tribal organization and semiautonomous villages. Fear of witchcraft and sorcery dominates their lives, and the danger of sorcery acts as a major factor in their social organization, for protection against it is thought to be found by gathering large numbers of kin to live together. Ritual propitiation of the forest is vital, and the Lele respond unlike the Bira, by segmenting forest and nonforest activities, reserving forest activities for the men. Division of labor according to sex thus becomes an organizational principle for the Lele.

While the villages of the Lele are built around a central dancing square, demonstrating considerable cohesion despite internal divisions within the village, the villages of the Bira are divided into small family nuclei, each with its own meeting place. Different from both in many respects, but still responding strongly to the forest environment, are the Kwele, on the far side of the Congo River. While the Kwele have faced similar difficulties, they have made a more successful and practical adaptation. Also an intrusive people, they have adapted to the forest while at the same time retaining their identity as cultivators. They hunt, fish, and forage for wild forest products and make maximal use of the environment to enhance their material comfort, maintaining relatively little contact with neighboring indigenous hunters, and not relying on them for essentials, as do the Ituri villagers.

The Kwele also cultivate plantains and manioc, as well as peanuts and peppers and maize. The two imported staples are nonseasonal, flourish readily in the forest, and are recognized as the major source of prosperity of the forest Bantu. While the work of cutting and clearing, which is done by men, is arduous, it does not call for much co-operation. Like most other forest cultivators, the Kwele are divided into a number of autonomous villages. Forced to move their fields every year or two, they have a social system well suited to a high degree of mobility, and their simple but highly artistic material culture reflects an essentially practical approach to life.

Cultivation in the forest is only possible under certain conditions; an iron technology is indispensable for cutting down trees and clearing the undergrowth. The iron that makes this work possible is used, in some symbolic form, as bridewealth, signifying the vital role of women in tending the fields their husbands have cleared. But the fields yield crops no more than two or three years in succession, and each time the laborious work of cutting and clearing has to be undertaken again. Then, as the fields move farther away, the village moves. Always the village plan reveals the same divided nature of Kwele society, groups of kin clustering together, each with its own "guardhouse" used as a meeting place. At each end of the rectangular village are more guardhouses, remnants of the old days when it was necessary to defend the village against attack by aggressive and feuding neighbors. But the Kwele did not let this necessity for defensiveness, nor the difficulties of their farming economy, lead them to evolve elaborate methods of ritual protection. A practical people, they have sought practical answers to their problems, and have come to satisfactory ritual terms with their world. Their system of belief shows little of the neuroses exhibited by cultivators like the Bira and the Lele, who have made less satisfactory adaptations to their environments. However, of the few rituals of the Kwele associated with subsistence, that connected with net-hunting is of major importance. The same is true of the Lele, whose communal hunt in the forest is primarily ritual in nature; this is reminiscent of the Bira, who attach so much ritual danger and impurity to the forest that they rely on Mbuti to get for them whatever they need, and remain isolated in their tiny cleared enclaves.

Successful as they were, either the Kwele kept their success within limits or it was kept within limits for them, and they did not develop any system of social stratification, although there were certain status positions that could be acquired. With regard to wealth, they were more concerned with material comfort than with the amassment of wealth for its own sake. Dr. Leon Siroto, from whom all these Kwele data are drawn, suggests that "prestige" is more of a Kwele concept than "wealth." In all of this they are different from the Bira and closer to the Mangbetu, another forest people.

Originating near Lake Tchad, the Mangbetu arrived on the northern edge of the forest a thousand years ago, but did not penetrate far, settling just within the forest fringe. Within the past few hundred years, they have been forced deeper into the forest by another powerful savanna people, the Azande. The Mangbetu had already developed a centralized state, which they were able to retain partly because their section of the forest favored the growth of the oil palm. This is a crop that continues to grow, year after year, without impoverishing the soil, and consequently the Mangbetu agricultural economy did not require constant shifting. Of all forest cultivators they are among the most sedentary. Other than the oil palm, the Mangbetu cultivate the banana, potatoes, manioc, peanuts, squash, and tobacco. They also gather wild sesame and eleusine. As with the other forest cultivators, the only fertilizer they use is wood ash, and the only water is the natural rainfall, which is evenly distributed throughout the year.

Mangbetu men and women also hunt, and from this advantageous economic position they do not have to assert control over the indigenous Mbuti, as do the Bira and others. The Mangbetu have an easy relationship with the Mbuti based on the barter of plantation goods for forest products that the Pygmies forage daily. But one of the most evident differences between the Mangbetu and other forest farmers is a high degree of specialization and a high level of craftsmanship. Due to the importance of iron for forest cultivation, and its consequent ritual importance, smithing is everywhere a specialized profession that accords its practitioners special status, whether they make ritual goods or common hoe blades. This is as true with the Bira as with the Mangbetu. But the Mangbetu also have skilled ivory workers (always men, as with smithing), and this depends on the existence and nature of the royal court. Men occasionally sculpt in clay, but most of the pottery is done by women. Both sexes work basketry in many forms for many uses, from beer strainers to hats. Men are the sole woodworkers, and the enormous wealth of material culture in wood alone testifies to the social distance between the Mangbetu and other forest cultivators. Even the size of some of the artifacts seems excessive, like wooden food bowls several feet in diameter, enormous benches, and chairs and stools. The degree of artistic ornamentation is much higher than elsewhere in the region.

This all relates to the presence of a King who is located in a central village, living in an elaborate palace surrounded by a court formed of his wives and ministers. The territory is divided into provinces within which each village, usually rather small in size, comes under the authority of lesser chiefs. The villages are not fortified, but are clusters of permanent houses set in valleys and along rivers to get the benefit of fertile land and for ease of communication. A good system of paths enhances communications, and the people block small streams with stones and earth to make dry fords wherever possible. Drums and trumpets provide a rapid signaling system by which complex messages can be sent from one end of the kingdom to another within a matter of minutes.

The villages have central meeting places. Isolation houses for the sick are off in the forest, perhaps indicating some remaining attitude of ritual respect for the forest. If anything the Mangbetu are even more practical minded than the Kwele, for while Kwele craftsmanship indicates a concern with both religious belief and temporal power, Mangbetu craftsmen work almost entirely within the framework of a secular court art. Ivory in particular is reserved for the royal court and nobility, and its possession is an indication of rank. Indeed, much of the ivory carving is in the form of miniature replicas of household furniture and utensils, and as such serves no useful purpose other than as an emblem of position in the social hierarchy.

Forest Fishers

Fishing, like cultivation, is in a sense a hostile act, and it brings its own psychological responses to the environment as well as its own form of social organization. African rivers, lakes, swamps, and coastal waters teem with fish, and although few communities devote themselves exclusively to fishing, it provides a vital source of protein for a third of the population. Unlike the cultivators, African fishermen have developed a wide variety of ingenious techniques for exploiting their economy to its fullest. Some techniques depend on the nature of the water, others upon its seasonal rise and fall and the spawning of the fish. Fishing societies organize themselves so as best to meet these demands and opportunities. The techniques used are often reflected in the social and political organization of the people: Some techniques call for considerable co-operation, others allow for individual enterprise.

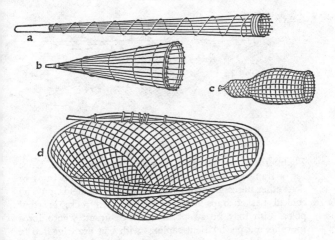

Figure 9. Three types of basket traps: a) Ndaka. b) Ndaka. c) Mangbetu. d) A Rega fishing net.

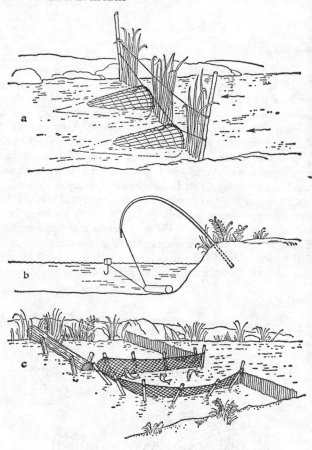

Figure 10. Most fishing in Africa is done with traps. Once set, a trap can be left while the owner sets more traps or does other necessary work such as tending his fields. a) The conical basket traps are wedged between rocks or stout poles. Fish may be swept in by the current, whose force prevents escape. b) Bent saplings with bait are triggered to fling the fish out of the water and onto the bank. c) Sometimes a small forest river is dammed, leaving a gap in the canoe-shaped cage into which fish are swept.

Intoxicants may be used to bring fish to the surface in such large numbers that men, women, and children must all combine to retrieve them before they recover and swim away. Dams similarly gather large numbers of fish, and while women and children scoop up the smaller fish with hand nets and baskets, the men harpoon the others. Sometimes fish are isolated in pools by reed mats and are fattened up with snails, manioc peel, and bananas until ready for eating. Communal fishing techniques bring in larger rewards, often creating a surplus for trade, but individual techniques free women for tending the fields and plantations that are usually also a part of the economic scene. Fishing villages vary enormously in size and organization; within a few miles of each other are the vast communal fishing grounds of the Wagenya fishers on the Congo River and the isolated dwellings of solitary fishermen living with their families in remote fishing camps where they have dammed some forest stream. Each brings its own rewards and its own problems.

Most fishing is done with traps, for once set, a trap can be left while the owner sets more or does other necessary work. Commonest are the conical basket traps that are wedged between rocks or stout poles and anchored by stones or vines. The current sweeps in fish and prevents their escape. In still water, fish are lured by bait into ingenious "no return" traps. Other automatic devices include underwater cages with doors, released when the bait is taken, and bent saplings with bait triggered to fling the fish out of the river and onto the bank. Sometimes a small forest river is dammed, leaving a gap through which fish are swept into a canoe-shaped cage. The owner collects his haul twice daily, walking out to the cage on poles so that he does not even have to get his feet wet. Techniques like this allow surplus fish to be dried and traded at leisure, to supply other needs. Individual families can then specialize in fishing as a full-time occupation, living independently of their kinsmen. This well suits the isolationist nature of some forest peoples like the Ndaka, neighbors of the Bira.

Rivers may be swept by nets supported by cork floats and weighted with sinkers, and the fish may either be brought in with the nets or speared or shot with bow and arrow in the water. Fishing by torchlight at night is done in the same way, the flares attracting the fish to men who lie in wait with spears. The valuable metal heads are often attached to the shafts with a length of cord so that if the fish breaks loose with the head embedded, it can easily be detected by the floating shafts and retrieved. Sometimes separate floats are used for the same purpose. But the use of harpoon or spear does not lend itself to individual effort; it is most productive in communal fishing. If conducted from a large canoe it is a technique that can be used against such heavy game as hippopotamus, the wounded animal towing the canoe behind him as he tries to escape, until he tires himself out. Harpoon and spear fishing, unlike trapping, bring the men of a village together, sometimes uniting several villages, while leaving the women free to care for the land.

In the same way that hunters think killing game is a dangerous act, for it is an offense against whatever power created the game, and that farmers surround their hostile acts of breaking the soil and reaping the harvest with propitiatory ritual, so the fishermen guard themselves against ill effects from their theft from the waters. At an annual festival, the coastal Ijaw of Nigeria, who depend to a large extent on fishing, don fishlike masks and carry regalia resembling fishing spears and paddles and go in procession to a shrine where offerings are made to ancestral spirits. Ritual prohibitions are often associated with fishing, though formal manifestations such as the Ijaw festival are more rare. It is common in areas where fish are scarce for there to be prohibitions against fishing; in this case they are often said to be a form of snake and will not be eaten even in times of hunger. In many other areas fish are associated with fertility and multiple birth, and pregnant women may be debarred from eating them, just as men are forbidden to have sexual intercourse while making or setting their traps. In these less formal ways, rather than in major religious festivals or cults, fishing ritual plays a valid and important role, reinforcing family and tribal values, uniting people otherwise widely dispersed in a single common act of belief.

Trade and Commerce

After the fifteenth century, the population migration from the North slowed down, and with the development of a stable forest agriculture, people began to agglomerate into larger political units. The Congo River basin is a massive complex of tribes of this order that have developed powerful states with complex kinship structures, side by side with less centralized but also powerful peoples. One such state grew into the great Kongo Empire, already in full flower when the Portuguese arrived in 1482. The contact proved fatal, however, for undermined by the desire for European goods, the Kongo resorted to selling their own people into slavery and finally fell to the Yaka, a much less organized neighboring tribe. The Yaka drove the Kuba peoples eastward, where they in turn founded a great empire based on riverine and overland trade, having first conquered the indigenous Kete. An exchange of goods and technology among these peoples led to an exchange of ideas and the weakening of divisive political and religious barriers.

South of the Kuba an even greater complex of empires arose, founded originally in the sixteenth century by the Songe, later taken over and developed by the Luba, who subsequently conquered the Lunda. To the north even the Chokwe and Pende were drawn into the imperial orbit. Riverine communication facilitated conquest just as it did trade, and the whole area is one full of cross-cultural influences. Despite this, tribal tradition is of such resilience that today the crafts of each people retain their distinctive styles while benefiting from this rich interaction.

During the sixteenth and seventeenth centuries, European trade routes, established throughout the Kongo Empire, converged in the area later known as Stanley Pool. From here the Kasai River formed a major artery in the exchange of goods between the coast and the interior. The tribes not directly under the influence of the Kongo, Kuba, or Luba, but in the vicinity of the river (such as the Teke), were drawn by this trade closer to one or other imperial center. Portuguese traders originally managed the caravan routes through the Kongo Kingdom, but before long, they entrusted them to Africans. Slavery became an essential part of the trade, for since there were no pack animals, goods that could not be taken by water had to be transported overland by human carriers. Once at the coast there was a ready market for the carriers themselves, for export to the Americas. This was the civilization the Portuguese brought to the Congo.

The overthrow of the Kongo Kingdom by the Yaka caused the European trade routes to move southward, into what became Portuguese Angola, outside the forest region. In the interior they were controlled by the Lunda Empire, which prevented the Portuguese from effecting a transcontinental route from Angola to Mozambique. The chief item of trade was ivory, with slaves as its inevitable corollary; beeswax and copper were also important. In addition, there was a lively trade going on between the Luba/Lunda empires and the Kuba, involving all kinds of locally manufactured goods. During the nineteenth century the importance of the transcontinental route waned with the drop in the demand for ivory, and with it waned the power of the Luba and Lunda. Arab slave traders managed to establish themselves in the interior with the help of the notorious explorer Henry Morton Stanley, on whose personal recommendation the Belgians appointed Tippu Tib, one of the most infamous of slavers, as first governor of what then they named Stanleyville, at the head of the navigable stretch of the Congo River directly in the center of the continent. The Arab slavers linked their headquarters on Madagascar with the Atlantic mouth of the Congo River, but with the abolition of slavery, they too lost their power. For a while rubber was an important export, but by the beginning of the twentieth century the days of long-distance overland or riverine trade were over. The once great empires broke up into their component parts, and colonial powers drew their artificial boundaries, sometimes linking traditional enemies at the same time that they divided traditional friends.

On a smaller scale, marketing had an equally vital role to

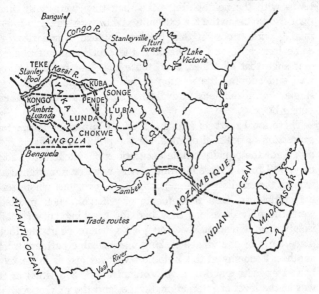

Figure 11. European trade routes, running throughout the Kongo Empire, converged in the area later called Stanley Pool. Caravan routes through the Kongo Kingdom were first managed by Portuguese traders. Slavery became essential: as no pack animals existed, goods not transportable by water had to be carried overland by humans. Once at the coast these carriers were quickly sold, for export to South America. Undermined by greed, the remarkably sophisticated Kongo took over both trade and slavery. The Arab slave traders later gained a foothold in the interior, linking their Madagascar base with the Atlantic at the Congo River mouth, but the abolition of slavery ended their power.

play in local political systems. In areas where tribes dispersed in a linear manner, as along a river or along the great slave route through the Ituri, adjacent tribes shared common markets and had an opportunity for an exchange of views there, so that tribesmen at one extremity were often on better terms with the neighboring tribe than they were with their own tribesmen at the far extremity, who were similarly inter-mixing with tribes on that border. Political boundaries be-came less rigid, and in the Ituri the process of interchange was such that all tribes, even those that had become Arab-ized and adopted the religion of Islam, became unified in a single central religious festival, the *nkumbi* initiation of their young boys.

These local markets also provided an important forum for expression of political opinion, for the public hearings of dis-putes, for the equally public accusations of witchcraft or sor-cery, and for the dissemination of any news of importance as well as the smallest item of gossip. In the regions where for-est cultivators lived in autonomous villages, such markets were the only occasions they had for breaking out of their isolation, and markets became places where courtship took place, boys of one village seeking marriageable partners from another. Economy at this humble level was just as intimately bound up with politics, family organization, and ritual as it was at the level of international trade, and the market served as such a powerful integrative force that in some of the new nations, where modern transport and trading methods and a cash economy have made many markets unnecessary, local governments are considering their reintroduction to prevent the loss of the vitality and all-encompassing character that was the nature of marketing societies.

Science and Belief

It is a widespread belief in traditional African societies that the world is permeated with a powerful force. It appears in stones and rocks and in all manner of inanimate or vegetable matter. It is also possessed in greater strength by animate beings, and is at its most powerful in the human form. This force can be trapped and utilized, for good or evil. What we might call magic, then, is science for the tribal African, for whether he is or is not mistaken in his belief, he acts in the belief that he is dealing with a scientific phenomenon. We should not discredit it; tribal doctors are well versed in effective herbal remedies, some of which are new to the Western world. Some of the preventative medicines we might scoff at, but in African experience they have proven effective, at least offering a sense of security. Some remedies we class as sympathetic because the appearance of the object, or the associated act, is similar to or is related to the end we wish to achieve. Thus rain medicine looks or sounds like rain falling, medicine for the prevention of theft looks aggressive, and protection against thunder and lightning is achieved by use of a vertical rod (much like lightning conductors: "It leads the danger away"). But whatever the appearance, all such medicines are considered to work by the nature of the force within them, without any spiritual intervention, through science and not through belief. To refer to them as magic is to misunderstand them and the attitudes associated with them.

Curing requires more "force" than preventing, as Western doctors know as well as traditional African doctors. Most medicines used in Africa involve living matter or represent (in the form of carvings or fetishes) animal or human life, the latter being the most powerful of all. Sometimes the various ingredients are combined, but still the resultant medicine or fetish is thought to have its own inherent power to work unassisted by supernatural intervention. Protection that requires particularly powerful force, such as the protection against household theft (including that most insidious form of domestic theft, adultery) or protection against the malformation of a fetus in the womb, calls for medicines of this higher, more curative order. The ailments that can be cured by this means are all physical ailments. Spiritual ailments that include social ailments demand a different kind of treatment, involving the use of *spiritual* force.

A central figure in any traditional African society is the diviner. He may also be the doctor, the priest, the chief, or all of them at once. All represent different aspects of the one essential need, the need for physical and social order. The term "witch doctor" is utterly inappropriate. The "doctor," as he should more properly be called, is there to cure. The diviner diagnoses the nature of the complaint, the doctor enforces the cure. First of all, however, there must be diagnosis, or divination. There are innumerable forms of divination, mostly involving actions and manipulations designed either to impress the gullible or to actually invoke spiritual assistance. Others may be "scientific" in that they are thought to rely on inherent qualities of objects (shells, stones, bits of wood) that always fall in certain patterns under certain circumstances. Sandals that can be listened to, however, imply the presence of spiritual beings who are talking to the diviner. A cupping horn when held in the diviner's hand sends him into a frenzy as he dances among the assembled villagers, and is thought to have the inherent quality of leading him to the culprit. A shrewd diviner, however, reads the eyes and actions of those gathered around him and can quickly detect fear and guilt.

The methods of diagnosis and treatment of symptoms usually associated with mental illness are also dealt with by the diviner and doctor. Many traditional African societies have a complex system of diagnostic categories not very different in content from those of Western psychiatry, and treatment varies from the dispensing of herbal medicines to something very much akin to individual and group psychotherapy.

The diviner is the center of all gossip, and if the problem brought to him is of a social nature, such as theft or adultery, he is likely to know the cause and be able to divine the culprit in a public hearing. If the complaint is of physical distress he will use his knowledge as a doctor, or recommend his client to such a one. If it is a minor complaint, he may recommend that his client go to the market and purchase the appropriate fetish, for protection or cure. If the complaint is more serious he then recommends that the doctor or a priest be called in, and when a situation moves beyond the possibility of scientific treatment and can only be handled by the priest, we enter the realm of belief.

The family itself is a spiritual entity, for the dead and the unborn are as much a part of it as the living in much of traditional African thought. In the same way that animals and humans have more "force" than inanimate objects, so spirits have more power than humans. A family may maintain a shrine to the ancestral spirits not only as a means of benevolent protection, but also as a means of securing specific aid on specific occasions. Such occasions generally involve the family as such; pregnancy, childbirth, sickness, adolescence, marriage, and death are all occasions on which the family spirits may be invoked. This cannot be done by anyone, but is usually in the hands of the head of the family, the senior member of the matriline or the patriline. Men perform some rituals, women others. Some rituals require the intercession of the local priest. Whatever the case, there is a clear division between the worlds of the natural and the supernatural, the material and the spiritual. This is not quite beyond the realm of science, for the people believe they are dealing with a force that, while spiritual, is still real and indisputable. The shrine figures indicate the difference in attitude; the preventative or curative fetish requires no manipulation by a ritual specialist—it is in itself powerful. This is not so with the ancestral figure. Even a fetish made in human form is different, and this difference is emphasized by incorporating in the carving powerful substances such as nail parings or human hair. An ancestral figure may be decorated with such charms; if so, they are incidental. The figure itself is not powerful; it has to be properly consecrated, and offerings have to be made according to ritual form to invoke the family spirits to inhabit the image and thus be accessible in times of need. These ancestral figures are not idols, nor are they worshiped. They are vehicles for spiritual power, and as such they are respected and treated with reverence.

It is only in times of the greatest crisis that the higher spirits are invoked, and this can only be done by a doctor who has been properly initiated and trained. Doctors of this high order are sometimes strangers to the community in which they work, so that they can be accused of no bias. Sometimes the office is hereditary, sometimes circumstantial. But it is only a properly qualified priest, living a carefully regulated life, who can invoke the most powerful spirits of all. The complaint can be either a physical or social disorder, the sickness or death of a great tribal leader, or the commis-

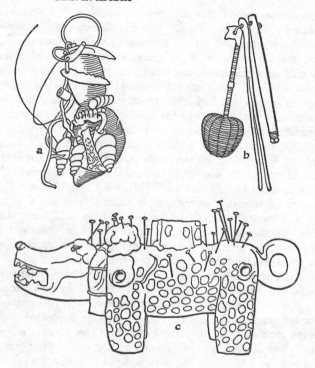

Figure 12. Many medicines used in Africa are represented in forms of carvings or fetishes. a) Medicine for protection against forest spirits. Mangbetu. b) Medicine rattle with tweezers and snuff holders. Mangbetu. c) Animal nail fetish for use in judicial procedure. The doctor/judge drives nails into the figure, and the guilty are automatically sought out and stricken. Kongo.

sion of a crime particularly heinous in the eyes of the tribal ancestors, such as incest. Or again it may be a crime by or against persons unknown, but the commission of which is plainly evidenced by a calamity such as drought or pestilence. In such extremes the doctor invokes the ancestral spirits, and calling on them to seek out and punish the culprit, whoever it might be, he may drive a nail into a fetish filled with the most powerful substance of all, known only to himself. This is thought to result in the sickness or death, often violent, of the culprit. Any guilty person, hearing that such a curse upon wrongdoers has been made, and believing in the efficacy of the curse, is likely to sicken of his own accord and even die of his fear and guilt. These special fetishes, sued for manipulating spirits to achieve goals of this kind, are guarded against falling into the wrong hands and against being used for antisocial purposes (sorcery) by the insertion of mirrors into the body of the fetish, so that any person attempting to use it for evil has the evil reflected back onto himself.

Only qualified specialists well versed in tribal lore and acting for the general good pass judgment of this kind. It has nothing to do with witchcraft. Witchcraft and sorcery both involve the use of supernatural force; but only the sorcerer uses it consciously and for antisocial purposes. The doctor uses it consciously for social purposes; the witch uses it unconsciously, usually for antisocial purposes.

Most often, witchcraft is conceived of as a substance in the body, lodged in the intestines or the stomach. When the host body, the witch, falls into a state of ritual impurity by committing some infraction against tribal custom, this substance becomes hot and activates itself. It either forces the body to perform antisocial acts, or it leaves the body by night, when the witch is sleeping and does its deeds by other means. A witch may be forced to go, in his body, and steal or set fire to someone's crops; or he may, while asleep, by his very impurity allow the substance to escape and bring sickness or bad dreams to others.

The witch then is not culpable for being a witch; he is considered as an unfortunate and sick person who has inherited an incurable malady. However, if he maintains ritual purity and undertakes certain additional and probably periodical purification rituals, he can keep his witchcraft substance inactive and continue to live his life as a full, respectable, useful, and honored member of society. He is only guilty if he fails to maintain his purity; the first time or two he will be adjudged of irresponsibility, but if he is found guilty again it may be said that he is deliberately, consciously manipulating this power and is guilty of the infamy of sorcery.

The manipulation of spirits does not necessarily imply, let alone constitute, religion, though religious belief is spiritual, and religious life in Africa centers on the belief in spirit. It is belief in spirit rather than belief in specific spirits that makes for religion, and the ultimate in the spiritual is the concept of godhead. While traditional African peoples acknowledge the existence of a supreme being, they think of him as remote and unapproachable, a creator who, having created, stands back and watches rather than participates. He is unknowable, but some believe that his intermediates are the ancestors. In this sense, involving a belief in God and a belief in some form of afterlife of a spiritual nature, Africa is well endowed with deeply spiritual religions that rise far above what we dismiss as magic and superstition, far above the mere manipulation of vital or spiritual force, and they represent: cunning, strength, swiftness, ferocity, and so forth. These spirits are not worshiped; they are respected and used. Worship is reserved for the ancestral spirits at the maximal extension of the lineage system, be it clan, tribe, or that offer each people a coherent system of beliefs that explain their world and answer their needs, that offer hope and encouragement and promise of an afterlife. It is a system that has roots in a deep spiritual conviction in the existence of a power greater than man.

Between this world of the living and the world of the unknowable Creator lies the world of spirits, and these spirits are, in varying degrees, approachable. Some are animal spirits that can convey something of the particular power nation. Craftsmen sometimes represent these spirits in the form of figurines or by a vacant throne or stool. In such a throne dwelt the spirit of the founding ancestor to whom all the living owed existence. His descendant, the living ruler of the people, might occupy the throne (though he was sometimes forbidden to actually sit on it), but he is no more than an

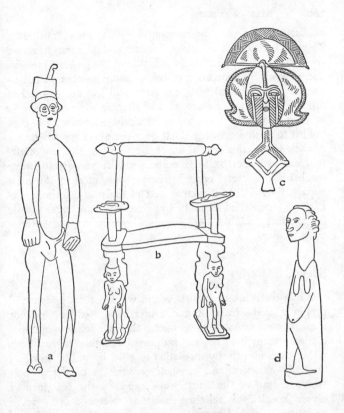

Figure 13. While many systems embraced a Creator God, few believed him directly approachable. Worship was only for ancestral spirits often represented by figurines and masks, or by a vacant throne or stool wherein dwelt the people's founding ancestor. a) Ancestral figure or *deble* of the Lo society. Senufo. b) Chief's chair. The human figures as legs and totemic birds for arms symbolize the pervasive presence of the invisible ancestral spirits. Senufo. c) Spirit mask. Kota. Guardian spirit, of wood covered with brass and ironfoil, used by placing above funerary basket containing ancestral skulls. d) *Nimba* fertility spirit. Baga.

official, the secular representative of spiritual authority. Though invisible, the spirits, human and animal, surround the living and see all they do. They have the power to punish and reward. By veneration of the ancestral spirits and adherence to the ancestral way, the good and just are assured of afterlife. The exact nature of that afterlife they do not pretend to know, nor are they particularly interested, for they hold it to be unknowable. That does not affect the religiosity of their belief, nor does it affect the fact that this essentially religious attitude to life is perhaps the supreme integrative mechanism of social order, often permeating even the most apparently trivial and secular acts of daily life, forming the basis of a powerful morality by which, by and large, people behave in a sociable way because they *want* to, not because they *have* to.

Sacred Societies

While there are specialists whom we can term priests and prophets, they are not found everywhere. Neither God nor the ancestors channel their power through solitary intermediaries except for special purposes. Religion is manifest, rather than by priestly mediation or even by public worship, by daily behavior and constant recognition of the all-pervasive nature of the spirit world, and by the existence of divers specialized religious societies better called sacred societies, though frequently called secret. The Yoruba of Nigeria have a highly developed and complex religious system within which operate many cults and societies. Sometimes the public is ignorant of the membership of these societies and of the details of the rituals they perform, but there is a general awareness of their existence and of the roles they play. The powerful *Ogboni* society, for example, plays a vital role in government and has in some cases adapted itself to modern conditions under which power has passed from the hands of the traditional Kings by becoming an effective instrument of contemporary local government. Other cults such as those of *Elegba, Shango,* and *Oshun* unite diverse groups of people in a series of interrelated common beliefs, all of which help to strengthen the governmental and moral systems. The existence of the cults alone is a check on the power of the political rulers, for it recognizes the existence of a superior spiritual power, and the loyalty of a cult member is often greater than that given his King. Whereas the King maintains political order, sacred societies maintain moral order and remind everyone that the King's authority derives from the spiritual realm, the ultimate source of all order. The King may have power, but it is an empty power unless reinforced by the higher spiritual authority of such societies. In extreme cases, if the Ogboni considered their King unfit to rule, they sent him a sign by which he knew that he must commit suicide or fear worse.

Figure 14. Left, mask of women's society. Senufo. Right, headdress worn during initiation of boys. Bambara.

Membership in sacred societies can only be acquired through initiation, which is given to those considered most fit. The initiations vary according to the function of the society, be it political, moral, jural, or economic, and while some test moral fiber, others test political ability, or knowledge of tribal lore. These initiations are followed by a period of training in which the desired qualities are further developed. Masks and figures serve as emblems of these societies and may indicate the rank or specific role of the holder. Through a complex symbolism with associated proverbs, they focus attention on the ultimate spiritual authority to which all men owe allegiance. Such societies often became the core of anticolonial resistance, for they resisted the abuses and crimes they found in colonial government just as they resisted any abuses they found in their own traditional form.

Initiation into a society unites new members in obligations toward each other. It creates new social horizons for its members, binding together people who might otherwise feel no special bond. It also places initiates under the power of the spirits, making them more apt to be stricken with disaster should they transgress the tribal law. In the case of occupational societies that act rather like trade guilds, initiation enforces what we might call fair-practice laws, ensuring quality of workmanship and mutual respect. The more specifically jural societies will be discussed in the section on western woodlands.

In the more complex Congo societies, such as that of the Rega in the East, where the people are ruled by a King, sacred societies are more like those in the western woodlands. The Rega are famous for their *Bwamé* society, which involves an elaborate hierarchical membership, each grade conferring specific duties and authority upon its members. Various emblems, all in ivory, indicate the grade of the holder. In the more segmentary societies the cults were far less formalized and existed for the more general purpose of maintaining social order rather than for a series of graded specific purposes. One of the more dramatic examples is the *anyota* leopard-man society of the Bali, in the Ituri Forest. Many other peoples take the leopard as a symbol of spiritual power

and either use charms of leopard teeth or skins to denote
membership or cult adherence, but there is no particular
unity to the many leopard societies scattered throughout the
continent; what is said for the anyota does not necessarily
apply elsewhere.

The anyota members are chosen from youths of out-
standing moral character. The act of initiation tests both this
and their physical strength and courage, and they emerge
scarred across the stomach as if they had been clawed by a
leopard. Thus they proclaim their membership openly and
proudly, as a high honor, and are known to be good men,
fair and just. But like the leopard they take as their symbol,
and with which they enter into a kind of mystical relationship, they must be strong and relentless and bringers of
death in pursuit of justice. They are the guardians of social

Figure 15. Nkumbi initiation (Zaïre). Wearing skin mask,
raffia armbands to represent mythical bird, and ankle rattle
to drive away evil spirits, initiator is painted with spots to
symbolize the sacred leopard. Dressed partly to frighten
noninitiates, he carries the bass stick of a portable xylophone called a *makata* and used only at initiations.

order, and their supreme function is in times of tribal crisis, such as when the tribe is rent by dissension over succession to the chieftainship. Any member of the society is then likely to fall into a trance, during a rite of identification, and actually "become" a leopard, exchanging his own personality for that of a leopard. As such he is a dangerous animal, and will not rest until he has killed and eaten. When he wakes up from his trance he may not know what he has done, for he will have divested himself of all his paraphernalia—the leopard skin that covered his body and face, the metal claws attached to his hands with which to rip the jugular vein of his victim, and the wooden stick whose end is carved so that it leaves an imprint all around the victim's corpse, like that of a leopard. But people know that the killing, often of one of their kin, has been done by one of their own, and the horror of the act together with the double horror of eating human flesh quickly compels them to resolve their differences and reunite, for they know the killings will continue until internal order is restored. This may seem like a drastic measure, but in a forest society such as that of the Bali, internal dissension was an invitation to annihilation in the old days when tribes were competing for land.

More common to these forest societies is a form of initiation often dismissed as a *rite de passage,* admitting a child into adulthood, but actually meaning a great deal more. It also initiates the child into a society every bit as sacred as the Bwamé and as political as the Ogboni or anyota, for it initiates them into an adulthood that itself is sacred. The *nkumbi* initiation does this for many of the tribes of the Ituri, and acts as the mainstay of society, without which social order would be unthinkable. It takes place every three years, taking boys between the ages of nine and twelve and circumcising them. The boy does not know what is going to happen, and the doctor dresses in a manner that is designed to frighten, but that at the same time symbolizes tribal totems —animals or birds that play a special role in the tribal mythology. The boys survive the shock of being carried off and the shock of the operation, which specialists perform with care and skill. Then follows a period of several months of schooling during which the boys gain strength and courage and become versed in the tribal lore that they will be expected to maintain as adults.

Many of the restrictions and ordeals they suffer during this time seem senseless, even cruel, to the outsider. But during those few short months the boys have much to learn, for they emerge as adults, with full adult responsibilities. This is another important feature of the nkumbi, and similar rites de passage—they publicly define the status of the individual, leaving no room for the doubt or ambiguity that exist in our more leisurely way of growing up. And while it is preparing the children for adult life, breaking them away from their individual families and introducing them to the wider family of clanship, even of tribe, it is achieving direct political goals for the society. It is at this time that different clans in these highly fragmented societies are forced to co-operate, breaking the otherwise autonomous isolation of each village. Each clan may have a specific role, as discovered by Towles,* and the correct performance of the ritual thus demands that at least once in every three years the clans come together in co-operative effort. Further, Towles found that this is a time when the political scene may shift, changing the locus of secular power by changing the locus of ritual authority, there being an element of competition among the various participating doctors for ascendancy during the nkumbi. The doctor who gains ascendancy over the others carries the weight of this prestige to his clan and to his kin, who for the next three years will have additional influence in village matters.

The initiation, then, is not only for the children's benefit, even at that given moment, it also allows for many other objectives to be achieved. While the children are being taught things they never knew before, the same things are reinforced for the men, for all adult men of the village are expected to take part in the teaching and singing and dancing. Throughout Africa dance is an intergral part of religious life and is used even on occasions that have a purely festive ap-

* Joseph A. Towles, field work undertaken under National Science Foundation grant No. 9536442 among the Bira and Ndaka of the Ituri, 1970–72.

pearance, to reinforce beliefs and values. The costumes may be symbolic, but they also serve to conceal the identity of the dancers, and rather like the mask, focus attention on the spiritual essence of the dance rather than the personality and skill of the dancer. In some cases the dancers have to be senior initiates, and in a special state of purity, for by donning the costume they invoke the presence of ancestral spirits. Secular dances, if they exist purely as secular dances, are probably hard to find in Africa. Even a dance of flirtation may be rich in symbolism, expressed at an unconscious level, but nonetheless present. Dance is yet another mechanism by

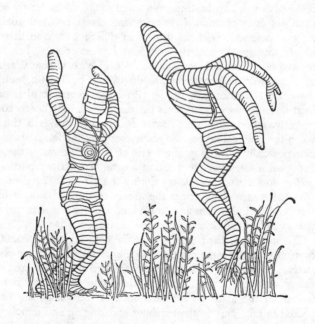

Figure 16. Dance and belief. As with masks, dance costumes may serve either to conceal the identity of the dancer or to symbolize a ritual change of role, as with these male and female initiation dancers. Cameroon.

which society is integrated as a whole and by which the all-
pervading presence of the spirit world, the world of the ancestors, is made felt.

Music

What is true of dance is also true of music, the role of
which goes far beyond mere entertainment, though even in
its most ritual forms it may be enjoyed by the participants.
One of the richest art forms on the continent, music is made
not only with the voice but also with an infinite variety of instruments. The instruments may be divided into four acoustic
classes: those in which the sound is made by a vibrating skin
(membranophone), a vibrating column of air (aerophone), a
vibrating string (chordophone), or a vibrating instrument itself, as with gongs, bells, etc. (idiophone). Every available
material is used—ivory, bamboo, wood, skin, metal gourds,
horn, vines, even stones—and African musical instruments
are examples not only of the African's determination to make
music but also of his genius for producing such a variety and
beauty with the simplest of tools and materials. Whatever
material was available to him, man in Africa made use of it
to make music, and we should not forget that he probably
started with the most basic instrument of all, the human
body. Still today he makes music with his whole body, dancing, stamping, and handclapping; and above all, singing.

Music, like religion, permeates the whole of life, and the
two are closely related. What seems to be pure entertainment
is often associated with specific social needs. Music and dancing often occur when the young meet each other. Parties set
out and sing and dance their way from one village to another
looking for marriageable partners. A dance may be held to
cement good relations with a neighboring village or tribe.
Significant events such as birth, initiation, marriage, and
death are commonly celebrated by music and dance that outwardly seems intended mainly to entertain.

Certain instruments appear only on nonritual occasions,
such as the *sanza*, or hand piano. But even it, rather like the

drum, may have a tiny pebble in it or a buzzer attached, to indicate that there is another, spiritual voice speaking with the instrument. Other instruments appear during work, and a special form of music is associated with work, reducing its tedium and effecting a necessary co-ordination in complex co-operative tasks. But music has a more direct link with economic life. Much of its origin may be due to activities inherently musical or rhythmic. The smith's pounding hammer exemplifies both music and rhythm, and he can be seen moving his bellows to create musical effects. Two or more women sharing a mortar touch their pestles in between their alternating and syncopated strokes to achieve an even more complex rhythm. Fishermen take the natural rhythm of their paddles and develop rhythmic and tonal variety by tapping or beating the sides of their canoes, perhaps to the accompaniment of song, or merely to signal up and down the river to other fishermen or back to their village. A cultivator chopping down trees to clear a field, a hunter listening to the uneven tinkle of the bell that tells him where his dog is, all live with music as they work. For the African, even the rhythm of walking is music and dance.

Music frequently plays a prominent role in the maintenance of law and order in African society. Sometimes plaintiffs sing their cases and the judgment is given in terms of whether he sang well, without referring to guilt or innocence. The idea there is to maintain order and perhaps reprimand a wrongdoer without branding him as a criminal, particularly if it is his first offense. The attendant ridicule on being judged a poor singer is usually sufficient punishment, and since the case is heard (and sung) in public, the ridicule is immediate and the offender is publicly revealed and must thereafter watch his step. In some places a tall rattle is used, shaped so that seeds at one end fall slowly through a series of bends and traps to the other end, to measure the time allotted for a man to speak in court. Far more important than punishment in African jural systems is prevention, and music is widely used, particularly in royal courts, as a means of perpetuating "the way of the ancestors" by singing of that way. Minstrels wander the countryside singing not only the news

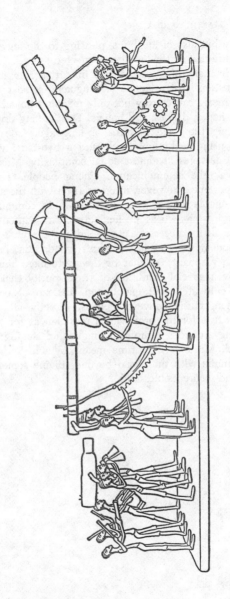

Figure 17. Dahomean representation of royal procession. Music was often used to attract the attention of subjects on festive occasions, and as an indicator of status and power.

of the day but also of all things pleasing to the ancestors, of the good life that all the living are expected to lead.

More than anything else, music in Africa is a means of communication. Just as much as language, some would say more so, music can convey not only meaning but also ideas, thoughts, hopes, desires, and beliefs. The "talking drum" can, by imitating the tonal patterns of language, "speak." The gong, by using a rhythmic code and a two-tonal variation, can send messages of almost equal complexity. Music helps in this way the communication among people. This is of minor importance, however, in comparison with the ability of music to enable man to speak with God. In communication with the ancestors, words are inadequate and without power. Music has all the necessary power, adding the vital force of the component parts of instruments (wood, skin, bone, the tusk of an elephant) to that of the performer, himself enhanced by a special condition of ritual purity that he has carefully cultivated and maintained. Instead of conveying words, then, music conveys feelings, directly and simply. This is as true for the professional musician as for the Pygmies sitting around a campfire at night and singing to their forest god. Music is the prime means by which the living may commune with the world beyond, divine something of its will, and secure its blessings.

CHAPTER 5

The day we die then the wind comes,
To wipe us out, the traces of our feet.
The wind creates dust which covers
The traces that were where we had walked.   (Bushman)

DESERT

IN the same way that the family serves as a model for wider
social relationships, so does the organization of man at the
simplest level of technology, that of the hunter/gatherer,
serve as a model in Africa for the more complex forms of social organization. The desert, superficially the most uncom-
promising environment of all, provides examples of both extremes of complexity and simplicity. In the Kalahari the
Bushmen roam in nomadic hunting bands, much as the Pygmies roam the forest. The technology of the Bushmen is minimal and their social organization is informal. Their adaptation to the desert is a submissive one: They accept what it
offers and adapt their life style accordingly. As with the Pygmies, there is an avoidance of individual leadership or any
form of centralized authority. Authority is dispersed throughout the band according to sex and age, each with its own
sphere of influence though without actual control. In this
way the band as a whole is *necessarily* a co-operative unit.
Any assertion of individual leadership would destroy this es-

sential co-operativeness which, in the marginal subsistence economy they practice, is their major source of security. Their sense of sociality is so great, in fact, that as a person becomes injured or ill while on the long trek from one water hole to another, he will voluntarily remain behind almost certainly to die, so that the others can go on unimpeded and reach the next water hole before being overcome by thirst. Water holes may be three days apart, and three days is the maximum that one can survive in the desert without water.

In the North African desert the Berber live a very different life, as camel herders and goat herders, with some seasonal

Figure 18. Often mountainous and rocky, rather than sandy, the desert may seem barren of ground cover but has patches of vegetation suitable for grazing sheep or goats. Grazing is soon exhausted, and Berber nomads such as the Ait 'Atta never stay in one place more than a few days as they exploit the limited resources south of the Atlas mountains. Camps are simple, temporary, and constantly guarded. Tea making and prayer (facing Mecca) are important rituals usually conducted while the camp is being set up.

mountain farming done by a caste of serfs. While the Berber spend some time each year in the mountains overlooking the desert immediately below, their world is that of the desert, over which they wander for the rest of the year in small familial bands with their herds in search of pasture and water. This dual form of existence, a form of transhumance, calls for a very special form of social organization that provides for order while fragmented and dispersed in their desert environment, and that will provide for order when in their highly concentrated mountain settlements. The situation is further complicated by population pressure on the land, and in the past by the threat of attack by neighbors and by the constant menace of the Arab invaders.

Organization for warfare has become a paramount necessity, yet the Berber have managed to keep a remarkably flexible social system that allows for this while at the same time corresponding efficiently to the simpler model we have seen established in hunting societies, forest and desert. Their kinship system is much more complex, to allow for the much greater complexity of interpersonal and intergroup relations, but instead of centralizing authority into a hereditary kingship (using the "father" model), as was done elsewhere, the Berber developed an electoral system, whereby authority is dispersed and rotated through various segments of the tribe, with geography as well as kinship defining the segments so that they crosscut each other and prevent abuse of authority. In this way no one family or no one segment can amass power for long enough to abuse it, yet power and centralization are provided for as required by the military needs. And the same system easily allows for the annual fragmentation of the tribe as it disperses into the desert. Even with the hereditary kingdoms in Africa, where power is centralized in a much more permanent manner, abuse is checked effectively by diverse social institutions, and it is frequently said that "the King is to be eaten," meaning that any wealth he amasses is for the consumption of the nation. The King's granaries, filled by tribute, are for distribution in times of famine, and any failure in this obligation or any abuse of his position of authority can lead to his removal from office and replacement by classificatory "kin."

Early Life in the Desert

The Sahara is the largest desert in Africa, and one of the most enigmatic. It has undergone many changes of climate, and for thousands of years was habitable to man; even today it, and other African deserts, gives life to those who have learned its secrets. Giraffe, elephant, and rhinoceros once roamed the Sahara, and rock paintings show man in pursuit of such game. The Maghreb, the northern tip of Africa, butts violently against the Sahara today and seems to be a totally different world, for the Maghreb enjoys a good rainfall and is Mediterranean in climate and vegetation. But pollen analysis shows that this same vegetation once covered most of the Sahara.

Archaeologists have uncovered abundant traces of early man, discovering man-made tools dating from the earliest times onward, such finds often being in places that today are uninhabitable. For most of the prehistoric period man obtained his food by hunting, but from about 6000 B.C. onward he adopted nomadic cattle herding as a way of life. In the southern Sahara, people depended on fishing in lakes that have long since vanished, leaving only the bone harpoons and fishhooks as witness to the past. By 500 B.C. the central Sahara had become a desert much as it is today, life being tolerable only around the oases. These oases became the center of life for semisedentary oases dwellers, also for nomadic herders, and were vital in making possible the trans-Saharan caravans that were to trade back and forth in the coming centuries. The Maghreb retained its abundant vegetation, and entered into history at Carthage, with the coming of the Phoenicians.

The earliest hunters probably used wooden spears, with fire-hardened tips much as do some of the contemporary hunters today, including the forest Pygmies. Remains of such spears have been found elsewhere in Africa, indicating a people living a similar way of life with a similar technology and material culture who may have migrated from north to south or the reverse. Digging stick weights of the type still used by the South African Bushmen have been found throughout the continent, and it is certain that the Bushmen are descendants of a very early hunting people, although the place of their origin is unknown. In terms of blood grouping, they are closer in kinship to the forest Pygmies of the Ituri Forest than to any other African peoples, according to tentative results of work being done by Professor Cavalli-Sforza. There is evidence that the Bushmen now living in the harsh Kalahari Desert were not always a desert people any more than were the hunters of northern Africa.

The Acheulian and Aterian tool-making traditions of the Old and Middle Stone Ages were common to both the Sahara and the Maghreb in the North, but the later Stone Age (Capsian) tradition is peculiar to the Maghreb. Elements of these Middle and Later Stone Ages were carried on into the Neolithic cultures that followed, providing a story of continuity in the northern desert, in spite of the drastic climatic changes taking place—a vivid testimony to man's adaptability.

After 6000 B.C. cattle raising became the predominant economy of the Sahara. Deep and rich deposits of cattle bones have been found in the Acacus Mountains of southwestern Libya, one of the most desolate parts of the whole desert. Many of the rock paintings show large herds of cattle, and it is possible that wild cattle were domesticated in this area, though cattle raising might have been introduced from Asia. There have been many discoveries of unstratified neolithic sites in the Sahara, suggesting nomadic herding rather than the more sedentary farming life we associate with the Neolithic, and even hunting was still an important activity, judging by the large numbers of arrowheads found at these sites. In fact, there is scant evidence of any agriculture at this time, the picture being one of nomadic herders supplementing their diet by hunting, though they may have practiced a limited form of vegeculture as well.

A Desert People: the Ait 'Atta

Even today the two great deserts of Africa, the Sahara and the Kalahari, are neither as inhospitable nor an impenetrable as they may seem. Historically the Sahara has always been traversed by innumerable caravan routes, and in both deserts people are still born, live full lives, and die without ever seeing anything of the grassy wooded worlds beyond. But the desert is a strict master, and it demands constant movement. All desert peoples are nomadic, living in small shifting groups rather than in large tribes. Among herders, laws are rigid, and penalties for infraction are severe, or survival would not be possible. Here alone is a major contrast with the flexible way of life in the grasslands and forests of Africa.

Given these restrictions, life is not only bearable in the desert, it also has a certain ease of its own. For one thing, there is little competition for desert lands, and desert people are mostly left to themselves; many of them moved into the Sahara from the richer land to the north for that very reason. They respect their solitude and have a passionate devotion to the world they live in. They herd flocks of sheep and goats and drive herds of camels across the desert, some of them living by trading or by guiding (or raiding) the wealthy trans-Saharan caravans. They may also deal with tribes of farmers in the savanna fringes, obtaining food supplies from them in return for trade goods from the North, but they regard the farmers as inferior beings, unfit for consideration as real men. The religion of Islam, which swept across northern Africa in the seventh century, sits easily among these austere nomads and adds to the sense of dignity they feel simply by virtue of being desert peoples.

The Berber inhabitants of North Africa strongly resisted the Arab invaders, but when resistance was no longer possible, many fled to less hospitable areas, particularly the mountains and desert to the south, where they could be free to continue their own way of life. If they adopted Islam it was sometimes a nominal adoption, particularly in the more remote rural areas away from urban centers of orthodoxy. In North Africa as in Arabia, Islam readily absorbed local beliefs, and the Ait 'Atta, a Berber people numbering two hundred thousand, are typical in that while they practice Islam, they also continue to practice many of their earlier customs and hold to many of their earlier beliefs. The two are not in conflict but have become an inseparable whole.

The Ait 'Atta are a transhumant people organized under a series of chiefs, the top one of which used to be the *amghar n-ufilla*, who was essentially a war chief responsible for intertribal relations. Today warfare has ceased, but there is still a top chief. The Ait 'Atta still feel themselves as a distinct people apart from other Moroccans.

Apart from the amghar n-ufilla were the clan chiefs, with more local responsibilities. Both these top chiefs and local clan chiefs were elected annually by a complex process involving divisions: for the top chief, the division of the tribe into five fifths, as described by David Hart*; for the local clan chiefs, a territorial division and a system of alternation that prevented any one individual, segment, or territory from achieving power over any other. So here, where a long tradition of warfare has demanded maximal centralization, yet the preferred nomadic way of life equally demands segmentation, and the Africa tradition of democracy is maintained.

Unlike the Arab system, the Ait 'Atta took care not to evolve a hierarchical system and have remained remarkably unconcerned with status, not even veiling their women when visiting Arab towns. Only in one respect are they status conscious, and that is with respect to the sedentary Haratin oasis populations who happen to be dark, while the other Ait 'Atta are fair, like other Berber. To dismiss this as color prejudice would be to miss what is probably far more important to the Ait 'Atta, namely that the Haratin farm, and the Ait 'Atta, like other herders, despise farming. The Haratin come under Ait 'Atta protection and work for them as sharecroppers in return for protection and for one fifth of the harvest of grain

---

* David M. Hart, "Segmentary Systems and the Role of Five Fifths," *Revue de l'Institut de Sociologie* (Université de Rabat, 1966).

and dates. Also, unlike the Ait 'Atta, the Haratin are formed into groups that are named after places (rivers) and not people. They do not have the elective chieftainships or the well-developed lineage system of their "overlords," or even tribal organization. In fact, this may be another relationship like that between the forest Pygmy hunters and their more centrally organized farming neighbors, where the group that seems to be in a subservient position by their lack of central organization manages to hold a good whip hand. It is, perhaps, better understood as a relationship of mutual exploitation than as one of domination and subjection.

Although they are transhumants, the Ait 'Atta build elaborate fortified citadels or *ksar,* which could shelter large numbers of people and livestock in times of war and which may serve as centers of government at other times. They wander from the high central Atlas Mountains, which can be farmed in the spring but which are covered in snow during the winter, down to the south across a stretch of desert to the Jbil Saghru Mountains, below which stretches the vast expanse of the Sahara proper. Their life is intimately tied up with their herds and flocks and with this wandering, nomadic existence. By comparison with others more acculturated to the Arab way of life in the North, their life is hard and frugal, but to them it is ample because it is their own. Although as transhumants rather than pure nomads they have bases between which they move, their material culture is limited, especially when on the move and they are living in tent encampments. But even there the Ait 'Atta are a generous and hospitable, gentle and kind people, welcoming strangers to their tents. They are without the hardness, commerciality, and narrowness of vision that characterizes many of their more prosperous compatriots to the north.

The Spread of Islam

Islam came to Africa with two distinct waves of Arab invasion. When it first swept across North Africa in the seventh century it encountered fierce opposition from the indigenous

Berber. The Arab soldiery established military bases that grew into towns and then into cities that were centers of trade. These centers spread the religion of Islam and the Arabic language, which became the language of the traders as well as of the government.

The second wave in the eleventh century was far larger and brought an invasion of Bedouin Arabs who, as true herders, had no use for a sedentary life and laid waste to towns and fields alike. Some of the indigenous Berber, converted to Islam, helped the invaders press on westward and up into Europe in one movement, and down the western coast in another. But while other areas were quickly pacified and converted to the new faith, North Africa remained a battleground for many years, and relics of the Crusades can still be found there as testimony to the threat posed to Europe in the Middle Ages.

On the eastern coast the Muslim invasion spread up the Nile to northern Nubia, where it was temporarily halted until the fourteenth century, but before long, Islam had spread throughout East Africa and Ethiopia by overland routes and by sea. Although it made less converts in the East than elsewhere, it nonetheless left its mark. Wherever it went it brought more than a new religion; it also brought new political, social, and economic ideas, and by the process of mutual exchange led to the flow of African influences beyond the shores of the continent. Just as Spanish influence exists in Africa, so African influence exists in Spain. Islam introduced notions of social hierarchy where none had existed, and unified small tribal groups into nations and empires—on the western coast as early as the first millennium A.D. Tribes now found allegiance on the basis of common religion rather than on the narrower basis of kinship. The introduction of Koranic schools provided formal education, teaching the writing and reading of Arabic, which further spread the Islamic faith. They also provided a means for some to climb higher than others and to aspire to a life of greater ease. In many cases this meant complete breaks with the past, but more often there was an easy adaptation. Above all the schools provided a class of elite whose interests lay in continuing the system and who were capable of entering into the new administrative posts. In this way the Arabs were quickly able to leave the business of government to their African converts. At the great trading center of Timbuctu in the state of Songhai, Islam gave rise to Africa's most ancient university. It became a place of such academic repute that scholars came from all over the Islamic world to consult its priceless library and to discourse with other scholars. This together with its commercial importance made Timbuctu one of the most important centers in traditional Africa. Timbuctu was a metropolis in the modern sense. It was a large condensed area that contained a heterogeneous population primarily composed of Berber, Tuareg, and Songhai. These cultures lived side by side but were socially separate, and came together in the marketplace for economic activity.

The *djihad*, or holy war, is a religious duty that every Muslim is obliged to fulfill when called upon. It ranks in importance next to the five primary obligations of professing faith in Allah as the only God and Mohammed as his prophet, praying, giving alms, and making the pilgrimage to Mecca if possible. The Fulani led a djihad against the Hausa of northern Nigeria, for instance, because the Fulani leader, Usuman dan Fodio, held that the Hausa had lapsed into paganism. In fact, following the djihads that took place in northern and western Africa, the religious zeal wore off, and many of the deeply rooted traditional beliefs and customs reasserted themselves. The basis of Islamic expansion became trade rather than war, and though the traders still proselytized and the Koranic schools further spread the faith, the conversions were not so deeply rooted. The new African Muslims, for instance, did not relegate their womenfolk to the same inferior status accorded them by the orthodox Muslims; nor did they adopt the same rigid and inflexible political life the characterized the orthodox law. The ultimate power of Islam in fact lay, and still lies, in its adaptability as well as in its lack of internal schism, and in the sense of pride and superiority that it instills in its converts. Certain elements were particularly attractive to the traditional mind, such as the Muslim notion of *baraka*, a special power that emanates from God. Muslim holy men had control of baraka and could perform miracles and accomplish cures and give protection by the writing of Koranic texts and enclosing them in leather bindings and using them as charms. This, to the traditional African, was identical to his own belief in vital force. Further, although Islam condemned the use of magic, it did not deny its efficacy, and the convert saw little contradiction between his old way of life and his new faith in Allah. A final factor in encouraging the wide spread of Islam in Africa was that the colonial governments not only tolerated it, but also often actively encouraged it. They saw in Islam a well-defined system with which they could deal. They could make use of many Muslim institutions such as the courts and schools, as well as the Muslim administrators. This gave a still higher status to Islam and encouraged a fresh wave of conversion as important, if not more so, than any that had preceded it. Colonial measures often broke down traditional institutions and beliefs, and the Muslims were quick to enter and replace them with their own, which were acceptable to both sides. The colonial era also brought greatly improved communications, and this was another major factor in bringing about this late spread of Islam. Throughout Islamic history the religion has spread along trade routes, and colonial expansion provided in this way a natural avenue for Islamic expansion.

While the Bedouin Arabs retained as far as possible their purely pastoral economy, rejecting even the semisedentary mixed farming of the earlier Berber populations, some of the Berber themselves turned away from their limited agriculture and, with Islam, adopted the aggressiveness of the invaders, their religion and the hierarchical nature of their social organization so foreign to original Berber life. Such were the Tuareg, whom the Bedouin invasion of the eleventh century displaced. Whereas some like the Ait 'Atta sought refuge in the mountains and northern desert, the Tuareg pushed right out into the desert itself and forged a new way of life that was neither Arab nor Berber but a synthesis of the two. The

Tuareg are part of a single but complex society made up of itinerant traders, nomadic herders, armed patrols, and sedentary cultivators. Up to the Middle Ages there were two distinct groups, but in the sixteenth century the southern Tuareg largely abandoned their nomadic ways and settled on the Niger River. The northern Ihaggaren Tuareg, relatively isolated, remained strongly feudal and kept the hierarchical social organization they had adopted, relegating certain types of work to menial classes.

Their hierarchically organized society related to their particular adaptation to the desert environment. They turned the demand for constant movement to their own advantage by combining four nomadic economies: the herding of camels, sheep and goats; the salt trade; the protection of trans-Saharan caravans; and the raiding of those caravans. The Ihaggaren confederacy consisted of three tribes, each headed by the chief of the noble clan of that tribe, and the total confederacy came under at least the nominal leadership of the senior of the three tribes, the Kel Rela. But for the most part the wide separation of water holes, and the sparseness of pasture, made it necessary for each tribe to break down into small nomadic bands, each to a large extent independent of the others, maintaining and protecting the water holes against accidental or deliberate damage, offering protection to caravans passing through their territory, and raiding those that spurned protection. The society was matrilineal, and women were powerful and free, going unveiled like true Berber women. Their husbands took pride in providing for their wives, particularly among the nobility, so that they had plenty of leisure for recreation, which included poetry as well as music. Servants took care of all household chores, and the Tuareg got what agricultural produce they wanted from the oasis cultivators, who came under their protection.

While raiding and protection have diminished in importance today, the Tuareg are still able to maintain their isolated way of life by continuing to herd and by their salt trade, involving a cyclic movement by which they supply the agricultural peoples of the western Sudan with salt, mined for them by their serfs. Salt is a vital dietary factor and is always in demand; in return for it the Tuareg receive subsistence commodities to supplement their own staples of dates and dairy products. During this cyclic salt trade the Tuareg move from oasis to oasis, some of which may be as much as five days apart. At each oasis they are again able to trade, or to provision their caravan with goods supplied by their Haratin agricultural serfs, mainly sorghum. This dual economy is in this way fully interlocked with that of the neighboring peoples on the fringes of the desert. The Tuareg are bound by various ecological factors to a fixed calendar for this trade; the mining of salt takes place in April and May, and it is then taken by caravan in July through Tamesna, which is rich in pasture and provides a good resting place where camels can be refreshed or exchanged for new ones. The next leg takes the trade caravans to the trading centers just north of Nigeria, the trading season beginning in October. As well as salt, the Tuareg do a lively trade in dates brought from the North, and in donkeys and camels. The return trip begins in January, stopping once again at Tamesna, reaching their northern homelands around March.

In earlier years the Saharan trade routes used to be divided, for purposes of raiding and protection, between the Tuareg in the southern section and the Chaamba, Bedouin Arabs, to the north. Apart from the salt trade, the Chaamba operated like the Tuareg, enforcing a toll system on all caravans and carrying out punitive raids on those who tried to pass without paying. Today the Chaamba continue, as do the Tuareg, to maintain their nomadic way of life, living by their herds and flocks, and doing a limited trade with the northwestern oases, bringing them grain and sugar. Raiding continued into this century, by both Tuareg and Chaamba, and the French colonial authorities played on mutual hostilities as well as the love of fighting and built up their camel corps of desert police, who were primarily Chaamba. This finally shattered the Tuareg confederacy and destroyed its military power. The independent spirit, however, remained unbroken, and even the Muslim governments of the new nations find their desert nomads difficult to incorporate, so effectively has Islam done its work, binding them in opposition to others.

Water and Politics

To say that water is the major problem the desert presents to man does not mean there is no water. On the contrary, there are vast reserves of it lying on bedrock deep below a sandy surface that helps protect it from evaporation. The problem lies in locating the water where it is close to the surface and accessible, and in devising means for raising it. That done, there remain the problems of distribution and of water rights. The supply of water involves problems that are technological, economic, and political, and it dominates the life of desert peoples. On a summer day when temperatures may reach 120 degrees, a man may easily die by nightfall without water. If the temperature does not exceed 110 degrees he may last two days. Water is the most precious commodity in daily life. Second to water in importance is the camel, which because of its remarkable ability to endure weeks without water and to carry heavy loads, enables man to move freely from water hole to water hole, even when they are days apart, watering himself and his flocks from hide water bags carried by the camels.

This all leads to various refinements in social organization, for human relationships have to be as carefully regulated as the distribution of water. In fact, they go hand in hand, varying as does the economy, with the readiness with which water can be made available. In the Nile Valley, for instance, where there is ample water in the river at all times of the year, the desert is usually within a mile or so of its banks, even under the best conditions. The problem here is one of how to raise the water, and because the ancient Egyptians solved the problem, agriculture became possible and Egypt became (and still is) a vast expanse of desert with one tiny narrow ribbon of fertile land flanking the riverbanks. The technology for raising and distributing the water was designed with irrigation in mind, and called for quite different techniques and organization than when the water is required solely for drinking purposes, and it led to the highly co-operative nature of peasant life that still characterizes Egyptian villages, though modern irrigation methods are slowly breaking down this ancient unity.

The problem of raising water depends on how far it has to be raised, and with a river such as the Nile, this varies from one part of the year to the next, depending on how far it is in flood. The ancient Egyptians developed two techniques to deal with this. During the flood season where the river overflowed the banks, nothing had to be done; the river did all the work, from moistening the ground to depositing rich layers of silt that gave new life to the poor soil. But once the water level began to fall, water had to be raised, and the simplest form—a bucket on a rope—was inadequate except for small supplies of drinking water. The major invention was the *shaduf*, which operates on the lever principle, one end being weighted with a mudball that bakes into hard clay and acts as a counterbalance to the other end, which holds the large water container. Conservation of energy is all-important under desert conditions, and with the shaduf a man could raise a continuous supply of water with a minimum of effort—the bucketful of water swings back on being raised, and tips into the canal or catchment.

Before the level sinks too low (when it is still only a matter of raising it a foot or two), the Archimedes screw, or *tambur*, can be used. This is a helix enclosed in an outer case, with a handle at one end. The lower end is dipped into the water of the river, or more often, a supply canal, and a continuous flow is produced by turning the handle. Both the tambur and the shaduf are as much in use as ever today.

When the water level falls beyond the reach of the shaduf, two techniques are employed along the river. One is simply to use a series of shaduf in chain, each raising the water and pouring it into a basin at a higher level, from where it is raised by the next shaduf until it reaches the upper basin or irrigation canal. This calls for co-operation between a number of people, each with his own shaduf, and the labor and equipment cannot always be spared. The second method is to construct barrages wherever possible, particularly during the lowest summer levels, so as to raise the water level to where

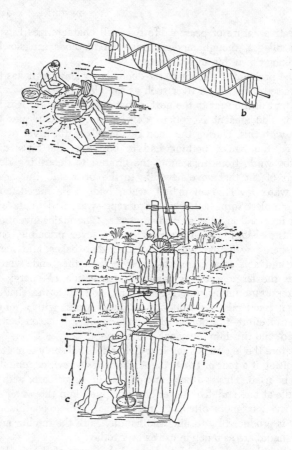

Figure 19. To find water hidden under the desert sand, tunnels (*foggara*) may be dug into slopes and sand drawn up to the surface through vertical shafts until water is reached. a) A *tambur* for raising water from canal to catchment basin. b) A closeup of tambur (a cut-away screw). c) The *shaduf*, for dipping water from river or well, is sometimes used in gangs when water level is low.

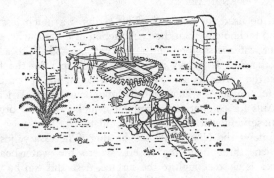

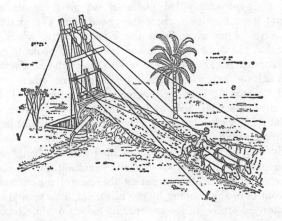

d) The *sakya*, or Persian wheel, needs less manpower and provides a continuous flow, raising water level four or five feet. e) From deep wells, water is raised on double pulleys; the lower pulley keeps the water bag closed until the end of the lift, when it is automatically released.

it can be used for irrigation. This requires a much less advanced technology than the construction of a dam, where the flow of water is stopped and a reservoir created. With a barrage, the flow is merely restricted enough to raise the level within the normal confines of the riverbanks, and it is a common technique of water control throughout North Africa. It also calls for co-operative effort for a higher level of organization, serving as it does a larger population.

All along the Nile, wells can be dug if necessary, just as they can throughout the desert, where the water-bearing bedrock is close enough to the surface. A shaduf can be used to raise water from a well if the water is not too far down, but an improved form of water raising was discovered early, involving what is often known as the Persian wheel or *sakya*.

When the water level was high enough, the engineers of ancient Egypt simply led water off at given points and brought it by canals to where they needed it. This practice may have begun as early as the First Dynasty, when we know that Menes began the task of building up banks to control floodwaters. The next step was to direct the floodwaters by canals or irrigation ditches to depressions where they could be stored. Then, with greater engineering skill, the later dynasties were able to lead the water away from the Nile at a higher level, and by using a reduced gradient bring it to places that might not have been reached by the floods. Slowly a system developed of running parallel banks and crossbanks all the way down the valley, cutting the land into vast checkerboards, thus ensuring the careful measurement and control of the flooding by use of sluices. This system still operates efficiently and economically today. Again, it obviously called for a high level of administration and co-operative effort, but it was not peculiar to Egypt. The same system is used along the less spectacular rivers and even the smaller streams of North Africa right into Morocco, and serves there both to supply the water to garden plots and to bind small groups of people together in co-operative effort, just as it binds much larger groups of people in Egypt.

Along the Nile, measuring devices were raised to compare each year's rate of rise with the previous year's, so that the flood level could be predicted and the necessary arrangements made in advance for the controlled flooding and irrigation of the land. Records were kept in the temples, and we can see the accuracy with which the water was conserved and distributed. In this system of basin irrigation some units were one thousand acres in extent and others as much as forty thousand acres. The land within each of these enclosures could be flooded to a depth of up to five or six feet and the water held there for a month or so until the ground was well saturated. It was then run off, and the ground was plowed and sown. This control of the inundation was then, as now, of national importance, though the filling of basins could be organized at a provincial level. The irrigation needed throughout the growing of the crops, however, in the dry months of spring and summer, called for organization at a more local level. This was not a problem peculiar to Egypt, and the Latin word *rivus*, signifying he who shares an irrigation ditch or water rights with another, is suitably the origin of the English word *rival*. But in northern Africa, although water could indeed be a cause of friction, even of warfare, it was seldom at the local level that people saw themselves as belonging to this water unit or that one, and where survival depended on each man respecting the other's rights. Just as today one well-placed bomb on Aswan High Dam could wipe out much of Egypt, so in the old days the careless closing of a sluice or the malicious breach of a canal wall or the greedy and thoughtless attempt to divert water belonging to another or to take more than one's share could spell disaster for an entire community. As a result, a rigid code of laws applicable to water usage arose, with severe penalties for infractions. Throughout the desert it is the same: Water sources are clearly defined property, and their unauthorized usage may be punishable by death.

The small-scale garden irrigation of the peasant communities was much like the basin system in that fields and plots were laid out in a similar checkerboard pattern, connected by water-supply canals running in one direction and ditches in another, each ditch leading water across a series of plots down to the lowest fields from where any runoff was

collected by another canal and led on in the same direction
as the main canal. Each man's field was allowed so much
water, measured by the amount of time for which he was allowed to breach his dike and allow the water to flood in from
the canal or ditch. Once his field was flooded, the dike was
rebuilt and the next field was flooded. Within his field a man
might have several plots, and these he might also divide
checkerwise, but since there would be no appreciable slope
for him to use, he removed water from one plot to the next
by use of either a *baddalah* or a *nattalak*—oblong boxes resting on a pivot with a nonreturn valve at one end. When the
device was rocked downward into the plot under water, the
water entered by the nonreturn valve, and when the device
was rocked the other way, the water simply flowed out of the
other end into the adjacent plot. This was an individual activity, but not everyone might own one of these devices and
might be forced to borrow or rent one.

Later Muslim law states clearly that only land that is properly watered can be claimed as property, implying that every
man's responsibility is the proper management of water.
However, water rights and land rights do not necessarily go
together, and a person could conceivably have title to land
but not to the water he uses to irrigate it, which he may have
to rent. Similarly, a man may own a certain allotment of
water from the communal supply but have no land, in which
case he may sell or lease or reallocate his share to another.
All the way along the south side of the Atlas Mountains, on
the edge of the desert itself, agricultural communities are
flourishing that depend on the control of the water that
comes down from the mountains in the winter and with the
summer melting of the snows. These waters are caught by
dams of stones and earth built right across the *wadi* beds,
just as the ancient Egyptians of the Old Kingdom did at
Wadi Gerrawi. In such ways a short but plentiful supply of
water can be made to last a whole season, and in the more
fortunate locations, units of measure can be as great as a half
day's flooding of a field. At the other extreme, when the wall
of a canal is broken to allow the water to irrigate a field, the
flow of the water may be measured by floating a metal bowl

in the water. The bowl is pierced with a small hole so that it will sink at a given time, at which time the canal wall is closed up again. Such measures usually allow for a flow of about five minutes only, but the number of measures allowed depends on several considerations. It is not only the amount of water that must be regulated (this may vary according to status and wealth), but also the time at which the water is distributed. Each man is allocated so much water at certain times of certain days in proportion to his rank, the size of his fields (or of his family), or according to what he has paid for.

Cultures that rely heavily on irrigation techniques for their livelihood usually exhibit highly centralized political structures. The entire process of the organization and allocation of water, based on status and wealth, is one that requires an elaborate and sophisticated kind of political organization. The emergence of dynastic Egypt illustrates the importance of this kind of centralization for the successful maintenance of river valley technology. Irrigation as well as most aspects of life must be highly organized under tight hierarchical control, and it is here that the river valley and its technology crystallize and permeate the entire nature of the culture.

Even at some of the oases, the water supply could be generous. At Kharga, 130 miles into the desert west of the Nile at Luxor, hydrostatic pressure causes the water to rise to the top of a deep borehole, and the artesian principle may well have originated in the oasis exploitation by early desert farmers. Date palms and orange and olive trees can thrive around an oasis, and the water makes possible the cultivation of crops such as rice and barley, even wheat and sorghum. In many cases no equipment like the shaduf is necessary; pools act as reservoirs, built up to allow sufficient water to accumulate and opened at specific times and for specific periods to allow for irrigation. Sometimes the community employs specialists to keep track of water usage, making sure that each person gets his due at the appropriate time. The community also joins in the work of cleaning out pools and repairing irrigation banks and walls. In other places water may have to be drawn up, and if it is from some depth, this may be done by an ox pulling on the rope attached to a bucket made of skin. Another example of labor-saving ingenuity is the bucket that has a flap at the bottom that holds the water in when being drawn up, and releases it automatically by ropes attached to the oxen when it reaches the catchment. The oxen, which may be trained to do this work on their own without guidance, then walk back up to the well, allowing the bucket to be closed, lowered, and filled again.

Where the bedrock comes close to the surface and bears water, springs may be opened to supply a continuous flow. To avoid evaporation, water can be led underground by the *foggara* system from a subterranean water supply to the fields. Shafts are dug in the hillsides, the dirt being raised from vertical holes. Once the water source has been reached, it flows of its own accord, but the tunnel must be kept clean, and after a while this becomes dangerous and impractical. Whereas the foggara cannot be practically used to lead water much more than two kilometers, canals or aqueducts (often made of hollowed-out olive trees) can be used over much greater distances.

Whether it is a question of remotely spaced wells that supply water for nomadic herds and for traders, and come under private ownership of Tuareg or Chaamba families, or whether it is a question of a communally owned and communally operated irrigation system, water supply in the desert is just as much a political issue as it is economic and is a strongly cohesive factor.

Savanna Cultivators

We often think of the feud in connection with desert life and desert peoples, but this does not mean that they constantly fight each other. Feuding is a system that divides even the tribe itself into small, effective, tightly knit groups, each demanding absolute loyalty, and each in opposition to others. It is a method of holding widely scattered peoples together in a system of mutual oppositions, and not merely as a means of ordering one's animosities or of guarding one's rights. Many of the laws pertaining to feud and many instances of feuding involve water rights in the desert, but there life revolves around such rights. When we get to the savanna fringes of the desert where cultivation is possible without oases or other localized sources, but where rainfall is still minimal, we see societies built up on a larger scale—unities, exceeding the family group or the co-operative peasant village, and foundations being laid for nationhood.

While there is a powerful sense of unity in the desert proper, no matter how divided and even hostile the people may be toward groups that are not of their own, this is not so when you reach the more hospitable fringes. The desert compels rather than favors a certain way of life, and with it goes a way of thought shared by all desert peoples in the Sahara, regardless of the degree of their conversion to Islam. Even when there is hostility, there is respect and understanding. It is as though the quest for water, which brings about such strong local political unities, brings about a spiritual rather than a political unity at a wider level.

The region of Lake Tchad typifies the diversity that exists in this critical intermediate area between desert and equatorial forest. The North is inhospitable, shady wasteland giving way in the center to a vast steppe of thorn and gum trees, a treeless savanna that in turn gives way to the lightly wooded savanna that impinges abruptly on the huge equatorial forest of Central Africa. The lake itself, a great fluctuating mass that is sometimes lake and sometimes swamp, is the dominant feature. Nilotics from the East, Saran or Charien peoples from the West, and Berber and Arab from the North all meet and mingle in the vicinity of Tchad, an intricate interrelationship among land, climate, and people.

The Teda and Daza pastoral nomads wander through the North, returning twice a year to harvest date palms, their major fixed landmark. Each of them leaves the limited cultivation of cereals and cotton to specialist castes. Cultivation becomes easier in the central and southern Tchad region, and although a limited caste system exists, it is mostly related to the working of iron. The Kanembu peoples both herd and cultivate, and among them the Danoa form specialized groups of blacksmiths, ritually respected and set apart—a respect the upper classes try to conceal as contempt. Millet and sorghum remain the major crops, though the cultivation of rice is spreading. On the Logone and Chari rivers fishing becomes the primary occupation, bringing with it its own form of social organization, its own way of life and thought.

While the degree to which a population is dispersed or nucleated as nomadic or sedentary is linked to the level of aridity, that is not the only factor. Lake Tchad is a major crossroads between the North and South and the East and West of Africa, and this results in an integration of the disparate peoples and disparate economies of the area and in a loose system of mutual interdependency. The over-all acceptance of Islam, except among the Sara cultivators, corresponds to and supports this loosely formed system. In intermediate savanna areas that are isolated, a different development can take place, as with the Dogon in western Sudan along the Bandiagara escarpment. This is an area in which an extremely early and indigenous development of agriculture may have taken place. It is now a great deal more desiccated than it once was, but cultivation is still possible, though difficult. The Dogon may represent a people who stayed in their ancestral homeland while others pressed outward in search of better arable land. The Dogon are a people with a long tradition of cultivation, to whom it comes easily despite the difficulties of their environment, and who have developed an agricultural system that relieves them of much of the worry that faces others. They are not concerned with expansion, nor are they hampered and dominated by an elaborate hierarchical system. They have a long and peaceful history of settlement, and are not overly concerned with economic factors; content with the stability and subsistence level that they have achieved, the Dogon turn their energies to a consideration of the source of being, and have developed an elaborate artistic expression of their belief in sculpture, music, dance, and poetry.

Where others, even their immediate neighbors and kin, concentrate on the problems of life and living, the Dogon concentrate on another realm of being altogether. The social system, which is organized only at the local level, runs parallel to the world of belief as expressed in Dogon myth. But Dogon myth is itself a dual system—an esoteric and an exoteric body united in a complex system of symbols that the living society and social organization represent. The thought binds them together; they have no need for a strong central authority. Their unity springs from the belief that God and Earth were lovers and that man is the seed of the universe. Social order depends on the Hogon, the ritual chief who controls the world and the universe, for the order of the one depends on the order of the other. Even the physical layout of villages and fields often directly reflects the spiral symbolism, implying continuity within the universe.

The Dogon divide into four groups, each with a specific function. Two of these tribal groups concern themselves with trades and craftsmanship. Ritual sanctions stress the equality of ironworkers with field cultivators, but separate the two realms of activity. This is much more likely to typify the position of smiths elsewhere, rather than the common simplistic assertion that they are either despised or honored. One of the other four tribes is concerned with agriculture and the fourth with ritual, including chieftainship, which is seen as a ritual activity. All four come under one supreme ritual leader, or Hogon. The life of the Dogon throughout the year is punctuated with complex ritual requirements that form the focus of their interest and concern. Their economic adaptation to the savanna is successful enough to allow them leisure for this pursuit of a sensitive religious life. Their religious thought, which stresses the reality and functionality of opposition, enables them to accept differences without seeing in this any necessary cause for disunity. On the contrary, though, the Dogon hold that part of man is in his opposite, and so in opposition they see complementarity rather than hostility, and their peaceful relations with their neighbors indicate that they find that it pays to practice their beliefs.

The immediate neighbors and kin of the Dogon, the Bambara, share both the early connection with agriculture with the Dogon and a related social organization under priest-chiefs. They credit their knowledge of agriculture to the ancestor whom they honor with the famous *chi-wara* antelope headdress that has now become the national symbol of the

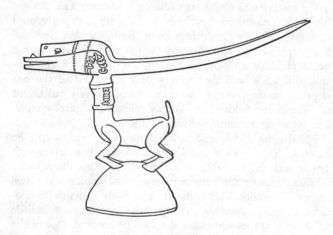

Figure 20. A *chi-wara* antelope headdress, now the national symbol of the modern nation of Mali. Bambara.

new state of Mali. They recognize their dependence on the land in both economic and religious terms, and each district is administered by a priest-chief whose prime function is ritual rather than political. Good order springs from good order, social and ritual; a defect in the one may induce a defect in the other, and by the proper observance of all necessary ritual, the priest-chiefs bring order to man and society, and prosperity to the fields. But their focus is more on the land, as distinct from the ritual, than is the case with the Dogon. They are as concerned with subsistence as with the source of the subsistence, and that is not true for the Dogon. They still have not elaborated any degree of social stratification, but they can be regarded as intermediate between the spirit-focused Dogon and the world-focused Senegambians. All three represent different ways in which man can adapt his thinking as well as his social structure within a similar environment—in this case the savanna.

The western fringes of the desert in places reach almost to the sea, and in others trail off through lightly wooded savanna into forest. The forest area is known as the yam belt, where root crops such as yams, manioc, and sweet potatoes are cultivated. The Senegambians—the Wolof, Lebu, and Serer—live north of this belt and cultivate sorghum and fonio, both indigenous, and the indigenous rice *oryza glaberrima* (though the latter is being replaced more and more by *oryza sativa*, introduced by the French and Portuguese).

The climate today is perhaps like what it might have been farther inland many years ago, and the Senegambians are less concerned than those in the drier savanna with either food or its origin. They take both for granted and turn their energies to the development of a more complex and highly stratified social organization, based on a more complex technology and made possible by the leisure afforded them by the way they live. Each facet stimulates the other; we have a social organization emerging not in isolation, but in vigorous contact with the outside world and adapting itself to the ever-increasing rapid pace of change.

The Senegambians recognize two main castes: free-born and serfs. Free-born are stratified into royalty, nobility, and peasants, and the serfs or lower castes consist of specialized groups like musicians, leatherworkers and ironsmiths, household servants, fishermen, and captured slaves. Status is important to them (a thought that would be foreign to the Bambara to the northeast and to the Dogon), and it is made outwardly manifest by various restrictions and injunctions on dress and ornamentation. Some of the finer status differences observed in this way include marriage and widowhood, old age, middle age, and youth (denoted by women's differing styles of wigs, adopted appropriate to their age group). The

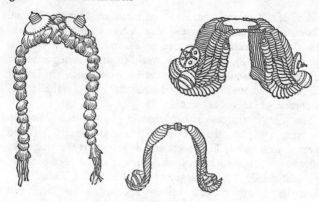

Figure 21. Wolof women wear these sisal and wool headdresses denoting their age and marital status.

Senegambians have largely adopted Islam, and this is in part responsible for their more secular approach to life, as it is for their status consciousness and their separation from certain specified classes of occupation. It is a development that is less African in nature and spirit, but represents what might have been a stage through which the diverse people of the western Sudan went on their way to becoming organized into the great modern states and nations of West Africa. It is a process of nucleation and secularization, and of increasing social stratification, which so far the Dogon and Bambara have managed to resist. It is one way to one form of progress, though a comparison among these three peoples shows the cost that has to be paid in terms of a life that is moral and religious as well as merely social.

Desert Hunters

The Bushmen of the Kalahari Desert have retained to the present day the hunting and gathering life of their ancient past. They are much like the forest Pygmies not only in that they are hunters, but also in that they have consciously rejected assimilation into what seems to outsiders to be a much easier way of life. This is not due to any deficiency in ability or comprehension, or to a truculent conservatism; they simply consider themselves better off where they are and how they are.

Their way of life today does not represent the way their ancestors lived in prehistoric times. Whereas the Pygmies have always been in the forest, the Bushmen have not always been in the desert. The Bushmen were forced into the Kalahari from the game-filled grasslands by waves of migrant peoples. Much of their contemporary social organization represents an adaptation to their new desert environment. Different conditions also persist in different parts of the Kalahari, and the Bushmen have found many ways to respond to them.

Throughout the Kalahari the environment is an exacting master; it would be so even if the people had an advanced technology, yet the Bushmen manage to find a livelihood where others would surely die. They create for themselves a life that is rich and full. Their nomadic pattern responds to seasonal variations that often place food and water as far as seventy miles apart. This would be nothing to the Saharan nomads with their camels, laden with skins full of water and with dates and other food supplies, but it is crucial to the Bushmen, who must travel on foot and carry their supplies themselves. In the Sahara the Dar Hamar are so careful of water that before shaving the heads of children they make them run around so that they perspire and the scalp does not need to be watered. If this seems excessive, it is nothing compared to what the Bushmen have to do to extract and conserve water. Far from running around needlessly, they conserve both their energy and their body moisture. In the heat of the day they may lie in shallow pits lined with pulp moistened with their own urine, the evaporation of which helps keep them cool and prevents their own dehydration. In such extreme conditions it is difficult to see how life can be either full or rich, by any definition, but it is.

As with the Sahara, the desert is not as waterless as it

seems, though it requires highly specialized knowledge to make adequate use of it for survival. Where it lies on bedrock it is sometimes close enough to the surface for the Bushmen to be able to reach down with long tubes, the end protected by filters, and suck up water, drop by drop, and feed it into ostrich eggshells for storage. It is not easy, and may result in painfully swollen and bleeding lips, but it does provide water. Then there are certain plants that can reach down through the loose sand with ease and draw up water into storage sacs, and others that convert water into melons and fruits that, regardless of taste, can provide man with that life-giving fluid. Certain kinds of trees, notably the great baobab, may collect and store water from the rare but stormy rainfalls, and when water itself is lacking there are always the juicy contents of any game that might be slaughtered. Nothing is wasted by way of either solid or liquid food among the Bushmen. Some tell a story of how originally man did not hunt and kill, but through a curse had to do so, and has been trying to atone for it ever since. One method of atonement is to waste nothing, but the story tells of how the gall always remains to remind man of his original sin and fall from perfection.

Their material culture, as for all nomads, must be kept to a minimum. It shows how carefully the Bushmen utilize every resource—not only the hide, sinews, horn, and bone of game killed in the chase, but also cocoons, made by men into dance rattles, and the nests of the penduline tit, which make tobacco pouches among the !Kung. Ostrich and tortoise shell are widely used for ornaments as well as for storage containers, ladles, and dippers. Wood, scarce as it is, is ample for the limited needs of these nomadic peoples, providing them with spears, bows, arrows, and digging sticks as the major items. Various root and bark fibers are twisted into strong cord and made into carrying nets and used in snares, and grass is an all-purpose domestic material used for providing shelter, stoppers for water containers, making toys, ornaments, and as bedding. There is little, in fact, that the Bushmen cannot use for some purpose or another.

They do no cultivation, though like the Pygmies and other

hunters, they may practice a limited form of vegeculture. The Naron burn the country wild grass at the end of winter, aware that this will help the fresh growth of the foods for which they will forage the next season. They wander in constant search of the edible roots and fruits and nuts with which the desert provides them, combining this with the search for game and the exploitation of known water resources.

Water may be found in a few widely scattered permanent water holes, but not every band will have such a permanent supply in its territory, and even those that do will only use it when other supplies have dried up. There are also semipermanent sources on which the Bushmen can rely with reasonable certainty at given times of the year, and a number of highly unpredictable holes. Vegetable supplies are rather more predictable, and with water as the major consideration, the Bushmen organize their nomadic life in a pattern that is not as haphazard as it may seem. Among the !Kung two major sources of food are *mangetti* and *tsi*, but these are at the greatest distance from the permanent water holes, and again, not every hunting territory is possessed of both, though all have at least one if not the other. Life for the !Kung, then, is a constant wandering to and fro between water and food supplies, sometimes days apart. To make it possible the !Kung fill their ostrich eggshell containers on setting out from the water hole and bury them in the sand at strategic intervals on their way to the gathering site. When they arrive they have just enough water left to enable them to gather food for the return journey to the water hole and back, and they return to the water hole drinking up their stored supplies as they go. They seldom stay in any one place more than three days.

While hunting ranks first in their ideology, it takes a second place to these basic gathering activities, for the presence of game and its capture are even less predictable. The Bushmen are excellent trackers, and the desert facilitates tracking. But the desert also favors wild game, which can go for much longer without water or food than can their trackers. A hunter may follow his quarry for as much as three days and fail even then. The desert does not favor large-scale co-operative hunts, and at best two or three trackers may set off together. The pursuit and kill are often done alone, and to be alone in the desert is dangerous. The hunter may get back to find that the band has already moved on without him, and he will have to follow as best he can; no concession is made for those who cannot keep up. So it is when someone falls ill, or when the old become too weak—they simply have to be left behind. For the whole band to stop might endanger the survival of all, and the person being left behind knows it. He or she is only alive, after all, because others have made the same sacrifice before. The person is left with whatever provisions the band feels it can spare in the hopes that he or she will recover and be able to join the others. Sometimes a perfectly healthy adult will volunteer to stay with the person being left, especially if it is his or her spouse. The others will help build a rough shelter of thorn and scrub against the predators that will surely come at night.

The Bushmen have a minimal social organization, just as they have maximal self-discipline. They need to be flexible at all times, and in this they resemble other hunters despite the relative poverty of their environment. There are no chiefs, among the !Kung anyway, and elsewhere it is only occasionally that a family head acts with more authority than others. It is more usual for individuals to be respected for their particular qualities, and the old, as such, are certainly respected for their vast store of knowledge. It is reasonable, then, for an old man to be listened to with care, but he does not do much more than wield influence, even as head of a family. Sometimes the critical issue of water is placed firmly in the authority of such a man, for there can be no dispute over its usage, and some form of authority is needed in that respect.

The process of growing up is not accompanied by elaborate rites of passage, though in one or two instances certain groups seem to have borrowed such rites from their Bantu neighbors. Adulthood is reached, rather, by the simple process of proving oneself capable of shouldering adult responsibilities. For a youth this means being able to hunt effectively and to provide for a family; for a young woman it means being able to gather effectively and to give birth to and care for children. Bravery, so much a part of initiation rites elsewhere in Africa, is not highly valued among the Bushmen. Bravery smacks of recklessness, and prudence is the wiser way in desert conditions. Rather than bravery the Bushmen appreciate other values that to them spell survivability, though for those living in more luxurious conditions they are scorned. Such values are trickiness and deceit, and what we would call cowardliness, but which is plain good sense in beating a prudent retreat whenever necessary. The Bushmen survive by not being fools and by not allowing personal vanity to interfere with the hard business of survival.

To outsiders they might seem rather submissive in terms of their reactions to hostility or challenge and in their willingness to conform and to enjoy the good opinion of their band as a whole. But these also are survival tactics—a band could not survive a week if it began allowing personal animosities to develop, or personal ambitions to lead to self-advancement at the expense of others. A very highly developed family sense helps to make communal living without dispute a possibility, and as with the Pgymy hunters, the band is considered a single large family regardless of kinship connections. It is bound together by ties that are emotional as well as economic, for there is a great deal of affection in Bushmen life, and this coupled with their singleness of purpose in the everlasting food quest prevents most minor disorders from developing beyond the level where they can be dealt with by group disapproval or by some informal mechanism such as ridicule. At the worst, an offender is exiled and must seek admission to another band.

To reinforce this familial cohesion there are various apparently insignificant devices, but these are just the kinds of things, in these loosely formed, hunting societies, that take the place of the more elaborate and dramatic social institutions. They are all devices that bring peoples together as individuals and as members of groups, in a network of interpersonal relationships. The Bushmen use a limited number of personal names, for instance, and people sharing the same name are considered under a special obligation toward each other. This is true of many African societies, but it is most highly developed under these conditions, where very real claims can be made, and will be honored, by virtue of common nameship. It is not merely an economic bond-friendship; there is an almost religious quality to it, a sense of identification, of the inextricability of the fates of those sharing the same name, as though by virtue of the fact alone they have some power over each other. Most of us, even with our more common names, feel something of the same thing and would feel a rather special feeling toward someone with exactly the same combination of names. This name sharing is not necessarily invoked all the time, but it is one mechanism by which temporary alliances and bonds can be formed when there is need, either to secure support in a dispute, or shelter or food in times of shortage.

Regulations as to the sharing of meat effect the same kind of network but link totally different persons and groups. Once again, the rules are strictly adhered to, but here it is more usual for the rules to be applied even if there is no need, so that one is constantly being given or having to give strips of meat to those related to one in the meat-sharing system. This is not wasteful, since every Bushman usually carries dried meat with him that he can eat in an emergency, such as if he is caught out while hunting and has to stay away longer from the band than he had anticipated.

The enforced sharing of meat is backed by a third mechanism, that of gift-giving. This may be informal borrowing and lending, of which there is a great deal, or it may be formal presentation, which creates formal obligations of reciprocation at some unspecified future time in some usually unspecified future manner. This again is a mechanism used in many other African societies to build up social interaction and create a sentiment of interdependence, but here it actually creates that interdependence. A man may give another his bow, but not the arrows, while another man supplies the arrows. The recipient supplies the hunting skills, so that if successful he is under additional obligation to share the meat with those who provided him with the weapons. These various devices cut across the strong familial obligations that in themselves enforce a truly communal existence, and bind the Bushmen in such an interlocking system of reciprocal obligations that government, in a formal sense, is not necessary.

And above it all, having mastered the art of exploiting their desert environment so that it always provides them with enough for their minimal needs and demands, and having mastered the art of living together without formal government, without law, without mutual recrimination or self-seeking, the Bushmen add something else to life, making of it something far beyond the mere business of survival. They add an incredibly rich belief, a religious belief in a kind of dream world that beautifies every insect, every leaf, every grain of sand, where stars become the hunters and the hunted of some vaguely perceived afterlife, and where every little thing around them is as great and as good as the heavens themselves—rather as the way the Dogon make of their real world a dream world in a complex system of symbolism.

Perhaps the very severity of their daily life leads the Bushmen to a greater awareness of the world around them. They see beauty where others would only see ugliness; kindness where others would see cruelty, for they understand it all. The Bushman sees himself as part of one single universe, kin not only to the animals he hunts (with reluctance sometimes) and to the birds and insects, but also to the rocks and stones, the trees and water, the sun and moon. How much closer, then, he must feel to his own family and those of his band, who share his world with him. In music and dance the Bushman communicates with the world beyond, the dream world he believes in and tries to express in the symbols of his mythology. Yet this does not remove the Bushman and make him in any sense "otherworldly." He is not concerned with living this life in an ideal manner so as to win for himself a better life in another world; he is concerned with living this life as effectively as possible. In this way many of his songs and dances are invocations for the curing of this or that, for the coming of rain, for the successful hunting of game. What his religious belief does for him (apart from uniting him with his fellows, as it does everywhere else when shared) is not to raise him from this world in brief moments of exultation, or make him a mystic living in another world; for the Bushman, belief brings his dreams down to the world he lives in, giving it color and shape and meaning, giving this life some special purpose and beauty, making it at the same time more livable and infinitely more worth living.

CHAPTER 6

Sing me a song, a song of death,
That I may guide it by the hand,
Sing me a song of the underworld.
Sing me a song, a song of death,
That I may walk to the underworld. (Ewe)

WESTERN WOODLANDS

WHILE MANY think of the Nile as having brought forth the only true civilization in Africa, several others were also linked with river valleys. The Niger, Congo, and Zambezi rivers all enabled civilizations to flourish, be it in desert, forest, or open grassland. Rivers allow for agriculture, the prime requisite for civilization as we understand it. Farming communities are no longer nomadic; they can produce a surplus for trade, allowing for specialization and technological growth accompanied by increasing organizational complexity. Rivers also simplify travel, and with it facilitate the process of economic and political expansion. Egypt, then, is only one of the African civilizations, unless we use the term in a very limited way. The Western woodlands were the home of several others.

The bend of the Niger saw an early beginning to agriculture, very likely simultaneous with that which took place in Egypt. We must speculate more about the exact course of the development, because of the lack of stone monuments. The Niger abounded with the wood that Egypt lacked, but wood rots and leaves nothing to tell us of what once was.

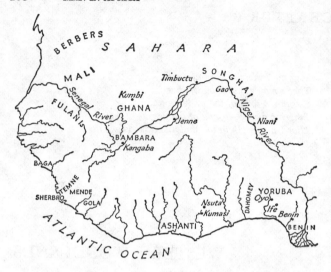

Figure 22. Many of the great West African nations of today owe their origins to ancient kingdoms and empires, some bearing the same names although in different locations.

Our knowledge of the Niger civilizations, then, really begins with early Arab documents, though archaeological finds are increasingly filling out the prehistory.

In historic times, gold was as central as agriculture in the rise of such great states as Ghana, Mali, and Songhai. And like the Nile, the Niger played a vital role in encouraging sedentary agricultural communities and then in facilitating both economic and political expansion. Far from its distant namesake of today, ancient Ghana was founded in about the fourth century A.D. in the heart of the area where agriculture had its first beginnings, at least in this part of Africa. It grew in size and splendor until it was renowned throughout the Middle Eastern world for its powerful and magnificent court. The King was, much as in Egypt, a divine King with secular duties and responsibilities. He was attended in affairs of state by his sister or mother. He had a monopoly of all the gold in his country and used it lavishly in the ornamentation of royalty and the decoration of royal possessions. Much of this is still true of the Ashanti of modern Ghana. The King's power derived from his divine ancestry, and while this was the source of his strength, it was also an effective check on his behavior. To this day an Ashanti chief who dishonors the stool or throne, in which the ancestral soul is thought to reside, proves himself unfit and is promptly "destooled."

Ancient Ghana eventually fell to a Mandingo kingdom, Mali, a Muslim state for which yet another modern nation is named. During Europe's Middle Ages these Niger kingdoms flourished as never before, dazzling the Arab world with their wealth and splendor as the center of a vast gold-trading complex. Timbuctu, one of the chief cities of the Songhai kingdom, was important not only as a transshipment point for trans-Saharan trade, but also as a center for learning. The Islamic university there acquired a magnificent library of rare manuscripts and attracted scholars from all over the Muslim world. The story is the same from the headwaters of the Niger to its mouth, west of which lay similarly great states such as Benin and Ife.

These civilizations were renowned not only for their wealth and magnificence, but also for learning, hospitality, courtesy, and justice, which qualities are particularly remarked upon by early Arab documents. Behind the façade of autocratic kingly rule lay a democratic political system in which order rested on moral behavior rather than on law and physical coercion. Civilization in Africa was not only a question of cities, or technological progress, but also one of human relationships. The present-day descendants of these ancient Niger states may be less able to dazzle the modern world with their wealth, but they still retain much of the character and quality that so impressed the early Arab travelers.

It is generally thought that following the development of agriculture in the Niger bend, the consequent population expansion reached across the southern desert in one movement, and down through the Congo forests to the southern grasslands in another. In the great Congo basin, with its network of tributary rivers, a diversity of states and empires arose including the Kongo of the coastal area as well as others farther inland, stretching through to nations such as the Kuba, Luba, and Lunda right in the heart of Africa. These states produced not only politically united and powerful empires, again ruled through semidivine Kings, but they also established long periods of peace during which they cultivated the arts, giving rise to courts of considerable splendor. This political unity was disrupted during the eighteenth and nineteenth centuries by the slave trade, which brought drastic changes to the traditional political system.

Trading Kingdoms

The introduction of ironworking, the development of agriculture, and the intensity of commercial activity in West Africa in the early centuries A.D. laid the foundation for highly organized kingdoms and city-states that rivaled Europe at the time. The early kingdoms of the Akan and the Yoruba kingdoms of Ife, Benin, and Oyo were trading from the thirteenth to the fifteenth centuries with the great city-states in the savanna to the north. These were part of the Muslim world and traded with Muslim North Africa over the trans-Saharan caravan routes. The western woodlands and forest zones exported gold, marine salt, kola nuts, pepper, Guinea pepper, and ivory. Kola nuts were much prized because they were one form of stimulant allowed by Islam.

After the arrival of the Portuguese in the late fifteenth century, woodland and forest trade flowed south instead of north, and changed drastically in character. Under incentive and pressures from the European powers, Benin, Oyo, and the states of Ashanti and Dahomey and others acquired increasing power and wealth by the export of slaves to tropical America. But the prosperity was short-lived, and the western woodland suffered the same decay and degeneration that accompanied the Portuguese arrival in the Congo.

While trade was flourishing and these great kingdoms revolved around elaborate courts, other parts of the western woodland and forest were untouched. Nsuta is a site on a hilltop in the western province of modern Ghana near the major trade route from Jenne to Benin. It dates from the fourteenth century and so was contemporary with bronze-casting Benin; yet stone tools were still being made and used at Nsuta.

Older than Benin was Ife, from which Benin is said by oral tradition to have learned the art of casting bronze and that first unified Benin under an Ife King. Unfortunately, neither oral tradition nor archaeological record gives us any clear picture. Ife as a kingdom reached its peak around the thirteenth century, and although we have bronze and terra-cotta figures from early Ife, we know nothing or little of their origin. The art style is probably indigenous and stretches far back to the much earlier terra-cottas of the Nok culture to the north, and the Yoruba do have a tradition that there was an early migration from the Nile Valley—another enigmatic and frustrating element connecting Egypt to the rest of Africa. Since there is evidence of an early contact between Indonesia and West Africa, the art style might derive from the Orient. The particular technique of casting, a complex method known as *cire perdue*, or lost wax, may well have come from Sudanic Meroë. Whatever the origins, there is little doubt that the growth of these states was based on indigenous elements and was not simply due to diffusion from elsewhere. The core of greatness was there, and while the states of the western woodlands accepted and modified foreign influences that came their way, they retained their own identity and developed in their own manner. Even though it is almost certain that Benin did in fact learn bronze casting from Ife, it developed a distinctive style all its own.

The Sacred State

While each of the many woodland states had developed its own distinctive identity, by the time of the Middle Ages of Europe, there was an over-all pattern based on the fact that despite the complex level of political development and organization, the family was still the basis of society, and belief in the ancestors was still the basis of the family. The states, though their wealth was due to commerce, were nonetheless sacred in that they believed their unity derived from ancestors whose souls guided their destinies and order derived from authority rather than power, from the sacred rather than the secular. It was not until the introduction of firearms that individual rulers were able to exercise any personal power over and against the will of the people. The Kings ruled by virtue of their descent from semidivine ancestors. As opposed to the more classical divine kingdoms like the Shilluk, these sacred states were militaristic, consisting of individual kingdoms that banded together for common defense. Such confederations became unified nations by creating the myth of a common ancestor from whom all descended. Whereas each lesser kingdom had seen itself as a separate "family" entity, it was this notion of family that enabled them to extend their horizons to larger organizational membership or contract them to suit the particular situation.

When the seven founding Akan principalities united for common defense agains the Denkera, they each felt divided by the family system, for each traced descent from a different ancestor, whose soul resided in the tribal stool and continued to rule his people. The chiefs met and decided that in reality their ancestors had all been brothers and were descended from an even earlier common ancestor; the question remaining was which of the seven chiefs was the senior. They decided to invoke the ultimate ancestor so that he could demonstrate his presence and show where seniority lay. A storm arose, and out of the sky came the Golden Stool containing the soul of the original ancestor, and it alighted on the knees of the chief of the Kumasi. In this way the Ashanti nation came into being, and its leadership fell to the leader of the Kumasi, who became the Ashantihene, ruler of the new confederacy. At whatever level authority was exercised in the sacred states, it was always in the name of the ancestors, and in this way they achieved a unity that was secular as well as sacred, a unity far more binding than signatures on a piece of paper.

While concern with the ancestors has its origin in the biological family, and is the basis of family organization, it is neither solely a domestic issue nor a religious one. It also operates on a political level to check the abuse of personal power. A King may rule by virtue of his descent, but if that descent is passed on in the female line, as it frequently is in West Africa, his own children cannot inherit his status, only the children of his sisters. His sister is then a more important person than he is, for the continuity of the line is in her power, not in his. Royal mothers and sisters have their courts and their own stools of authority. They may advise or counsel the King, and their word will carry more weight in state matters. Yet, like him, they derive their power from the ancestor that is father or mother to the nation, and this power is held in sacred trust. Among the many onerous duties shared with the men of the royal clan is the ritual propitiation of the ancestors. While the male in any line might hold the temporal power, the ritual authority was in the hands of the female, and this division made for order and justice. Veneration of the ancestors, which was as much a duty of the commoner as of the King, was a constant reminder to both rulers and ruled that the ultimate authority was divine.

Of all the various insignia of authority held by virtue of descent from the founding ancestors, none is so significant as the stool. The Ashanti believe the stool contains the kra, or soul of its departed owner. The King never sits on the highest stool of all, the Golden Stool—it is the real ruler, the soul of the nation working through him. As the representative of the ancestors, the King is semidivine. His feet must always be clad in slippers for fear they will be polluted by the dead buried beneath the soil, which his feet may never touch. Gold is his personal metal, and gold is the symbol of the sun. All gold in the nation belongs to the King, as does the power, but like the power the gold is also held in trust. The King used to have special police at the markets to confiscate any gold that was allowed to fall to the ground, indicating disrespect as well as irresponsibility, and return it to the national coffers. Just as gold is the symbol of the sun and of the King, so silver is the symbol of the moon and of the Queen Mother. The rich symbolism of the Ashanti helped create a moral force that encouraged order and social responsibility among rulers and ruled; ritual restrictions and obligations heightened this, and to further ensure a minimum abuse of power, the rulers delegated much of their authority to others, either as the province of certain souls, and so hereditary, or according to individual ability and so within the ruler's power of choice.

The Benin kingdom of the Niger delta emerged sometime during the thirteenth century and reached its peak during the fifteenth century at the same time that Portuguese explorers discovered the kingdom. The Niger delta provided a myriad of inland waterways some 100 miles inland and 250 miles along the coast—a network of rivers and canals that facilitated continuity within the kingdom and provided easy access for trade to the north. Benin was largely a conquest kingdom led by a succession of warrior kings whose headquarters at Benin City have been described by Portuguese documents as the most grand and elaborate in all West Africa.

One of the most important crafts was brass-casting, probably introduced to Benin from Ife, and the bronzes produced by this select guild of craftsmen were considered the most valuable of both Benin religious art and secular art. The Oba, the sacred King, was the organizing political principle around which the kingdom revolved, and the Benin bronzes could only be ordered and distributed by him. The Oba had ultimate control over the kingdom; he was supreme judge and retained the power of life and death, although in some instances his power was limited and tempered by councils and lower courts. In many cases the Oba's decisions had to be approved by his council.

The kingdom itself had an elaborate political hierarchy to

collect tribute, organize government labor, recruit soldiers for military service, and issue laws and dispense justice over specific geographical units. These administrators received their authority from either the King directly, or in the case of low-level administrators, from one higher up on the pyramid. The delegation of administrative authority was based on both hereditary and clientage appointments. In either case the political organization of the Benin was highly personal and particularistic. The hereditary positions emerge from the web of kinship and clientage positions from the Oba's personal preference of an individual, usually in terms of allegiance, support, and ability.

This sophisticated and complex political structure was flexible enough to continually incorporate smaller states into the kingdom. Their intense trade and commerce, together with their indigenous markets, crafts, and urban centers, indicate a dynamism that was often characteristic of these traditional West African kingdoms.

The extensive growth of such West African kingdoms as Benin, Ashanti, Dahomey, and Ife provided an urban base in West Africa. The cities of these kingdoms, such as Benin City, Kumasi, and Oshogbo, often numbered well over thirty thousand people and were the focus of all political, religious, and economic activity. In addition to their importance as the capitals of the kingdoms, it was their importance as trading centers that primarily contributed to their development. Most of these urban centers can be found either on the coast or along important riverway and caravan junctions. These cities were traditionally heterogeneous in terms of social segmentation and contained both residential and commercial areas.

Social and economical segmentation in these cities often took the nature of secret associational-type groups somewhat similar to guilds, and functioned to regulate the conduct and behavior of its members. The organizational process of these secret societies was largely surrounded by ritual initiation and categories of myths, which served as unifying agents. Their influence was, and still is, extensive as a supervisory agent and presents an additional level of symbolic representation of group membership that unites people both economically and politically.

The origins of the ancient kingdom of Ghana, the first large-scale kingdom of West Africa, dates back to the fifth century. The kingdom began as a small state and owes its development to its geographical significance for trans-Saharan trade. The core of the kingdom was situated at a midpoint between the coast and the Sahara Desert between the Niger and Senegal rivers, quite far to the west of where the modern state of Ghana is now located. The capital of this ancient kingdom was Kumbi; it became the go-between for commercial activity between North Africa and the coastal area, and by the twelfth century it was the largest city in West Africa.

During its development, the kingdom expanded politically by incorporating neighboring states and is regarded as the first kingdom in West Africa to reflect intense stratification, a highly developed bureaucracy, and a centralized and unified system of government with a sophisticated system of taxation and military organization that enabled the kingdom to assume such control.

Wealth was accumulated through the imposition of taxes on trade, and gold was the principal export. The King had complete control over the mining of gold and regulated its production to ensure a satisfactory price. During the eleventh and twelfth centuries, Ghana experienced increased hostility from the neighboring Berber and Fulani peoples. In the political chaos that ensued during the twelfth century, the Mandinka of the small neighboring state of Kangaba along the Niger River emerged as the successor to the crumbling kingdom of Ghana. The Mandinka were also involved in gold trade, but on a much smaller scale. Under the Islamic emperor Mansa Musa, the Mandinka proceeded to gain control over most of the gold-producing area, and the empire of Mali emerged. Mansa Musa expanded his control north and ruled over a vast territory from the capital city of Niani. The empire of Mali eventually suffered the same fate as Ghana. By the fifteenth century, Mali was far larger than the kingdom of Ghana had been, as Mali expanded north to incorporate the Saharan trading cites of Jenne, Timbuctu, and Gao. This vast area was difficult to control centrally, and it began to tear apart from dissident groups who no longer saw any advantage in remaining part of the kingdom.

A third ancient kingdom of West Africa was Songhai, an Islamic people centered around the commercial city of Gao along the Niger River. During Mali's disintegration the Songhai, under the capable leadership of Sunni Ali, began to push outward and expand their political control, and by the fifteenth century had within their control a vast area stretching from what is now Mali to what is now Nigeria, incorporating the other two major cities of trade along the Niger River, Timbuctu and Jenne.

During the final years of the sixteenth century, Songhai was invaded by Moors from the North, and its ascendancy ended. It is also during this time that trading activities began changing focus from gold, salt, and ivory to slave trade on the Atlantic Coast.

The kingdoms of Ghana, Mali, and Songhai stretch over ten centuries and the entire area of West Africa. They owe much of their success to their geography, for it was these kingdoms and their natural resources of gold and ivory that provided the motivation for the intense trade with the North. Through them we see the emergence of stratification, concepts of aristocracy, and a centralized government based on a highly developed bureaucratic system. While in any large kingdom there are impositions placed on the populace—for example, taxes, tributes, and military service—the indigenous social structures of the various cultural groups brought under control were largely left untouched, as were many other cultural patterns. Rather than forced cultural assimilation, these kingdoms tolerated pluralism, demanding only political loyalty and in certain cases loyalty to Islam.

Trade too played an important social role within these kingdoms, bringing much diffusion of cultural items, patterns, and ideas. Ghana, Mali, and Songhai represent not only the development of political and administrative sophistication, but also the evolution of material culture such as architecture, as reflected in the great urban centers of Kumbi, Niani, Jenne, Timbuctu, and Gao. The refinement of ideas and learning were also present in the development of these kingdoms culminating in Timbuctu, which under the Songhai empire became one of the greatest centers of Islamic studies.

Sacred societies are common phenomena in West Africa and can be found among peoples from Senegal to Cameroon. These societies are concerned with social control, the regulation of conduct, general training, and the perpetuation of tradition.

Sacred societies traditionally play a significant role in the life of the Mende of Sierra Leone as well as the neighboring groups, Temne, Sherbo, and Gola. The two principal sacred societies concerned with general training among the Mende are the "Poro" for males and the "Sande" for females. Initiation into both usually occurs at the time of puberty, and for both males and females is characterized by a training period. For young men this period indoctrinates them into the principles of Mende culture—custom, law, and concrete training in competency in specific areas such as farming, craftsmanship, and song and dance. For the females the training period is characterized by learning domestic duties and etiquette.

The initiation period is accompanied by much seclusive ritual and grounded in a magicoreligious context, and the emotional identification within these societies is established through secrecy, seclusion, circumcision for males, and in traditional times excision of the clitoris for females. The initiates are sworn to secrecy regarding the rituals, and the supernatural and mysterious qualities of the ritual emphasize not only the spiritual nature of the society but also the importance of the society in Mende life. Its political importance can be seen in light of the controlling influence it has on lawmaking and regulating trade and is the main means for entering the political arena.

Other sacred societies among the Mende are the Humoi and the Njayei. The former is a society that regulates sexual and social behavior, and the latter is one that is concerned with the treatment of mental illness. Membership in both societies is either hereditary or by initiation. The Humoi demands strict adherence to sexual rules and regulations, such as relationships with one's in-laws and maintenance of the incest taboo. Both the Humoi and the Njayei practice medicine, as most illness is seen as connected to breaking a social or religious regulation.

Of the various functions that sacred societies fulfill, the Mende sacred societies illustrate two central concepts: Sacred societies are sacred in that they constitute the main vehicle for the transmission of cultural values and ideology unique to that group, and in that they provide a hierarchical status system that acts as a springboard for political and religious authority; they may also be secret in that they are often cloaked in an elaborate symbolic and ritual system. They emphasize the importance of the accepted cultural patterns and establish an intense emotional identification with them, while allowing for their modification, and exert political and religious control by virtue of their sacred nature and the hierarchical status system they provide.

Totemism

A widespread form of symbolic representation in Africa is what we loosely call totemism. A totemic symbol operates much as heraldry did in Europe—distinguishing different family groups by descent and relative status. Animals, birds, and sometimes fish and plants may be used as totemic symbols, and in the western woodlands and elsewhere, nations became associated with certain totems drawn from the animal world.

The leopard and lion of Dahomey, the snake of the Baga, the antelope of the savanna Bambara, and the hornbill of the Senufo were all symbols of unity in the midst of diversity. These symbols were repeated not only in national shrines or on royal regalia, but also in everyday carvings and household furniture and utensils, bringing the concept of the nation into the humblest home.

The totemic system itself reached down into the home also, for clan and lineal subdivision also had their own totems, and any one man might respect a number of different totems, each appropriate to a different level or set of circumstances. It was a way by which people from all over the nation could determine their relative rank, their social distance from each other, or the degree of consanguineal relationship, and so be able to act toward each other with proper respect and in observance of recognized obligations. It enabled them to see themselves as belonging to separate groups, but at the same time it bound them together in a single system of belief and behavior.

Totemic origins vary greatly, and one of the most common explanations for this is that the totemic animal in the distant past helped the clan or tribal ancestor, who in return vowed that his people would never hunt or eat the flesh of that species of animal. This occasionally becomes blurred into a belief that in the even more distant past the distinction between animals and humans was not so great and that they lived and walked together and intermarried—thus the ancestor might have been an animal. In any case, African peoples accept their totems much the same as Europeans accepted their heraldic emblems. There is one difference, however, and that is where the widespread belief is held that the relationship between the totemic species and that family or other kin group is so close that ancestral spirits may either commune with these animals or even inhabit their bodies. This belief increases the respect of the living for their totems, but it also increases their incentive to good behavior, since they never know when they are being observed, if their totem is one of the more common species. Among the Fulani herders, although cattle are not totems, the cattle are respected in this way, and it is thought that cattle have the power to observe "their" humans and to judge them by their actions.

Masks and Social Control

Another form of animal symbolism prevalent throughout this area is the carving of animal, bird, or fish forms into masks. The same mask may assume different functions on

Figure 23. Left, brass mask. Some masks were not made to be worn, but rather held or displayed as symbols of authority. Cameroon. Right, *to la ge,* "the executioner." Mask worn by high official when seeking or judging a major criminal. Mano, Liberia.

different occasions, or when worn by different individuals; others are more rigidly restricted both as to role and to ownership. Some masks are meant by their appearance to convey a certain feeling of awe, fear, respect, veneration, humor, or ridicule. Others assume their particular character by virtue of the character of the owner and the special way in which he uses the mask in dance, or however. Most, if not all, are a part of a total costume designed to conceal the identity of the wearer, so that his actions, which may be offensive, are not taken personally; this is particularly necessary where masks are worn by judges, much as in Western courts judges wear wigs or other special clothing to dissociate their individual personality from their role as judge. The idea is that it is not one individual passing judgment on another, for no human is perfect enough to do that, but rather the society itself is thought to be the judge, and is merely activated by the human wearer. The mask itself is possessed of vital force, and the animal form in which it is carved adds to that force, as does the addition of animal fur, whiskers, or skins.

Whether the mask is used to condemn a murderer, to extract compensation from a thief, to bless the fields, to offer thanks for a harvest, to secure protection in times of war, or to ridicule minor offenders, no one man has the right to judge others or to exercise a solely individual authority. All authority is held in the name of the ancestors, and all judgment is given in their name. Where sacred societies have specific roles, each society is likely to have its own totemic symbols, and represents this in the form of a mask that is worn when the society takes action. At times the disguise afforded was essential, for otherwise feuding could result between the families of those passing judgment and the families of those condemned. Liberia is wealthy in a variety of masks, and even within any one tribe, the diversity is great. Among the Gio, for instance, there is much variety in mask style and usage. The masks may represent a founding ancestor, or may be portraits of great people recently dead, or they may be totemic or simply represent certain animal qualities that are called for by given occasions. *Di kela* is the goddess of victory and is worn to honor successful warriors; *to la ge* is the executioner and is worn by a high official when seeking a major criminal, on which occasion he is accompanied by respected elders; and *klu ge*, in the form of chimpanzee or part chimpanzee and part man, is a lesser form that is said to come to town to help celebrate the rice harvest.

Craftsmanship and the Divine Presence

Behind the masks was the maker, the craftsman, and the elaboration of craftsmanship into art was a process confined to the West Coast states and some of those in the Congo. The distinction between craft and art is not an easy one, and the two are not mutually exclusive; it is more a question of em-

phasis. With simple tools the African craftsmen have for centuries worked the most unpromising materials into objects
that were beautiful and useful, emphasizing the utility. In
many African languages, the notions of goodness and utility
and beauty may be represented by a single word, for if it is
the one then it is the other two as well. Proportions of carvings of human figures, for instance, are not determined by reality nor by aesthetic considerations so much as by the quality that the craftsman wishes the figure to represent, such as
wisdom, strength, devotion, or humility. The figure of a
warlike ancestor may be given a tiny head and enormous
body, emphasizing physical strength; that of a wise King
may have a large head and relatively small body, and so
forth.

We can admire the technique and skill with which the
craftsman carves, molds, or casts, but in admiring beauty we
often admire what we alone see. African art is better understood as craftsmanship, as the successful attempt to achieve
certain practical goals. The most beautiful figurine will be
thrown away as useless if it fails to provide the protection it
was intended to provide, while one of much inferior artistic
quality will be retained as long as it can be shown to be successful. For success fine work is not always required, and the
resultant object may appear crude. Alternatively its crudity
may convey the intended quality and help achieve the desired results. There is little of what could be called decorative art—objects designed purely for decoration. The best-
known example is the Dahomeyan brass-casting of human
and animal figures, but in its present form it is recent, and
we know little of its origins except that, like other decorative
art, it is associated with the elaborate court life. And even
here in such decorative work as we can find, the simplest geometric designs may have symbolic content and thus be functional and craft rather than art.

This does not mean that there is no sense of beauty, no
concept of the aesthetic. African life is full of beauty, as seen
in their poetry and music and often in their very style of living. What it does mean is that their concept of beauty is not
ours, and does not form an isolated category in their lives, as

it so often does in the Western world. An African concept of
beauty involves not only the appearance of an object or the
sound of a song, but the touch of the one and the sonority of
the other, the intent and perhaps the purity of the carver and
the same of the singer, and the success with which the one
averts theft and the other famine. Beauty is functional as
well as sensual. Craft can be as beautiful as art can be ugly.

The elaborate courts of the western woodlands and in the
Congo were often generous patrons and encouraged crafts to
the point where guilds proliferated and the status of craftsmen rose to considerable heights. Even in the most secular
context, however, religious considerations were ever present,
and craftsmen had to observe additional ritual taboos and
maintain a certain distance from all impurity. While they
were privileged in some respects, they were restricted in
others. One graphic example of the interrelationship is the
well-known Ashanti gold weight. Craftsmen made these
weights of brass, and the nation used them for weighing gold
dust when that was its currency. The craftsmen used the lost-
wax method of casting: First they made a wax model or a
clay core with a wax model around it, then they surrounded
it with fine clay to take the impression of the wax. This they
built up with coarse clay to make a heavy mold. Then they
poured molten metal in through holes, by which the gases
and liquid wax escaped. After the metal set, they broke the
outer mold, revealing a metal figure, inside which the clay
core remained. Sometimes a real object served as a core, such
as a beetle or a nut or a claw. It was a process that called for
great skill and that allowed the highest level of craftsmanship. The variety of the weights is incalculable. The simplest seem to be counting devices, simple brass squares or
rectangles with bars running across from one bar upward.
But we have lost the key to the more complex geometric
symbolism. Only certain symbols can still be interpreted, notably the sun and the moon. The swastika is in evidence also,
and some symbols, such as that for water, are curiously
reminiscent of Egyptian hieroglyphs.

Apart from the geometric weights there are those representing animal or vegetable life; those representing items of

household furniture or material culture of any kind, including state regalia; and those representing Ashanti proverbs. In a way this consecrates all the elements so represented by bringing them into contact with the sacred metal of the King and the nation—gold—and at the same time it places a similarly religious sanction on any dealings with the animal and human world so represented. The weights could simply have been lumps of metal carefully sized to give the required measures, but instead an elaborate symbolic system introduced a religious element into what otherwise should have been a purely commercial transaction.

The weights representing proverbs tell us most clearly about Ashanti thought and ideals of human relationship. Two crocodiles formed with a single stomach represent the ideal of family unity; an antelope with long horns reaching right down to its rump reminds one of the necessity of knowing what is going on behind one's back (and alternately, that regrets are in vain and what is past is past); a snake shown with a hornbill in its mouth indicates that the impossible

Figure 24. The Ashanti brass weight for weighing gold is remarkable both for the "lost-wax" casting technique and for the richness of its religious symbolism. While some weights were used for actually weighing gold dust, others seem to have served more as status symbol or as ornaments, charms, and fetishes.

does not exist. The many proverb weights can still be interpreted today, since the proverbs have remained, and even though much of the significance of the geometric weights has been lost, enough remains to indicate that this was perhaps an even richer category, telling us about Ashanti cosmology and belief just as the proverbs tell us about their everyday life and thought.

The Ashanti still refer to the swastika as the hand of the colobus monkey, which has only rudimentary thumbs. It may have to do with left-handedness and therefore femininity, in Ashanti symbolism, which might explain why it was branded into the stool of a chief turned traitor. Two different kinds of crosses symbolize Nyame and Nyankopon, the female and male principles. Nyame the female is the creator and ruler of the universe consisting of sky, earth, and the underworld. Spirals of various kinds are known to have female significance associated with the moon and with conception, and a circle may represent the sun, and therefore the kingship, with its life-giving rays.

These are only a few examples of the wealth of symbolism involved in one particular craft form, but they help to illustrate its direct relationship to a religious belief that with the powerful and militaristic Ashanti nonetheless permeate their lives. Some weights were perhaps used not so much for weighing as for status symbols, and certainly they were used as ornaments, charms, or fetishes. Thus the weights, in daily use, through their symbolism reminded the people of the omnipresence and omnipotence of the divinity from which the King derived his authority, for the King's gold was the emblem of the sun, and it reflected the light and the life of the nation.

The elaboration of these precautionary measures indicates that internal order and cohesion needed considerable support. This was an inevitable corollary of the increasing complexity of state structure where the distance between the rulers and the ruled become greater and the concentration of power (particularly following the introduction of firearms) led to additional dangers of the abuse of authority. Social responsibility was on its way to becoming, at best, legal conformity. The next step was to be the introduction of physical coercion, but meanwhile the divine presence was all the more frequently invoked, and craftsmen helped to remind the people of their mutual responsibility and oneness of belief. But against all the evil of slavery, even the divine presence was powerless, and the European slave trade began and

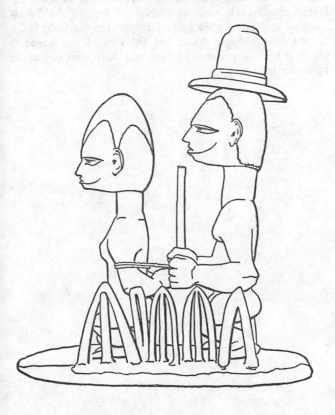

Figure 25. Headdress. Inland trade with Arabs was quickly replaced by the establishment of the European coastal slave trade, an institution recorded in various traditional ways such as dance costume, of which this is a part. Ibo.

flourished with the Portuguese in West Africa as early as the middle of the fifteenth century. The misery and blight that this enterprise brought, first along the coast and later inland, was hitherto unknown in West Africa. But it was not until the seventeenth century with the European development in the West Indies of the labor-intensive activity of growing sugar, that the slave trade reached its peak and attracted the Dutch, the French, and the English as well as the Portuguese. The demand grew and stretched from the Gold Coast to east of the Niger delta, and the cost of the havoc it wreaked in both personal and cultural disruption can never be accounted for.

CHAPTER 7

Obi n'kyere obi ase.
(No man should disclose another's origin.) (Akan proverb)

SLAVERY

It is sometimes said in defense of the European slavers who plied their trade in West Africa that the Africans themselves were already practicing slavery. Even if this were true it would not be much of a defense, but there is no evidence for its veracity at all. The slavery brought by Arabs and Europeans was of a totally different order from anything that existed in Africa before that time. As with many misunderstandings this one arises from the loose and sometimes willful usage of a word, and it is useful to make the distinction between slavery and serfdom.

Slavery and Serfdom in Africa

Even serfdom with its connotations of oppression does not describe what probably existed in Africa prior to the Arab and European slave traders. But the significance of the distinction is vital, and holds true—namely that while a slave can be bought and sold as chattel and his descendants held in perpetuity, a serf is merely bound to his master by certain bonds that can, by his own efforts, be negated. Whereas these bonds might be such that there is little chance of a serf achieving his freedom, this was not always true, even in Europe, where serfdom approached slavery in brutality.

African and European serfdom were responses to different conditions under different circumstances. The degree of bondage was different, as was the ease or difficulty with which a serf achieved freedom. There was also a difference in the way in which a man or woman became a serf or a slave. This is supported by written documents from ancient Egypt and from early Arab travelers and geographers. Even the Egyptian system, which may have come closer to slavery than was true in early West Africa, had laws to protect the health and well-being of the slave. In most cases, however, the system was more one of indentured labor, and the stories of the capture of peasants and their enslavement and exploitation for the building of the pyramids and other monuments are untrue. Peasants were used for this work, but under very strict conditions governing working conditions, even diet, and it was the workers' right to strike if these regulations were not properly fulfilled. Further, this work took place during the annual inundations when the peasants had no other employment, and it *could* be considered, in a way, as a relief system. Similarly, the excessive tribute that had to be paid to the Pharaohs in agricultural produce or labor was not intended as exploitation for individual gain, though it may have been in some cases, but as part of a national defense system under which the royal court acted as a central bank from which relief could be allocated to any part of the nation in need. This is equally true of the heavy tribute paid to many of the traditional African Kings farther south, to which the pharaonic system bears a striking resemblance. Our own taxation system is a comparable institution.

Serfdom in Africa came about in a diversity of ways. It was frequently a way of working off debt, as it was in Europe; it was a way of paying for some crime; it was a way of dealing with captives from warfare and raiding. Warfare and raiding did not take place for the specific purpose of ac-

quiring slaves until slaves became a commodity, which they
only did with the advent of Arabs and Europeans. The nature of traditional society was such that there was no need
for a labor force, cheap or otherwise. Warfare and raiding
took place largely for economic reasons and as land pressure
increased, and in the process captives were taken. Serfdom
was an alternative to their slaughter. Similarly, serfdom was
also a sensible and essentially humane attempt to cure a
criminal, rather than punish him. In both bases the system
reincorporated those who were temporarily outside society,
within its bounds.

Captives from other tribes had no kinship connection and
as such were outside the all-encompassing family system of
their captors. As such they were not even bound by the sanction of belief, for their belief was different. There was no
way of effectively relating to them and bringing them into
the over-all system of interpersonal relationships except by
adoption, and that is what serfdom in Africa often involved.
The same was true of criminals. However, it would be better
to refer to criminals as the sick, for social behavior is considered normal in Africa, and antisocial behavior is abnormal—
induced by witchcraft or by being cursed. Lesser cases are
settled locally; the criminal is restored to society, to his family, with restitution having been made and the spirits propiti-
ated. But in cases of murder, adultery, or incest, the offense
may be so severe that the continued presence of the offender
would be a constant source of friction. He may then be removed, or remove himself, and seek admission to a new family elsewhere.

Adoption of criminals or captives as serfs was a way of in-
tegrating them into the social structure in such a way as to
place them under social and ritual sanction and bind them to
social behavior. Through adoption criminals and captives
acquired full status as familial members, with the responsibilities of maintaining certain taboos, observing certain
rites, and performing certain duties. In their lifetimes such
individuals might acquire complete freedom, but it was not
something that could be bought, as could freedom from a

debt. Freedom could only come with complete integration, and that generally came with the next generation. As part of the family, the serf married and reared children within the system appropriate to that family, and only then was the integration complete. This explains the wonder felt by Europeans who much found the same system still in practice. MacLean, governor of the Gold Coast between 1837 and 1843, marveled that the "slaves" were regarded as members of the family, not even as servants, and were able to accumulate considerable wealth and even inherit from their "masters." MacLean missed the point that these were people who had actually *become* members of the family and so were inheriting not from masters but from their fathers or mothers. Slaves were frequently dressed with exceptional finery and adorned with expensive jewelry, and even more significantly were frequently given highly responsible posts. They had the advantage of being family members, and therefore were bound by all the ritual bonds of loyalty, but they were of foreign origin and so had even wider social horizons. Even in the royal courts, slaves were able, like any other, to climb the ladder of success, though frequently there were special posts reserved for them that opened the way to even more rapid promotion. Such men were often close to the King, acting as responsible officials in the army, the court, and the royal household, having the ear of the King and acting as his advisers in certain affairs. In the great Akan court the hammock of the King's slave had to be carried by the royal princes, and there were legal injunctions against disclosing any man's origin. Elsewhere there was no attempt to conceal origins in serfdom. Where the hierarchical system was less rigidly developed and there was less of an aristocracy, it simply did not matter.

This then was the "slavery" known to traditional Africa. Just as MacLean marveled at this system in the early nineteenth century, so Arab travelers marveled nearly a thousand years earlier at the magnificence of the West African courts, their opulence and splendor and the justice of their rulers. Even more than the opulence, it was the association of justice with power that struck these travelers as remarkable. The

Arabs themselves, though they had a well-defined system of what can more truly be called slavery, still did not develop the form slavery took, later on, in the Americas—the most brutal and vicious system the world has ever known. The Koran, for instance, encourages manumission as a godly act, and for those held in slavery laid down a number of exhortations. A child born to a slave woman by the master is born free, and freedom should also be accorded the mother. A child born of slaves within a household is to be regarded as a member of the household and should not be sold, unless because of gross misconduct. Masters were bound by religious considerations to care for slaves in their sickness and old age, and to maintain their wives and children, and were subject to criticism if they did not offer opportunity for self-redemption or for purchase out of slavery. I have myself stayed in an Arab household in North Africa and mistaken two slaves as members of the family. There was no attempt to conceal their status, it was merely considered irrelevant; to all intents and purposes they *were* members of the family. Further, they intended to maintain the status, since in this way they had security both for themselves and for their children, for whom the master was obliged to provide education, care, and finally employment. Slavery in this form is still practiced in the Arab world, and the slave trade from Africa to Arabia continued until the 1950s, when slave traders in Saudi Arabia enticed Africans to join them on an alleged pilgrimage to Mecca.

Earlier the Arab traders had not been so gentle. One of their mainstays was ivory, carried from the interior to both coasts (but mainly the East Coast) by African porters, who were then themselves sold as slaves. The East African trade supplied slaves to Egypt, India, Arabia, and Persia; the West African trade sent slaves to the North African coast across the Sahara and thence to Turkey. The extent of early Arab slaving in Africa is not know, but their main commerce was in gold and ivory—slaves being an incidental commodity until the introduction to Africa of the European and American notion of slaves as chattel, for usage as free labor.

This marked the beginning of slavery as most of us think

of it. The gold and ivory trade dwindled, and American slavery, operating through the offices of Portuguese and British, opened up a new market. To protect themselves against enslavement many Africans became Muslims, for as such they could not be enslaved by the Arabs; or else they sold their services to the slavers and helped capture their fellows so that they themselves would not be caught. The result was a rapid and terrible degeneration of all that had gone before. The scramble for survival was matched by a scramble for wealth, and the greed and inhumanity brought by the European slavers quickly spread throughout what became known as the Slave Coast. The rich and the powerful prospered briefly, but only outwardly. Their prosperity and success were the seeds of their downfall, for it destroyed the essentially democratic traditional form of government just as it destroyed the essentially egalitarian traditional economy. Unities built up over the centuries broke apart, just as families broke apart, and the divinity that had been the source of so much greatness became a tragic myth. Had it not been for slavery, the sacred states of West Africa and the Congo might have continued to the present day, but the trade that brought prosperity and power to the Americas brought impoverishment and foreign domination to Africa. In an odd way, the only ones to escape were the slaves, for they did not suffer the ultimate degradation of dealing in human flesh either as sellers or buyers or as intermediaries. They were the victims, and whatever humiliation they suffered was not of their own making. The slaves who were exported to the Americas were Africans before they were slaves and Africans afterward, and their descendants are still Africans today. The slaves took with them, perhaps, something of the past greatness that was to become lost in its own homeland and preserved it on foreign shores, so that Leopold Sadar Senghor of Senegal could sing of the Black American troops:

"... Behind your strong face, I did not recognize you.
   yet I had only to touch the warmth of your dark hand—
      my name is *Africa!*
   And I discovered lost laughter again, and heard old voices,
      and the roaring rapids of the Congo. . ."

Oh, black brothers, warriors whose mouths are singing
  flowers—
Delight of living when winter is over—
You I salute as messengers of peace!"*

The African Tradition in the Americas

The slaves, exported at the rate of about a hundred thousand every year during the eighteenth century, left behind
them a continent in decay. There was the psychological im-
pact of slavery that in itself undermined the entire traditional
system, and there was the corruption that spread with this
breakdown of tradition and coupled with the new opportunities for individual advancement at the cost of others. Survival, which had once been a social matter, had now become
an individual matter. A major factor was the introduction of
firearms, originally to make the capture of slaves possible, for
enormous numbers of slaves were required (the twenty million or so who arrived in the Americas represent only a small
part of the total number captured), and traditional weaponry
simply was not designed for this kind of activity. The
firearms so introduced placed a new kind of power in the
hands of the rulers. Whereas formerly their power had
derived from ancestral authority, and was unsupported by
the wherewithal to effect physical coercion, the rulers were
now in a position to maintain and exercise almost unlimited
power by virtue of gunpowder alone. Force replaced morality, and the essentially social, familial nature of African society, where touched by slavery, broke down. This is all
quite apart from the impoverishment of West African and
Congolese societies by the forcible removal of so many of
their healthiest men, women, and children. The greatness
that might have been Africa's had it not been for the slave
trade is incalculable, but at least some of it was transplanted
with the slaves and continues to thrive today in South and
North America.

Unlike those sent to North America, slaves sent to the

* "To the American Negro Troops," *An African Treasury,* ed.
Langston Hughes (New York: Crown Publishers, 1960).

southern part of the Western Hemisphere were able, for a diversity of reasons, to keep much of their culture intact. Just as the policy in the North was to prevent slaves from uniting and challenging their owners in any large-scale uprising, so it was in the South. But whereas in North America this was achieved by splitting families, destroying any sense of continuity with the past, and by splitting tribal groups so that wider traditional bonds were equally destroyed, and thus placing them under the necessity for learning and speaking, even to each other, in English, in South America the same goal was achieved by just the opposite policy. It was common there for slaves to be deliberately kept in tribal units, and the Portuguese encouraged *batouques,* which were periodic displays of tribal dancing and drumming, thus playing one tribal group against another and creating divisiveness and even animosity among the slaves.

Slavery reached south on the coastal areas as far as Argentina and as far north as Canada, but it has notably been in South America and the Caribbean that African tradition has survived in an easily recognizable outward form. This was mistakenly taken to indicate that it had not survived in North America. Although slaves were drawn from almost all over the African continent, in the Caribbean and South America distinct tribal pockets developed and preserved tradition that even in some cases was later to be lost in Africa. We have Dahomean culture in Brazil, Ashanti in Surinam, Yoruba in the Caribbean. Those in Surinam were exceptional because when the British transferred the colony to the Dutch in the mid-seventeenth century, many of the slaves fled to the inland bush and fought for their independence until finally it was granted little more than one hundred years later. From then on, divided into six separate tribes, they were able to flourish, retaining such of their past cultures as suited their new surroundings and conditions.

But cultures cannot be chopped up piecemeal, preserving a bit here and dropping a bit there, and changes in any one element must necessarily mean changes in other elements. There is the danger that when we find outward similarities between the African cultures of Surinam and those of the

Ashanti and Yoruba that we assume there has been more continuity of tradition than where there are no such outward manifestations of transfer. The material culture of the Djuka of Surinam does indeed resemble in remarkable detail that of the ancient Ashanti, and so do the shrines and rituals of the Yoruba descendants bear witness to their past. These elements could not have remained in isolation, but unfortunately few early studies were made of the total social organization of these peoples, so we know little of the process by which their past culture survived and changed.

In North America there are no such dramatic evidences of survival, and only in a very few places, such as on the islands along the Georgia coast, are there groups of people who can with reasonable certainty trace their tribal origins. There is little resemblance in material culture, and still less in ritual practice and behavior. This is not surprising, since the system split tribal groups, clans, and families, so that no community of belief or practice remained except with relation to their newfound status as slaves, and their newfound language and religion, English and Christianity. But closer inspection shows possibilities of survivals just as significant, perhaps more so, than can be seen with greater ease and certainty in South America. To start with, the depth to which the process of acculturation reached should be questioned. The nominal acceptance of a language or a religion does not necessarily indicate that the same thoughts and concepts are evoked by the same words or ritual acts, and the general lack of effective communication between black and white in America would indicate a wide difference there. Nor does an apparently willing, even cheerful, acceptance of an assigned position necessarily indicate a negation of the past. The assumption of English speech and clothes, of the Christian religion, could be as much a façade as the assumption of that mien by which the black slaves in America were so often characterized—happy-go-lucky and carefree. It is a measure of the arrogance and stupidity of the slave owners that they could mistake the singing and dancing for servile acceptance. During World War II prisoners equally enslaved in concentration camps also assumed a forced air of gaiety and even

fraternized with the guards they knew to be waiting to exter-
minate them. Such façades are essential, under such extreme
conditions of stress, for psychological survival, and just as
they conceal the despair and bitterness that lie below the surface, so could the outward acceptance of defeat conceal a pa-
tient vitality, and the appearance of acculturation conceal a
vibrant continuity of Africanness. Due to the North American system of separating family and fellow tribesmen, apart
from those few isolated enclaves such as the coastal islands,
the continuity of any one tribal tradition was made almost
impossible. However, there is a level of generality at which
one can meaningfully talk about an "African tradition" and
more particularly a "West African tradition," and it is at this
level of generality that we might expect to find continuity in
North America. If there, obviously its potential for unity is
far greater than that of the more tribally oriented Black
South American, and the current fervor of the Black nationalism in North America indicates that this might well be so.

Tribal survival was discouraged, not only by division of
families and tribal groups on landing, but also in subsequent
sales and by the relatively high mobility of slaves in North
America. The sale notices and posters of the day indicate
clearly enough what the condition of the slave was, and this
we *must* understand if we are to discover what remained of
Africa, for whatever remained had to relate to their new circumstances. The "Negroes" were considered as legal chattels,
classed together with other agricultural livestock. They were
inspected, as contemporary pictures show us, and assessed by
their prospective buyers, just as a farmer inspects a cart
horse or a prize bull. Breeding was encouraged, even super-
vised and controlled, as part of the commercial enterprise,
for a slave woman's children belonged to her owner. Contemporary documents only give a hint of the stark horror and
tragedy of life for the slave in those days. At first they were
allowed to have souls, but then as they became more com-
mercially exploitable and valuable, it was decided that they
did not have souls and so did not need to be treated like
human beings—similar to the dogma that white South Africans today find so convenient in justifying their apartheid

practices. But even when owners were finally persuaded to allow their Black slaves souls (for primarily political reasons) and thus opened the way for their conversion to Christianity, although the owners permitted Christian weddings, they still found it possible to tolerate separate ownership of bride and groom and continued to buy and sell slaves like any livestock (one system being to pay so much "per inch").

However, although the conversion of the slaves to Christianity may not have made much immediate difference to the owners, it made an enormous difference to the slaves, who suddenly found themselves repossessed of an old, familiar source of unity—a unity that transcended all familial divisions and that was able to thrive and bind the slaves together despite the fact that the family still could not exist, in many cases, as a viable social and biological unit. The slaves already knew of their brotherhood in misery and recognized a common kinship at least in opposition to the common kinship of white ownership; but now, once again, they found community of belief and made of their new religion what they had always made of their old, a central pillar around which their lives and deaths revolved. This new religion was the source of a new identity, and the slave owners lost their greatest advantage in that one fact, for a man deprived of his identity is nothing. And although the new religion was foreign, a white man's religion, what the slaves made of it was very African, as the Black American church today continues to demonstrate.

This was far more significant than the few elements of material culture that remained to remind us of his African past, though such elements were not so few as at first supposed. There were close parallels in fishing nets and fishing techniques, also in culinary techniques; the mortar and pestle has persisted up to the present day in form that is recognizably West Africa. A few wood carvings, some of them startlingly reminiscent of specific tribes, either by style or content, so also with metalwork and pottery—all contribute to the growing feeling that there was more continuity than originally supposed, not continuity of tribal culture but continuity of a sentiment that is purely Africa. But while this increasing evidence shows continuity of the African tradition in material terms, it can be seen or felt even more strongly in subtleties of attitude, social relations, and religious belief, even in political activity. The Black American music that is often said to be so "African" though it is almost impossible to detect any African rhythmic or melodic or harmonic structure, least of all in that purely Black American creation, jazz, *is* African, but not in form. It is African in content, in attitude, and in usage. Functionally it is African, and again the white slave owners of the old days missed the message entirely when they indulgently watched their "happy" slaves singing and dancing. It even became consciously what it already was unconsciously—a form of a secret language. So with their religion, they made of it more than it seemed, adapting it to their needs, emphasizing the Old Testament with its accounts of delivery of the oppressed from bondage.

At the same time, elements of the various traditional religious beliefs seem to have survived to a small extent, perhaps fed, particularly in the southern states, by immigrants from the West Indies. The religious attitudes having been preserved, and faint memories of a tribal past even, it is no wonder that in recent times there has been a major swing to Islam and the religion of the Yoruba, the latter with a strong Cuban drive behind it. From the purely religious aspect many of the Black Muslims uphold the strict moral code of Islam with greater fidelity than some of their African counterparts, for they have taken to the religion for different reasons, to escape from the last vestiges of slavery rather than to escape from the danger of enslavement. So also with the growing number of converts to the Yoruba religion, for the purity of ritual practice in Harlem may well be greater than that to be found, say, in contemporary Lagos, and at a time when many a sophisticated Nigerian of Yoruba origin denies his tribality, insisting on his nationality, consequently losing something of enormous value, some Black Americans are proudly proclaiming themselves Yorubas, not merely in name but also in belief, and are renouncing the non-African world of the whites just as their African brothers are embracing it.

This does not mean that Black Americans are Africans, necessarily, in terms of nationality or loyalty, but there is an increasing number who are recognizing that they always have been Africans in other respects, in terms of their beliefs and attitudes, in terms of their integrated way of life, which their utter repression and enforced poverty only helped to strengthen. This shows nowhere more clearly than in the Black American family. Once again too much has been taken at surface value, such as the matrifocus of the black family, which it has been alleged, with naïveté, derives from its African past. Matrilineality is common on the African West Coast no doubt, but it is a part of a total functioning system, and this system was utterly destroyed by slavery, for the slaves. The matrifocal family that later emerged in North America was not so much due to continuity of tradition as to specific circumstances relating to the different opportunities available to men and women, and the fact that it was generally the woman who had a fairly steady job and was the main provider, while the man was a migrant worker. Other circumstances added to the viability of this kind of family, which is then Black American rather than African in origin. But very strongly African is the family *feeling* and the functionality of the family, be it matrifocal or anything else. This is a strictly African characteristic: Security is found in the family, not in material wealth. Certainly for the Black American, who had no material wealth from the very outset, and who in any case regardless of what his tribal origins were, would have had a fluid sense of "family," family has remained a constant source of strength and unity. Even in the earliest days, it was only the biological family that was destroyed by the slaving practices of separating spouses from each other, and parents from children; the sense of family was never destroyed, as could be seen in the usage of kinship terms, manifest once again today in the almost mandatory manner by which Black American youth greet each other as "brother" and "sister," calling upon the family ideal of unity to bring about a much wider political unity.

And once again, as the Black Americans are discovering in their Africanness a new source of strength, a new pride in an old identity, many in Africa are abandoning their African identity, albeit unconsciously, in the mad scramble to emulate the Western way. And while the Black American is finding that he can be both African and American, for his very bondage kept alive all that was left to him, his African soul, the African is in danger of losing his Africanness except in terms of geography, for the conditions of slavery that kept it alive for the Black American do not exist in Africa; neither does the colonial regime exist to fulfill a similarly integrative role. Most of the new nations have committed themselves to the goal of progress as defined in Western terms; by the time they discover what progress means, in those terms, they may have lost something of much greater value. The Black American is in the happier position of having known both worlds, and seems to be making his choice, soberly and wisely, keeping at least something of the heart of Africa alive so that others too, perhaps, may benefit.

One of the most significant trends occurring in our own culture today is a change largely contributed by Black Americans. The disparity of being adrift in a sea of urban anonymity felt strongly by so many is being challenged by Black Americans in their attempt to develop, within education, housing, and business, new levels of community integration: levels that can supply people with feelings of community, neighborhood, and group such that an individual can understand and see himself as a vital part of the social whole.

CHAPTER 8

Listen more often to things rather than beings.
Hear the fire's voice.
Hear the voice of water.
In the wind hear the sobbing of the trees,
It is our forefathers breathing. (Birago Dicop)

AFRICA TODAY

WHEREVER one looks in Africa, at whatever level of organization, then, certain fundamental similarities emerge. There
is a focus on social personality rather than on individual
identity. This is learned in the normal way as a member of a
biological family that is itself almost invariably a co-operative
economic unit. This same family also serves as a model for
wider social relationships, ultimately embracing the whole society, be it a band, tribe, or nation. This feeling of "kinship"
is complemented by a sense of spiritual unity brought about
by the focus of ideological attention upon the natural environment, whatever that might be, taking *it* also as a model
from which to fashion social and intellectual order. This all
leads to societies that are, while by no means perfect or free
of disorder, essentially democratic and essentially egalitarian.
They are, however, relatively small societies or they are, in
the case of the larger states and nations, broken down into
smaller societies within which the concept of familial unity is
at least approached by the actual knowledge of biological
kinship. Almost everywhere you travel, within such a society,
you are likely to find biological kin, each with its own sepa-

rate circle of familial, economic, and political relationships. So everywhere you go, the myth of the tribe as a single biological unit is reinforced by a measure of actuality, and the ideal of familial relationships of obligation and privilege—and affection—is maintained.

It is in part a measure of the size of modern Western society and of some Eastern nations that we have lost this "natural" social order where physical coercion is unnecessary because of the inner, moral coercion that springs from a live sense of social identity and unity. And it is in part a result of our enormous technological complexity, which we are pleased to call progress, that we have been forced to abandon a social personality in favor of the new ideal, individuality, with security resting in a bank balance rather than in one's neighbors and kin. These are some of the essential differences between the traditional African way of life and ours, and this is one major lesson to be learned from a study of the peoples of Africa.

Africa and Change

It may seem a long step from the Kalahari Bushmen to the Africa of today, the Africa of modern cities, industries, and commerce, but it is not. They live next door, and both are the Africa of today. Land that once belonged to the Bushmen has been taken wherever the nation of South Africa found it had value, whether it was the rich grassland and farming country where they once hunted with ease and comfort, or the desert into which they were driven, but where it has been found, as it has on the Atlantic Coast, to be rich in diamonds. White South Africa has long robbed the Bushmen and exploited them by rounding them up in press gangs and forcing them to work as farm laborers. That is one way that change has come to Africa, but happily it is not the only way. Elsewhere, albeit reluctantly, the colonial powers have mostly either bowed out or been driven out, and Africa is once again African, but with a difference. It has been touched by the magic wand of progress, and we have yet to see the result of the spell. It may turn Africa into something great and powerful, or it may reduce it to impotent mimicry of a world that can never be its own. Or, perhaps most hopefully, it may have little or no effect at all, and Africa will continue to be Africa.

Change is nothing new to the continent; from ancient times it has been wracked with changes, yet man survived them all by constantly adapting and changing himself, devising new life styles to suit new circumstances. In historic times the continent had been invaded by foreign peoples and foreign ideas for thousands of years before Western colonial powers played their short-lived game, and Africa always emerged as Africa. In more recent times Africa has taken Islam and made something of it that is African. It has taken the less adaptable religion of Christianity and is making something African of that, in usage if not in form, but frequently both. The Western powers left behind political structures and institutions modeled on their own, but one by one these have shaken off the spell and have reassumed an African character. So with the family, to a large extent, though here, and in economic life, there may lie the greatest danger, for what has been introduced is so drastically different from anything traditional that adaptation seems too slow and feeble to meet the challenge. The new African family, in assuming some of the outward trappings of the old, may think it has become African again; but insofar as this new family rests on the new economy, the typically Western economy of individual enterprise, individual advancement, individual gain, and individual security, then the family is nothing but Western also.

An understanding of traditional Africa is essential for an understanding of the Africa of today, and it may help us to a better understanding of ourselves. We have tried to give a very general descriptive account of major elements of what are really a large number of African traditions, but certain common themes constantly arise that are part of one over-all tradition: the unity of the family, the communality of the economics, the democracy of government, and the integrative power of religious belief. Before taking a last look at these and trying to relate them to contemporary Africa, let us consider two examples of the practical problems faced by modern African governments, which are confronted with the enormous problem of creating new nations out of divers peoples speaking several hundred different languages, pursuing as many different cultural traditions, often rent by internal oppositions that had developed into open hostilities with the coming of the new spirit of commerce and personal greed, and which had been suppressed and compelled into unwilling unities, called colonies and protectorates, only by the presence of armed force and the willingness of colonial governments to use it.

I choose two examples here because they are personally known to me, and because they involve populations that, from the point of view of the governments concerned, are small and economically and politically insignificant, but about which the governments feel "something has to be done." Both, like the Bushmen, are hunting peoples, and so have the greatest technological distance to travel and the greatest conceptual gap to bridge. Both, like the Bushmen, find their own way of life preferable to anything the new government can offer them, and are steadfastly opposed to the kind of total change envisaged on their behalf, usually couched in terms of "educating them" or "teaching them how to be civilized" or, more subtly, "giving them the full rights of citizenship." As a result both are populations that are not in anything but name integrated into the new nations, and however small and insignificant they might seem from afar, this is obviously a situation that no national government can tolerate.

First the Ik, once known as the Teuso, but that proved to be a term applied to them only by their neighbors and foreigners. They live in the north of Uganda, on the borders of Sudan and Kenya, but their original hunting area included both these other countries from which they have since been excluded, sometimes by force of arms, since the formation and consolidation of what are now the new national boundaries by the colonial power of Britain. Since all three terri-

Figure 26. Caricature of a British administrator with gun. In carvings such as this, African "art" becomes social comment and should not be considered merely decorative. Yoruba.

tories were under British control, in latter days, a certain amount of wandering back and forth did not matter too much, particularly as this was an area left rather severely alone by the respective colonial administrations, being remote and unproductive. So the Ik continued much as ever to hunt and gather. They are very reminiscent of the Bushmen, even physically, and must have had a somewhat similar kind of loose organization, held together by bonds that were informal rather than formal, and by a strong sense of family and the necessity for sharing. Their homeland is mountainous and arid, but like the Bushmen they had an intimate knowledge of the environment and knew how to supply all their needs and wants.

Rather than the kind of shuttling back and forth described for the Bushmen (only one kind of subsistence pattern out of many), the Ik followed an annual cycle that centered on the Kidepo Valley, their major hunting ground, stocked with every kind of game. Although rainfall in the area is sparse, when it falls it comes in deluges, and the Kidepo Valley gets more than the mountains around it, and the runoff from the surrounding mountains floods down and makes the valley floor sodden, so that heavy game moves up and out. At this time the Ik moved also, and followed the game into the Didinga Mountains of the Sudan, around to the east, and then for the honey season they came down into northern Kenya, just west of Lake Rudolph, back across to the escarpment and up into the Morungole range in time for the next hunting season in Kidepo. It was a cycle that brought them into contact with a number of different Karimojong peoples, the great cattle herders of the region; the Dodos and Jie of Uganda, the Toposa and Didinga of Sudan, the Turkana of Kenya, and occasionally the southern neighbors of the Turkana, the Pokot. With these herders the Ik exchanged the products of their hunting and gathering and tobacco that they grew on the mountain slopes, for dairy products and for some trade goods. The Ik also got iron from their neighbors to the west, in Uganda, and worked this into knives and spear blades, both for themselves and for the Karimojong. This would be much as Ndorobo hunters do elsewhere in

enya and Tanzania, and it might have been an important
dditional facet of traditional Ik economy.

All this came to an end with the freezing of the interna-
onal borders and with increasing tension among the three
ations. The Ik were confined to the Morungole range,
aching to the escarpment above Kenya, and were forbid-
en to hunt in Kidepo because it was being made into a na-
onal park. Hunting in the barren mountains was totally in-
dequate, as was gathering; both had required in this hot,
ry country, a nomadic pattern extending over many thou-
nds of square miles for the tiny population of a few thou-
nd. The few thousand were easily enough confined to the
ortheastern corner of Uganda, as far as space went, but
eir economy could not be so confined. They took to a vigor-
us form of terraced farming, which suggests that they must
ave practiced some limited cultivation before (certainly
ey practiced vegeculture), but with the scant rainfall and
ith a drought coming an average of once every four years,
ultivation proved inadequate, except as a subsidiary econ-
my. The Ik needed something more reliable, and utilizing
eir intimate knowledge of the mountain ranges and their
gility and mobility, they sold their services to the Kari-
ojong herders as guides and spies and intermediaries in the
usiness of cattle raiding.

Suffering from the same extreme aridity, the herders in this
rea needed to raid much more frequently than did those liv-
g in the more fertile grasslands, but the Ik, in order to sur-
ive, encouraged raiding even beyond its normal proportions.
hey played one Karimojong tribe off against another, en-
rging on traditional hostilities and jealousies as well as tra-
itional alliances. The Ik plotted the movements of herds,
d sold their information and led the raiders to the most
uitable place for attack; then they helped the raiders escape,
ading the cattle through passes well known to the Ik and
rough country that otherwise would have been inaccessible
the Karimojong. The Ik had strategically placed cattle
amps to receive and hide stolen cattle until the hue and cry
as over; then they delivered the cattle and received their
hare in payment.

When I arrived to do field work among the Ik in 1964, virtually nothing was known of them except that they were there, known as Teuso, and that they were involved with the cattle raiding. The local administration was further aware that they were poaching in Kidepo (if you can poach by taking what belonged to you before it was arbitrarily taken away from you!) and suspected that they were also going back and forth between Uganda and the Sudan, which, at that time, was engaged in open warfare against its southern peoples all along the Uganda border, which the Ugandan authorities had sought to close tightly. In point of fact, the Ik were leading refugees into Uganda, they were poaching only to a limited extent because of the presence of armed guards in the park, but they were organizing raids on a much larger scale than the administration realized, and further they had developed yet another subsidiary economy, reviving their old profession of blacksmiths and making fresh spears for the Karimojong as fast as the administration confiscated the old spears.

In spite of this the Ik were starving, and the population was reduced by a half while I was there, over a period of two years.

Two things are important: One is what happened to Ik society and social organization under these conditions of stress, faced by this abrupt and drastic change brought to their world, however unintentionally, by government measures; and the other is what should and could the government do, its business being to govern. What happened to the Ika is a story I have told elsewhere.* The effects had been accumulative, and when I arrived the Ik had just had a year of drought, which continued for another year, so that for two consecutive years their fields brought no crops at all. Their subsidiary economies all combined, even with a good harvest, would have been barely adequate, and alone the Ik were simply starving to death. But they had been starving for a generation, and to combat this situation drastic changes had taken place in their social organization. Due to the adminis-

* Colin M. Turnbull, *The Mountain People* (New York: Simon and Schuster, 1973).

trative measures that confined them to a limited area, and prevented them from hunting and gathering, the population size was no longer in proportion to their environment, and had to be reduced. I do not say this was done consciously, but it was done, and the Ik were conscious of what was happening. They would say, "Why give food to the old? They are going to die anyway and they are useless, they cannot even give us any more children." So the Ik let the old die simply by not feeding them, and the old were too weak to feed themselves under those harsh conditions where, much as with the Bushmen, food and water might be days apart, and where mobility in those precipitous mountain ranges required strength and agility. So the old died, in their houses or in the open. And when that was not enough the Ik said, "Why feed the young? If they can't look after themselves they won't survive anyway. In any case, we can always get more children if we need them, so we (the breeding group) are the ones who should have the food and stay alive." And so it was that the young, healthy breeding group did stay alive, and the old and the young died, except for those children who had survivability.

Survivability, the Ik shows us, is the ultimate quality, and it is not a very pretty one. But it works. It is humanity and human society shorn of all its trimmings, shorn of the luxuries that we tell ourselves are necessities or that we claim to be fundamental aspects of human nature. In fact they are nothing of the sort: Generosity, kindness, compassion, considerateness, affection, even love—all are luxuries with which we can make life more agreeable when we can afford to. But the Ik could no longer afford to, and every luxury fell away, revealing man at his most basic. Ultimately even the family disappeared, for the Ik had developed their survival organization to the point where family was replaced by system. Mothers gave birth to children, with ill humor, and not very frequently. Having done so they breast-fed them, with equal ill humor, and gradually weaned them, until at the age of three the child was turned out to fend for himself and the mother heaved a sigh of relief. After all, if you yourself are starving and weak, another mouth to feed and an additional burden to carry are not likely to be welcome, particularly since the Ik dispense with both affection and love and can expect nothing in return except some possible convenience should there be a harvest, when children are useful in keeping birds and baboons out of the fields as the children run loose among the crops, stealing what they need. "The children do less damage than the other animals," the Ik say.

The children form into gangs for mutual protection, and roam the countryside scavenging. There are two age groups: the three-to-seven-year-old gang, and the eight-to-twelve-year-olds. You do not make real friends in gangs, nor are there co-operative activities; you merely scavenge together for protection. The youngest survive on figs that have been half eaten by baboons, then spat out. The older children are big enough to climb fig trees and compete with the baboons for the uneaten fruits. As you reach the upper age limit of each group your gang turns on you and throws you out, so that at thirteen you become a man or a woman and you are entirely on your own. It is not much wonder that a child feels little affection for his parents, and does nothing for them when they grow old and feeble. The parents in turn, having been through the same system, are not foolish enough to expect help. Society itself has died, and a once warm, human people have been reduced by administrative acts, done in the name of progress, to naked animality. One thing, however: The Ik have no hatred and no bitterness. And they still have their homeland. I am afraid, however, that they have no hope; they have forgotten what that is. They have learned how to survive, in the new Africa that has come to them, and they accept it.

All this was unknown to the administration, it certainly was not foreseen. But what can the administration do? When it learned of famine it instituted famine relief at once, which would seem the normal and right thing; but these were not normal or right circumstances, and the result was that the fat just got fatter, for only they had the strength to come down from the mountains to get the relief. Even when it was sent as close as possible, by a very difficult and dangerous mountain track, only the healthy got any. By then the old had all died anyway, few were left even as old as forty, and most of the weaker children had died. And still the food was rationed out by their system, going to those apparently least in need. And having seen famine relief, the Ik abandoned their fields entirely. Even in the following year when the crops suddenly sprang to life and offered rich harvests, the Ik let their fields rot so that they could claim famine relief. They saw a parasitic existence as being superior.

They continued their political machinations with the Karimojong, they continued venturing into the Sudan, they continued undoing all that the government was trying to do by way of reducing the raiding and killing, continuing to forge new weapons for the herders. The government tried to relocate them, but it failed, for the Ik just would not be relocated, always returning to their homeland. The only possible answer was one the government rejected, which was to round them up and disperse them to different parts of Uganda where, as adaptable as they were, they would have quickly become integrated into new societies. The breakup of the tribe would have meant nothing, any more than would the breakup of the families, for both units, great and small, had ceased to exist.

But the government would not accept that the situation was so extreme, and tried to keep the Ik together as a people in the hopes that things would improve. So far things have not changed; perhaps they only will when the last Ik is dead. The irony is that by trying to deal with the situation in a humanitarian manner, the government has condemned the Ik to a continued existence that is nonhuman.

I use that example to illustrate the extremity of change that can come in entirely unforeseen ways, in consequence of apparently minor, even well-intentioned acts. It also illustrates something of the dilemma of a government that must uphold the interests of the nation above all else. The Ugandan Government requires, for the country, peace and prosperity. The Ik threaten both. The Ik not only encourage but also instigate fighting that is at an international level. At one point they encouraged Turkana to invade Uganda with some twenty thousand head of cattle, and graze in Kidepo National Park. They threaten national prosperity because the park is an integral part of the national economy. It attracts tourists, and tourism is one of Uganda's major industries. To say "it is wrong" to stop the Ik from hunting is all very well, but it is equally wrong to prevent Uganda from benefit that accrues from the park. It is a situation the African government inherited from protectorate days. It has tried to deal with it humanely, with famine relief, with generous offers of relocation in areas where farming has proven to be productive, but so far has not been able to find a solution. Yet if it took the solution that seems sensible, if it tested and accepted the fact that it would do no violence to Ik society as it finds itself today by dispersing them, even splitting "families" if they cannot be rounded up together; and if it so rounded them up (as it would almost certainly have to) in a kind of military operation, the foreign press, politicians, academics, and laymen, would all decry the government's action as inhuman. Yet, by such action, the Ik would be saved, at least as individuals, from the conditions described, and the newborn would have a chance to grow up as human beings, if not as Ik.

A somewhat similar but far less drastic problem faces the government of the Republic of Zaïre with regard to the Mbuti Pygmies of the Ituri Forest. But here the problem is reversed, being based on a superabundance rather than on want, and having to do with a social system that even today is adequate and self-sufficient and unopposed in any way to the new nation. The problem is also different in that its solution, the integration of this forest population into the nation as a working, productive, responsible part, offers great possibilities of capitalizing on traditional resources, social as well as economic. The crucial similarity, however, is that the Zaïroise Government, like that of Uganda, consisting of men who have been educated in colonial schools, and who to the extent that they have been so educated have also been colonialized, is somewhat out of sympathy with tradition, and conceives of tradition as inimical to nationhood and progress; and it conceives of progress in the Western sense, deny it as it might. The country is well embroiled in the international economic and political scene, and it is difficult to see how, for a long time at least, it can do more than follow on the heels of the West in whatever direction the West is heading. Yet again the government is in a dilemma, for progress has been defined for them, and is demanded by the people. If the West itself is not so sure, any more, about just what is meant by progress, this new enlightenment is something yet to reach the colonialized minds of many of Africa's leaders. So completely have they adopted the values of their colonial teachers that many, if not most, are openly ashamed of their "backward" peoples, particularly if they are naked.

A head of state like Julius Nyerere openly enters the fray against nakedness and tries to force the Masai to wear trousers. The Uganda Government, similarly, has taken arms against the nudity of the Karimojong, just at a time when the Western world is discovering that the human body is nothing to be ashamed of after all. It is deplorable that energy and money should be wasted on such an insignificant thing as the satisfaction of personal prudery, but it is tragic to the extreme that Africans, with their traditional closeness to nature and life, with so much richess of tradition behind them, with a vital humanity and with a vital form of society still within their grasp, should turn to such pettiness and ignore such great potential.

Governmental policy of many African leaders is more attuned to their own "acquired" Western values than to the needs and desires of their people, and in the leaders' quest toward rapid Westernization, they set standards that the general population neither wants nor can bear. Change is not a unitary process nor is the concept of progress an absolute one. The innovative and discreet introduction of modern technology and the creative modification of traditional culture are the kinds of concepts that need more often to be incorporated into the African sense of nationhood.

Zaïre is in a strange position, and nobody can tell how things will turn out, but Zaïre may well hold the key as to whether Africa is going to continue to exist, or whether it will become another Coney Island. What may prove to be

Zaïre's greatest blessing has been held to be the greatest defect of the Belgian colonial system, the lack of any substantial body of educated elite. There were little over a dozen university graduates for a country almost the size of India when the former Belgian Congo won its independence. That means, however, that there were only little over a dozen colonialized minds. And such a mind, once colonialized, has to be extraordinary to escape from its fate and to regain its original Africanness. Nehru bemoaned this fate, recognizing that the British education that raised him to the leadership of the Indian people also divorced him from those people. He required a Gandhi to make the contact. Kwame Nkrumah suffered similarly, but was perhaps more successful in regaining his African identity. Had he regained it entirely, however, he would not have fallen the way he did.

But the leaders and administrators of Zaïre are mostly either military men with minimal Western education and maximal Africanness, or else they are men who have undergone rudimentary school level education in mission schools that, whatever else they have done, have not encouraged political and economic aspirations as a life goal, and have not divorced their students from their homeland. The Roman Catholic missions in particular, happily a large number in Zaïre, have been understanding and even appreciative of traditional African values, and while they have not been able to create an elite at university level, they have and still are creating a body of educated men who are still Zaïroise. Where the colonial power was more diligent in "educating the natives"—and despite protests from other British East African territories, the Ugandan protectorate had a fine school system and an excellent university for all East Africans—the result might in the long run not be as beneficial as once thought. Such educational systems were, like other transplants, of temporary utility, and the rejection process has already begun in some places. In others the transplant seems to have taken; the damage done, unless it can be excised. In Uganda the school system is becoming more suited to Ugandan conditions, and the new generation of elite may well be more African and Ugandan than their fathers, and may know better how to deal with the Ik and the naked Karimojong. Meanwhile the leadership remains largely colonial in outlook.

The attitude of the government of Zaïre is ambivalent. It is aware of the dangers of too eager a pursuit of Western goals, yet it is reluctant to forgo the benefits. It is charmed by certain of the graces that adorn Western life styles, yet it is too close to the heart of Africa to be unaware that its own life style is somehow more vital and more deeply satisfying.

So when faced with a population of some thirty-five or forty thousand seminaked Pygmies, living in the Ituri Forest and doing nothing to help the new nation, and in turn having nothing done to help them, the national government expressed an interest in this segment of the population and said that it was concerned with their future. It was wisely noncommittal. But at the local level, with less wisdom, individuals took this to mean that the government wanted the Pygmies to be civilized, like everyone else, and leave that backward forest life and live out in the open, and wear clothes, and hoe fields instead of hunting. They wanted to remake the Pygmies in their own image, and since none of the local administration came from hunting peoples, they all wanted, and thought it right, to make the Pygmies into farmers. That was progress, as they saw it. Others, not knowing how rich and healthy and abundant life was in the forest, for the Mbuti, interpreted the governmental expression of concern as a desire to "help" the Pygmies by taking them out of their "harsh" environment, where it was thought they lived a life of terror and poverty, and by introducing them to the benefits of a life of ease and plenty. Several projects were started, officially and unofficially, all designed either to help the Pygmies from their poverty, or to civilize them from their ignorance and backwardness, or simply to compel them to contribute to national prosperity by planting crops that, in fact, did nothing but contribute to economic impoverishment in the area. The results were uniformly disastrous. As soon as the Pygmies, so civilized or helped toward progress, saw what was happening to them, they fled back to the forest. Fortunately only a few were involved, but even so, the attempt to settle them in permanent villages, for instance, led to sickness and death, for a system of hygiene that was perfectly proven and adequate in the forest was totally inadequate in a settled village. Similarly, a social organization well suited to their nomadic hunting life proved utterly ineffective under the new conditions, and the Pygmies became disputatious, immoral (by their own standards as well as by those of the village world), thievish, deceitful, and parasitical. They were on the road to becoming Ik, for they were unable to survive in this new world to which they had been introduced.

The government of Zaïre did not behave like others; it was not too proud to listen to unsolicited criticism or advice, it was not too arrogant to abandon a given course once undertaken. When it learned of the difficulties being encountered in the well-intentioned "emancipation" of the Pygmies, it called a moratorium on such attempts, arrested one well-wisher who was suspected of lining his pockets in the process of enlightening the Pygmies, and co-operated with an international conference called to discuss the issue. The findings of the conference were the findings of scholars, including Zaïroise, well used to the intricacies and subtleties of this kind of situation, and it is likely that those findings, subsequently presented, may have seemed devious to a down-to-earth government. But insofar as the findings stressed the enormous potential value of the Pygmy population not only as a source of knowledge about an almost entirely unknown forest, the proper exploitation of which is yet unknown, but also because of its highly integrated social organization, which in fact gives the Pygmies just those qualities demanded for responsible citizenship, the government listened with African ears, and heard. Some at least of the recommendations were accepted, and the government may still initiate a research program to see just how tradition can be adapted, not just to fit in with national needs, but also to actively support them. This field of research could be of vital importance for the whole of Africa and help prevent the irretrievable loss of its own identity.

The Power of Tradition

One of the great assets of traditional African society is that it is self-regulatory. It is only with the excessive rapidity with which change is taking place today that it cannot cope. Otherwise it is highly adaptive and flexible, even where it presents a somewhat rigid appearance, as exemplified in the traditional family structures. From the least complex and formal societies of hunters and gatherers to the most complex and formal states and nations, the family is the basis of traditional society, and society itself is a complex and intricate system of interconnections among the divers aspects of social life. The structure is such that change cannot come to any one aspect without, in some way, affecting all the others. It is this close interdependence of the four major facets of social life—domestic, economic, political, and religious—that gives life, for the individual, its cohesion and coherence, that creates order. We have only tried to form a general picture, but it will help, by way of summary, to look at these four interconnecting facets with a little more attention to detail.

The family is the basis of traditional society, and it helps to understand the central nature of the family if we realize the great complexity of the divers kinship systems that can be found in Africa, and if we realize the importance placed upon kinship structure by the traditional African himself. It is not just the idea of family, it is the form that family takes that is important as well. At the root of all society, except the non-society of the Ik, is the concept of family; of parents and children and grandchildren and grandparents, extended upward and downward to include ever-widening and narrowing social horizons. Above the family is the lineage, several lineages form a clan, an several clans form a tribe. Above the clan level the actual relationships are not known in the sense that they can be traced through known ancestors, rather they are guessed at or supposed, or even created as a convenient fiction. But the relationship between clan ancestors is supposed to exist, at least. So also, then, this system has within it the seeds of extension to the national level, and was used to this effect by the Ashanti, as we saw, and as could be used today, as demonstrated by Nkrumah first and then others, assuming the "father of the nation" image.

To get some idea of the complexity and of the importance placed in traditional society upon formal familial relationships, we need only look at a few examples. A family, for instance, may or may not consist of parents and children; it always consists of adults and children, but the adults may be sociological parents rather than biological. A family may trace descent, for purposes of inheritance, for instance, through both male and female lines or through either one or the other. Bilateral systems are most common among the hunters, where there is little to inherit either in terms of property or status, and where marriage does not have such far-reaching political consequences and is sufficiently regulated, for the purposes of the society, if a child avoids marrying anyone he knows to be related to either parent. In this way he is sure of broadening his social horizon, and that of his family and band, to mutual advantage, creating new ties and bonds in the over-all network. The direction, for nomadic hunters, does not matter too much.

For herders and farmers, however, with increasing adoption of a sedentary life and increasing accumulation of wealth and status, direction does become important. Other factors enter into the picture that cannot be dealt with here, determining whether it is more advantageous for a given society to trace descent in the male line (a patrilineal society) or in the female line (a matrilineal society). Herders are almost invariably patrilineal, though not some of the Berber. Men are dominant in the relatively tough life that herders have to live, with its demands for long-distance travel and the ever-present possibility of raiding. A patrilineal family consists of a man and his wife and their children, at its most basic. As we saw with the Nuer, this is expanded into a man with his brothers, and perhaps their father, their wives and children, the wives of their sons and *their* children. This is the easiest form for us to understand, since it corresponds to our own concept of family, except that we do not extend it as traditional African society extends it.

Among cultivators we find many matrilineal societies, with descent traced through the female line, and in that case the basic family still consists of a man and a woman and children, but instead of being the father and mother, it is now a man, his sister, and *her* children; the husband/father is not part of the picture, for his family is with his own sister and her (their) children. This, for instance, is what the Ashanti mean by *abusua,* just as we mean the other, patrilineal form when we say "family." The matrilineal family can be extended in just the same way as the patrilineal. It provides equally for inheritance, it provides equally for child raising, for the giving of education, of affection, and of discipline. In fact, whereas in a patrilineal family a son may almost fear his father, for his father is the disciplinarian, in a matrilineal family the son will be much more free with his father, and will feel restraint rather with his mother's brother, from whom he eventually will inherit and from whom he can expect discipline.

Neither patrilineal nor matrilineal systems are usually exclusively so; frequently certain kinds of things may be inherited in one line and other kinds in the other. Thus the matrilineal Ashanti inherit *mogya* from the mother and *ntoro* from the father. Mogya is conceived of as blood, and it is this that determines descent for purposes of inheritance of status and wealth; ntoro is spirit, and in the male line certain ritual obligations are passed. The one line gives you membership in a blood community, the matriclan; the other gives you membership in a spiritual community.

Both patrilineal and matrilineal societies provide a system by which descent can be reckoned and inheritance properly ordered. Both provide a sense of community at different levels, according to whether you are working in the house of your mother's brother or whether you are attending a meeting of clan elders or "washing" your ntoro (in an Ashanti community). Both also provide a means by which authority can be centralized and segmented, according to the needs of the particular society. A patrilineal system can systematize authority among the highly segmentary Nuer just as satisfactorily as it can in a patrilineal kingdom, where having centralized it in the person of the King, it can decentralize it according to clan and lineage or by allocating various areas of authority to nonroyal lineages.

The political and economic implications of kinship are further heightened when direction is given to marriage as well as to descent. Apart from individual direction, according to the needs of the moment and personal taste, there are certain preferred forms of marriage within which people are expected to marry, and other restrictions that are mandatory, but within these restrictions a great deal of freedom of individual choice still remains, the individual being restricted as to the *group* into which he may or may not marry, not with respect to another individual. The mandatory demands are usually exogamy and endogamy; thus you are compelled to marry within the tribe, perhaps, but forbidden to marry within the clan. The clan is exogamous, preventing incestuous relationships, and the tribe is endogamous, preventing foreign "pollution" and maintaining cultural unity.

Preferential forms of marriage are often stated in terms of cousins, this being a critical relationship that some consider to be too close for marriage to take place without being incestuous, but that others regard as ideal, since cousins are far enough apart, according to their thinking, for marriage *not* to be incestuous, but close enough together to maintain essential family ties or to keep property or wealth or status within the joint domain of two clans. The two forms of cousin marriage are crosscousin and parallel cousin. Crosscousin marriage is between the children of siblings of that man's sister; and parallel cousin marriage is between children of siblings of the same sex, two brother or two sisters.

There are all sorts of combinations according to whether such marriages are matrilateral or patrilateral, and these have different imports as to whether they take place in matrilineal or patrilineal societies. A crosscousin marriage, in the example given, relates a man in a matrilineal society to both his father's father and his mother's mother, in common membership of the same matriclan. In a patrilineal society, crosscousin marriage can lead to a permanent relationship between two patriclans. If it were necessary to enforce clan endogamy (unusual but possible), then patrilateral parallel cousin marriage in a patrilineal society, or matrilateral parallel cousin marriage in a matrilineal society would achieve it. Crosscousin marriage always enforces clan exogamy, the more usual pattern.

Yet another possible pattern, often favored in bilateral societies where ties of personal affection and friendship are as important or more so than any question of descent, is sister exchange, though this is not a hereditary pattern since that would lead to crosscousin marriage, which is generally avoided in such societies. It does, however, retain the strongly effective ties that exist between brothers and sisters, which otherwise may be broken by marriage and consequent separation, and it enables two friends to add to their bond of friendship by becoming affines, brothers-in-law or sisters-in-law.

These intricacies are related, as well as to problems of inheritance and authority, to lines of tension, and serve as ways of alleviating such tension and even preventing dispute at certain levels. Between kin where there is likely to be friction, such as between a man and his mother-in-law, there may be avoidance relationships, the two being forbidden to even see each other in some cases, in others merely forbidden to talk to each other; or it may be a joking relationship in which they are obliged, if they talk, to talk in prescribed manner of excessive familiarity. This same kind of avoidance or joking relationship serves as the model for voluntary relationships between nonkin who find themselves in potential friction. And it is most common for people who call each other by a certain kinship term, such as brother or sister or brother-in-law, or whatever, to come under certain prescribed obligations simply by using that term. So if two people call themselves brothers, whether they are actually brothers or not does not matter—they owe each other the same bonds that any consanguineal brothers would. Further, when two individuals become related, either by adoption or through marriage, that relationship affects not only them as individuals, but also their whole families; it becomes a group relationship involving whole groups, whole segments of the total society, in reciprocal obligations and responsibilities.

From this sketch of some isolated examples of the ramifications of "family" it can be seen how this one basic biological unit is made, in Africa, to serve as a model for a whole host of sociological relationships, and how in fact the sociological relationship is much more important. It is considered irrelevant to discuss physiological paternity; whoever the genitor was is secondary if another claims sociological paternity and adopts, with the child, the corresponding responsibilities. But this is what is in danger of breaking down in Africa today, and with it the whole strength of traditional society will crumble. One of the major forces responsible for this is economic development and the introduction of a cash economy. This has enabled individuals to store wealth in a way that was never possible before, and to provide not only for future years, but also even for future generations. Under such circumstances a man does not need kin; his bank balance is his substitute, his security. Under traditional economies a certain amount of wealth could be inherited, but it was seldom portable wealth; it was rather in land and in family, or in cattle or in water rights, or in hunting territories. Such inheritance, rather than freeing him from dependence upon others, merely enhanced the system of mutual dependencies, for the obligations that went with his inheritance bound him to others all the more firmly the larger the inheritance. It is said that a chief inherits a whole tribe, he is responsible for them all. So under widow inheritance does a man inherit his dead brother's wife and children, not as property but as a responsibility, to be cared for as though they were his own.

Today when men work apart from their families, at a desk or in a machine shop or in a presidential office, they are paid salaries for their own efforts, and they feel an essentially non-social right to that salary, that wealth—an *individual* right. It is a far cry from the days when they called on kin and friends to help clear a field or harvest a crop or build a house or stop a bush fire, a far cry from when sharing was a way of life, when societies consisted of people bound to each other because they needed each other. The new spirit of individualism, come with the new cash economy, has destroyed the necessity for co-operation, except in the most depersonalized ways that carry no sense of mutual obligation, for each is merely doing his own job for which he is paid, and therefore under no obligation to anyone except to his employer, and then only for the correct fulfillment of his allotted task. With the consequent breakdown of the family, however, the wider notion of social responsibilities also begins to break down, for society, traditionally conceived, is a mere extension of the family. There is the danger then that the new nations will be comprised of mere amoral individuals, bound to each other by no more than adherence to a common law. A judge or a President, once he loses the respect due to him as a senior member of the family, becomes no more than a paid servant, to be used rather than respected. Authority tends to become synonymous with power. The traditional lines of descent, through which authority was regulated, avoided much dispute; with the passing of the family this vital conflict-avoidance mechanism also passes, and with it passes stability and security, unless these are secured by the imposition of force.

It goes beyond the conflict that a matrilineal family feels when the father of children, as a wage-earner, wishes his biological children to inherit, rather than his sociological children, born of his sister. This causes internal difficulties, and it is more and more of a common problem in countries like Nigeria, where the Western way is so eagerly emulated, Christian marriages becoming more fashionable, matriliny being abandoned together with polygyny. Despite this façade, many an urban family modeled along the acceptable Western pattern of monogamy and patriliny has its matrilineal double in the country, and a common and good solution is for the traditional wealth, the wealth of the land, to go to the matrikin, and the fruits of wage labor to the patrikin. Certainly urban dwelling is not suited to the needs of a full working extended family life or even to polygyny, though the more imaginative Nigerian architects have tried to design apartment buildings to allow for the continuity of the old family traditions. With the cost of urban living, and the increasing cost of rural living, with new demands for cash to pay for taxes and school fees, clothes and school books, and for imported foods and trade goods to replace local goods no longer produced or made, the old communal life with its correlate, an egalitarian economy, are gone, and with them have gone the stable political structure based on family, with its flexibility and adaptability. Gone also is the traditional jural system, which again depended heavily on mutual need and mutual respect, working together to create mutually compatible behavior, so that order was maintained without physical coercion. This only exists in the tribal areas, the "backward" territories from which tourists are excluded.

These traditional pockets are often held to be hostile to national development, just as tradition is often held to be inimical to nationhood. But neither the people nor the tradition are opposed to the idea of nationality; it is old hat to them, and given the right incentive they could, with traditional flexibility, expand their social horizons and swallow up the whole continent if necessary. But the problem is to convince them of the necessity or desirability, for as long as they consider themselves as distinct, or are so considered, there is no common system of values on which they can come to terms with the nation. The offer of economic aid alone will do nothing toward this, any more than famine relief did for the Ik. What the tribe has seen of central government often does nothing but impress them unfavorably, for it is seldom that administrators come from the tribe they are administering, and they bring with them their own previous tribal prejudices or "civilized" notions of what is right and progressive. Yet these administrators frequently find they have to come to terms with the tribe and use its political machinery, for instance, if only as a vehicle of communication. Many a rural people will listen to their traditional chief and unquestioningly do what he says, but would politely refuse to do anything the administrator asked, even if it were the same as asked of them by the chief, simply because he does not have the authority, in their eyes. The only time they will heed the administration is when force is brought to bear, the threat of a fine or imprisonment. The traditional leaders themselves are caught in a dilemma when approached by the national administration. The traditional leaders want to help their people, they may themselves see the necessity for integration into the national framework, though by no means always is this so, yet simply by becoming spokesmen for the administration they begin to lose the respect of their people, their authority, and with it their power. They are like the divine King who sneezed, and therefore demonstrated that he had lost his divinity.†

What is required is a change of belief, for it is belief that ultimately unites or separates. It was a change in belief that united the Akan and formed the Ashanti confederacy, and belief that transformed the confederacy into a nation. It was a growing belief in Nkrumah's mystical connection with the supernatural, if not with some vague original ancestor, that for many in Ghana demanded the kind of adherence they would only have given their own tribal chief before.

But Ghana is a relatively small nation, and to ask the same thing of Zaïre may seem to be asking for the moon. Belief, however, is no respecter of distance. Mobutu, in a few short years, acquired a wide following even in the remotest forest areas; there was probably not a Pygmy who would not claim, with tongue only partway in cheek, that Mobutu was his father. Mobutu carefully assumed the role, dropping the military uniform and status as soon as conditions permitted. The stability this one act alone brought to a volatile and basically disunited country was remarkable. Unfortunately, it is a form of stability that can be upset at any moment by some power-hungry malcontent, or someone not satisfied with a relatively slow rate of progress, or frustrated by the caution exercised by a government not given to sweeping radical changes.

What we have seen of traditional belief in African society shows that while it is most frequently associated with the ancestors, as expressed in ritual, and so is intimately connected with the concept of family, it is also associated with a belief

† It has been said of the divine kingship of the Shilluk that if the King sneezed he was put to death as unfit to rule.

in vital force and spiritual power, a sort of divine essence that pervades the world. It is a belief in the natural goodness of things; anything that is not good is not natural, a kind of disorder, a malfunction of the divine system. I use the word "divine" not to imply that there is an active belief in a Creator God; on the contrary, where such beliefs exist they are usually not active. But there is, nonetheless, an awareness of another, spiritual level of existence, and of a power that is greater than man's; and this is spread firmly throughout the whole of Africa. We misunderstand and misinterpret it as magic, witchcraft, and sorcery, dismiss it as superstition, but it is there in the land itself.

And *there* is the source of the greatest unity, and at the same time the greatest source of local unity, the connection between this belief and the land; for the land is Africa. Hunters, herders, and farmers alike all sing to the land—grassland, forest and desert, river and lake and mountain and valley—all in traditional African thought, are inhabited by spirit as well as, often, by spirits, a much lesser order of being. This spirit, this spiritual or divine essence, manifests itself through the traditional subsistence economies of Africa, where the land, in one form or another, provided the necessities of life and where the manner in which it did so could be seen and understood and respected. One could not barter and haggle with the land, cheat it or be cheated; the hunters lived with it, the herders lived on it, and in a sense the farmers lived in it—in different degrees of intimacy, of submissiveness or aggressiveness, but always with understanding. To all of them the land, eventually, was father or mother, and the leader of the people, be it family elder or Emperor, was himself one with the land. The many titles accorded by different societies to their kings and queens and chiefs make this connection between life, their life, and the land; it is a spiritual connection, religious rather than merely ritual, and as rapidly as the world is changing around them, for most Africans, the belief is still there. It is in the speeches of the politicians, in the acts of the local administrators, and in the hearts of the people. All that is lacking for it to become a unifying force is its formalization, for the old religions and rituals that could have done it have been supplanted by Christianity and Islam, and the one is more divisive than unifying, and the other is often more secularly militant than spiritual. However, there is the possibility that either, given a prophet or a head of state that assumes the guise of a prophet or is cast in that role by his people, might provide a new source of unity in the growing nations. Once the essential spiritual unity is recognized between adjacent tribes, conflict will vanish between them and the state. There will then remain the technical task of how to construct a single society, a unified social organization, that will make use of the truly vital traditional elements and judiciously combine them with such Western elements as are compatible. In this way Africa may create a new form of society that will avoid many of the dangers and weaknesses inherent in our own, yet which will not be isolated from the modern technological world. It is just possible that if it can retain enough of its past that it may once again show that order, in human society, is possible without law, that government is possible without abuse, and that the family of man is more than a myth. These things were not all true at all times in all African societies, and no future society is likely to be perfect; but the traditional Africa that is still so recent was abundant in these qualities and came nearer to combining them all in a single society than we can imagine in our far from satisfactory world. Such societies were small in size, which helped; since the world around seems to have favored vastly larger societies, perhaps one way for Africa to go is the way of federation rather than unification. This would be nothing new to Africa, and would make good use of the tradition of opposition without hostility, allowing for the vigor of local loyalties while uniting them all in a single wider belief.

Some, at least, of the new nations of Africa are searching for such a direction, involving a new sense of identity that will integrate them with the rest of the modern world and at the same time provide them with a sense of continuity with the traditions of the past. If it is not found soon, Africa will have irrevocably committed itself to the Western way, for good or bad, and the old Africa may cease to be anything but a memory of richer days, when the world was *not* all alike. The power of tradition is the power to keep Africa alive, and that may prove to be the power to add to the richness and well-being of the rest of the world.

ACKNOWLEDGMENTS

THIS BOOK is the result of work done, while at The American Museum of Natural History in New York, on a new permanent exhibit called "Man in Africa." Much of the research was done at that time, and during three major field trips made with the help of the Emslie Horniman Foundation, the Voss Fund of the museum's Department of Anthropology, and the Wenner-Gren Foundation for Anthropological Research. For all these sources of financial support I am most grateful.

I am also much indebted to Professor Harry L. Shapiro (then the department chairman) for his continued encouragement, and to my other colleagues at the museum for their help. Everyone who worked on the hall in any way, from the carpenters and electricians to Planetarium curators, gave something not only to the physical hall but also to the whole body of ideas that went into it and to their manner of expression. In particular I must mention Henry Gardiner who, as chief designer of the Exhibition Department, worked closely with me over a number of years and contributed more than I can say to the success of the hall and to my own thinking. I would also like to thank Peggy Cooper, for in the process of editing hundreds of labels she helped greatly in clarifying the essentials of what we felt should be said about such a vast continent and divers peoples. Much had to be left unsaid, as it is here, because of shortage of space. Peggy Cooper and Henry Gardiner, through their sympathetic understanding, helped in the unenviable task of selection and in creating a common sentiment, if not a common theme, that ran throughout the hall and that I hope continues to make itself felt in this book—the remarkable dignity of man in Africa and of his relationship with the natural world around him, and the essentially humane nature of the divers African cultures.

A word about the designing of the hall is not out of place here, and will help explain the nature of the book. There were a number of vital and inescapable factors that guided our planning. Obviously the museum's collection was one such factor, but rather than start with the collection (one of the largest in the world) and exhibit it for its own sake, we ignored the collection almost entirely in the initial stages and planned what, theoretically, we would like to say about Africa, and how we could best make use of the space available—another major limiting factor. The main hall was long and narrow and badly needed breaking up into sections planned so as to prevent visitors from simply walking in one end and out the other. We were able to acquire additional space at one end and in the middle, where wide corridors led off. This all fell perfectly in line with my feeling that the environment should be the underlying unifying theme that should run throughout the hall, for both man and society are inescapably and intimately bound to the natural world around them in Africa. This relationship is as obvious as it is fundamental in terms of material culture, which of course forms the bulk of any ethnographic exhibit, but it is equally vital in terms of social organization, economic and political structure, and religious belief and practice.

The hall was divided into sections, then, that were designed to hint, in terms of color and lighting (and by lowering the ceiling in the forest section), at the major environmental divisions of Africa into grassland, river valley, forest, desert, and woodland. The entrance at one end was given to a brief discussion of the beginnings of man in Africa, and at the other end to an even briefer (regrettably) discussion of Africa today. But we felt that as a museum our prime concern should be, as it is here, with a presentation of the rapidly disappearing past, without an understanding of which there can be no adequate understanding of the present. We decided to include a small section in the corridor leading off from the center of the main hall (appropriately directly facing the western woodlands exhibit) devoted to slavery, both in Africa and in the Americas. This was intended to be a prelude to a broader treatment of the African tradition in America, a subject still requiring intensive research.

With this broad division in mind we then had to plan the content of each section. Just as the face of Africa can change from snow-capped mountains to blazing desert within a few miles, and the desert just as abruptly give way to grassland and forest, so does man in Africa change. He changes not only in appearance, but also in his material culture and social organization. While environment does not determine the form of man or his culture, it plays a large part in the shaping of mankind. Man is, after all, an inseparable part of nature. Rather than use a tribal format, presenting each people and their culture in turn, and rather than taking a culture area approach, both of which would have meant a certain repetitiveness from section to section of the hall, we decided to let certain organizational aspects determine the content. In the river valley section, it is the emergence of civilization in response to an increasingly dense and stable population that is given prominence. In the grassland section, political considerations are paramount; in the forest section, religious belief dominates, whereas in the desert section, the major consideration is economy. Naturally, all aspects are dealt with to some extent in each section, for they are quite inseparable, but when we came to look at the collections we found that they strongly supported the general outline we had arrived at in our original thinking. The magnificent wood carvings and metal casting in bronze and gold from the river valley states sit well in an exhibit that discusses the reasons for the emergence of what we call "civilization." The status symbols, in clothing and furniture, that in themselves may not always qualify for exhibit as "works of art" nonetheless are admirably suited to illustrate any discussion of political organization, and our collection from the East and South African grasslands was replete with such insignia. So our collections from the tropical forest regions, while illustrating the ingenuity with which local materials can be adapted to divers economic needs, were particularly rich in items of religious content, and the themes of magic and religion are central in the life of most forest peoples in Africa, as we shall see. Our collections from the desert regions of Africa (both the Sahara and the Kalahari) supported a focus of interest on economy, though a discussion of Islam falls into place here, equally.

Finally, in planning the exhibit, we established a large diorama in each major section of the hall in which we depicted the life of a single people typical of that environmental area, and discussed that one people as fully as possible. In the desert we chose the Ait 'Atta, a Berber people; for the forest it was the original forest dwellers, the Mbuti Pygmies. The Pokot pastoral cultivators were chosen as representative of grassland peoples. In the river valley section, instead of a diorama we built a scale model of a tomb (actually a composite) of an ancient Egyptian King, which enabled us to discuss life in ancient Egypt, the growth of the state, and the emergence of an African civilization.

The plan, like all plans, had its weaknesses, one of which was a certain fragmentation of individual cultures; but in the exhibit this was offset by the design, the lighting, and the color coding, which kept the theme of environment in the mind of the viewer, even as he was reading labels. In keeping the same outline in this book, which in essence is a presentation of the exhibit for those who cannot see it for themselves, we do not have the benefit of the museum's exhibit techniques, and the reader will have to keep the over-all theme in mind. I think the effort is worthwhile, for as a result, a much wider unity results, a feeling that one can, after all, discuss "Africa" at a certain level, with meaning and significance.

In all of this we were fully supported by friends of the museum, especially Mr. and Mrs. Gaston de Havenon and Mr. and Mrs. Gurnee Dyer, not only in terms of their gifts to the collections but also through their enthusiasm. The then administration, especially the president, the late Mr. Alexander White (although already seriously ill), and the vice president, Mr. C. de Wolf Gibson, saw to it that no help or support was wanting on the museum's side. The very genuine interest of the museum at that time led to our receiving voluntary help from a vital section of the public, Black America. The section on the African tradition in America was almost entirely researched by Mr. Joseph Towles on time taken from his own studies, and the American Yoruba shrine was presented, installed, and documented by Mr. Chris Oliana. Many others contributed with their ideas and criticisms, and while the result is far from perfect, it was the willing help and participation of so many Africans and Americans of African descent that has given the hall the success it has enjoyed.

While I have drawn as heavily as possible from my own field experience in the Congo basin and in East Africa, and from shorter field surveys that I have made in other parts of East and Central Africa, Ethiopia, Egypt, and North and West Africa, many colleagues specialized in other geographical and theoretical areas contributed directly to the hall, and so to this book. It would be impossible to mention all, and I hope others will forgive me if I single out those who actually worked with me on the exhibit: Jerry Bernstein, who as a student aid did much of the painstaking detailed checking and routine work; Shirley Blancke, for her work on the archaeological sections; Jennifer Chatfield, for research into the literature for areas not known to me personally, especially that relating to women; Frank Conant, who gave all the material on the Pokot and documented it for us as well as giving material and documentation on the virtually unknown peoples of northern Nigeria; David Hart, who provided us with material and vital information for the Ait 'Atta display;

Walter Fairservis, who worked on the ancient Egyptian section; Lucy Wood, who worked for us in Egypt itself, on contemporary village Egypt; John Middleton and Leon Siroto (who gave us a fine collection from the Kwele), who both spent much time inside the hall as it grew, offering over-all advice and criticism on material and theoretical content; Tamara Northern and Judith Randall, who gladly gave much of their time and knowledge; and finally Lenny Kooperman, in helping with the present manuscript, who brought yet another point of view to bear.

These names may not be significant to the average reader, but the diversity of areas of specialization they represent *is* significant, for it would be an impertinence for one person to attempt a book on Africa without such assistance. These days we are all overspecialized, and while we pay lip service to the interrelationship of our specialities, we all too frequently present data from our own exclusive and narrow field as though we were presenting a totality. The reality and intricacy of the interrelationships is such, indeed, that any attempt to present such a study faces almost insurmountable organizational problems. Both the hall and the book had to face these problems, and in the hall we had the additional complication of the stimulus offered by the very presence of such a vast collection. Sometimes when rambling through the storage areas in search of something with which to illustrate a chosen concept, either Henry Gardiner or myself, or one of the many others who helped, would suddenly see a piece that simply in itself seemed to demand to be exhibited. We would then have to think how and where we could squeeze it in, and thanks to the reality of the interrelationships we were almost always able to do so—a hoe has just as much to say (if not more) in a case on religious belief as in one on economics; ritual mask of figurine has equally as much to say in a case on economy or politics. In the end we decided to suggest these theoretical interconnections throughout the hall through case titles (such as Women and Land, Water and Politics, Masks and Social Control) and *not* try to force it elsewhere. In the hall the objects, certain types of which make themselves evident by cropping up in a number of different cases dealing with a diversity of themes, also suggest the interconnections to the viewer. I have tried to retain this pattern in the book, for to suggest one specific interconnection is to exclude others, and all are likely to be valid. Certain sections of the book may seem to stand in isolation, as do certain exhibits in the hall; they can be read as such, for they have a value in themselves, or the reader can, like the viewer, perceive similarities elsewhere and himself seek the connection. In a sense, then, the collection itself should be thanked for offering ideas of its own, and the limitations of space should be thanked for forcing us to abandon any attempt as a scholarly or encyclopedic coverage of all the major African cultures in favor of the technique of suggesting an underlying unity through the presentation of significant parts. Many well-known African peoples are not even mentioned, or barely mentioned, while prominence is sometimes given to small and seemingly unrepresentative groups. This again is a function of having to work with a single collection, and it all helps to show that perhaps we have been too occupied with the diversity in Africa and have paid too much attention to the great states and empires, very likely because they most closely approximated our notions of progress. For, thanks to all these factors, the unity emerges on its own.

It has been a privilege to work in Africa with the African people; in our less than easy world it has often been a comfort and an inspiration, a constant reminder of the great human potential for humanity. My last word of thanks must be to Africa, and to Virginia Commonwealth University for having allowed me the time to put into words the experience of trying to compress the whole of Africa into a single exhibit.

INDEX

Acacus Mountains, 135
Acheulian tradition, 135
Adultery (affairs), 37, 191
Adzes, 92
Aerophones, 127
African Treasury, An, 195n
Age and age grouping
   (sets), 13, 35, 41–50,
   95ff., 157. *See also* Old
   age; Youth; specific
   peoples
Agriculture. *See* Cultivation
Ait'Atta, 132, 136–38
Akan, the, 170, 192, 227;
   proverb of, 189;
   uniting of principalities,
   172–73
Allah, 140
America, 63, 111, 170,
   193–202; plants from, 94
Amghar n-ufilla, 137

Amun, 80–81
Ancestors, 12, 39, 41, 49, 60,
   62, 119, 120, 172ff., 182,
   183, 219 (*see also*
   Religion; specific peoples);
   family shrines to, 115,
   116; and totemism, 179,
   180
Angola, 110
Animals (*see also* Herding;
   Hunting/gathering;
   Masks; Totemism; specific
   animals): brass castings
   of, 183; early, 2–3;
   Egyptian gods, 80–81;
   fetishes, 116; for irrigation
   implements, 85, 118;
   spirits, 120
Antelopes, 179, 185;
   headdress, 156
Anuak, the, 51, 53

Anyota leopard-man society,
122–24
Apartheid, 198
Apes, 2–3
Apis bull, 80
Aqueducts, 152
Arabia, 193
Arabs, 29, 30–31, 63, 111ff.,
136ff., 168ff., 189, 192–94.
See also specific countries
Archaeology, 1ff., 22ff.,
92–93, 134–35
Archimedes screw. *See*
Tambur
Argentina, 196
Army (military), 17, 177.
See also War; specific
peoples
Arrowheads (points, tips), 4,
8–9, 21–22, 135
Artesian principle, 151
Artisans, 75ff. *See also* Crafts
Ash, wood, 103
Ashanti (people and nation),
169, 170, 172, 173, 175,
220ff., 227; culture in
Surinam, 196–97; gold
weights, 184–86
Asian plants, 93ff.
Aterian tradition, 135
Atlantic Ocean, 110, 111
Atlas Mountains, 134, 138,
150
Aton, 63
Australopithecus, 3;
africanus, 3; *robustus*, 3
Authority, 9, 12–13, 225.
See also Age and age
grouping; Government;
Kingship; Social
organization; specific
peoples
Avoidance relationship, 223

Axes, 4, 6, 21, 92
Azande, the, 103

Babies (infants) (*see also*
Births; Children);
mortality among, 91;
protection against
malformation of fetus,
113; and Pygmy magic, 99;
slings for, 98
Baboons, 100
Baddalah, 150
Baga, the, 119, 179,
BaGanda, 62
Bakwanga, 93
Bali, the, 122–24
Bambara, the, 121, 156, 158,
179
Bananas, 94, 103
Bandiagara escarpment, 154
Bands, 4. *See also*
Hunting/gathering;
specific peoples
Bantu-speaking peoples, xii,
38, 93, 94, 101
Baobab, great, 160
Baraka, 141
Bark, 98, 99, 160
Barley, 151
Barrages, water-control,
146–48
Basketry, 85, 104
Baskets, miniature, for girls,
99
Basket traps, 105ff.
Batouques, 196
Beans, 100
Beat hunt, 9, 96
Bedouin, the, 139ff., 143
Beer, women and, 40
Beeswax, 110
Begbe. *See* Beat hunt

Belgian Congo, 216. See also Congo
Belgians, 216
Belief, 112–20, 227–28. See also Religion
Benin, 169ff., 174–75
Benin City, 175
Berber, the, xii, 132–33, 137, 138ff., 141, 153, 176, 220
Bigo, 30
Bira, the, 100–1, 102, 125
Birago Dicop, 203
Birds, 97 (see also Masks); Egyptian gods, 80; honey guide, 11
Bird's nests, 160
Birth control, Mbuti and, 91
Births: fish associated with multiple, 108; Ik and, 211; music and dance and, 127
Bito, the, 30
Black Americans, 199ff.
Black Muslims, 200
Blacksmiths. See Iron and ironworking
Blood, bleeding cattle, 11, 13, 16, 35, 51, 65
Boats, reed, 74
Bolas, 4
Bone tools, 8, 21, 134
Book of the Dead, The, 82
Borers, 21
Bornu, 63
Bows and arrows, 8–9, 24, 34, 95, 96, 160 (see also Arrowheads); miniature, 49, 98
Boys. See Age and age grouping; Children; Youth
Brain power, 4
Brass, 174, 183–86; mask, 181

Bravery, 163. See also specific peoples
Brazil, 196
Breasted, James Henry, 68
Bridewealth, 28, 38, 102
British, the (Britain, the English), 55, 188, 194, 196, 206, 208, 216
Bronze, 30, 171
Brothers, 220, 224
Brothers-in-law, 223
Bull, Apis, 80
Burial, 24, 66, 73–74, 80, 82–84, 93. See also Funerals
Bushimai River, 93
Bushmen, xii, xiii, xiv, 8, 22ff., 31, 131, 135, 158–66, 204; quotation of, 131
Buttocks, steatopygial, xii
Bwamé society, 122

Cages, fishing, 106
Camels, 132, 136, 142ff.
Cameroon, 126, 178, 181
Cameroun mountains, 63
Camouflage, 24
Camping holidays, xvi
Canada, 196
Canals, 174. See also Irrigation
Cane, for weapons, 9
Canoes, fishing from, 108
Capsian tradition. See Stone Age
Captives (prisoners): in Egyptian army, 78; and serfdom, 191, 192
Caravans, 110, 111, 134, 136, 142, 143, 170, 175
Caribbean, the, 196. See also West Indies

Carpenters, 75, 85. See also Wood and woodworking
Carthage, 134
Carvings (figurines, statuettes), 80, 83, 116, 119ff., 183. See also specific materials, objects
Cash economy, 224, 225
Castes, 16. See also Classes; specific peoples
Cattle, 11, 13, 14, 19, 29, 30, 31, 34ff., 51, 64ff., 134, 135, 180, 209, 210, 213 (see also Herding; Oxen); Apis bull, 80; women and, 39
Cavalli-Sforza, Professor, 135
Cave paintings. See Rock paintings
Caves, 4, 93
Central Africa, 92ff., 153. See also specific peoples, places
Cereal crops (grains), 94 143, 154. See also Cultivation; specific crops
Chaamba, the, 143
Chairs (stools, thrones), 118, 119, 172, 173, 186
Chaka, 63
Channeled ware, 29
Charcoal, for wire making, 25
Charien peoples, 153
Chari River, 154
Charms. See Magic; Medicine
Chellean Man, 3–4
Cheptulel, 32
Chiefs. See Kingship
Children, 36, 37–38, 62, 173, 220–21 (see also Age and age grouping; Babies; Families; Inheritance; Youth) ; cattle game, 67; Egyptian, and Islam, 87; Ik, 210–12, 213; Pygmy, 95ff.; shaving heads of, in desert, 159; slave, 193, 198
Chimpanzee mask, 182
Chinese, 30ff.
Chinese yam, 94
Chisels, 92
Chi-wara antelope headdress, 156
Chokwe, the, 109
Chordophones, 127
Christianity, 82, 197, 198ff., 205, 225; Roman Catholics, 216
Ciga, the, 25–28
Circumcision, 124, 178,
Cire perdue (lost-wax) casting, 171, 184–85
Citadels, 138. See also Fortresses
Civilization, 68–71
Clans, 12, 39, 54, 60, 62, 219 (see also specific peoples); and exogamy, 222; and totems, 180
Classes, 16, 139; in Egypt, 74ff.
Cleavers, 4
Climate, 2. See also specific areas
Clitoridectomy, 36, 178
Clothing, 24, 215; gifts to wives, 38; and increasing age, 50; Pokot, 34; Pygmy, 98; rations by Egyptian government to workers,

76; Senegambian, 158; slaves and, 192

Clover, 85

Cocoons, 160

Cocoyam, 94

Cola acuminata, 94

Cola nitida, 94

Colobus monkey, 186

Colocasia esculenta, 94

Colonial powers, 54–55, 110, 141, 143, 205ff., 214ff. *See also* specific places, powers

Commerce. *See* Trade

Communication, 54, 104, 109, 141. *See also* Drums and drumming; Language

Communities. *See* Social organization

Companionship, 7

Congo, the, 92–93, 94, 109ff., 122, 183, 194, 195, 216

Congo River, 70–71, 106, 107, 109ff.

Cooking, 37; baking, 24; Black American culinary techniques, 199; resin for, 98; vessels, 8 (*see also* Pottery)

Copper, 29, 110

Corn, 85. *See also* Maize

Cotton, 85, 153

Courts (*see* Justice); royal (*see* Kingship)

Cousin marriage, 222–23

Cowardliness, 163

Crafts, 16, 39, 74ff., 85, 109, 155, 182–88. *See also* specific crafts

Crime, 116–17 (*see also* Justice); and serfdom, 190–92

Crocodiles, 185

Crops. *See* Cultivation

Crosscousin marriage, 222–23

Crusades, 139

Cuba, 200

Cultivation (agriculture, farming), xiv, xv, 8, 13, 14–15, 18ff., 31–37ff., 47, 51, 53, 54, 64ff., 71ff., 84ff., 88–94, 100–4, 109, 136, 137–38, 141ff., 167, 209, 220 (*see also* specific countries, crops, peoples); savanna, 152–58; vegeculture, xiv, 85, 92, 135, 161

Cults. *See* Religion; Sacred societies

Culture, difference in, xii–xiv, xv–xviii. *See also* specific peoples

Currency (*see also* Cash economy): iron, 28

Cushitics, 64

Cwezi, the, 30

Dahomey, 129, 170, 175, 179, 183; culture of, in Brazil, 196

Dairy products, 143, 208

Dams, for fishing, 106, 107

Dance (dancing), 125–26, 158, 181, 187, 196, 197, 200; Bushman, 165; Egyptian women and, 77

Danoa, the, 154

Dar Mamar, the, 159

Date palms, 151, 153

Dates, 143

Daza, the, 153

Death, 24, 115ff., 218 (*see also* Ancestors; Burial; Inheritance; Suicide; Widowhood); and age sets, 49–50; in Egypt, 73–74, 80, 82–84; Kikuyu and, 65–66; of King for sneezing, 227; leopard-man society and, 122–24; Masai and, 65; music and dance and, 127; and unauthorized usage of water sources, 149

Debt, 190

Deceit, 163

Democracy, 16, 137, 194, 202–4, 205

Denkera, the, 172

Descent, 39, 220ff. See also Ancestors; Clans; Families; Inheritance; Lineages; Tribes; Women; specific peoples

Desert, 131–66

Despotism, 63

Diamonds, 204

Didinga, the, 208

Didinga Mountains, 208

Digging sticks, 160; weights for, 22, 93, 135

Digitaria exilis. See Fonio

Di kela, 182

Dinka, the, 51, 52–53, 57

Dioscorea alata, 94

Dioscorea cayenensis, 94

Dioscorea esculenta, 94

Dioscorea rotundata, 94

Disease. *See* Sickness

Diviners, 113–14; women as, 40

Djihads (jehads), 63, 140

Djuka, the, 197

Doctors, 113ff.; and initiations, 124, 125; women as, 40

Dodos, the, 208

Dogon, the, 154–57, 158

Dogs, and hunting, xiv

Donkeys, 143

Dream world, Bushman, 165–66

Dress. *See* Clothing

Drought, 116

Drums and drumming, 104, 127, 196; "talking drum," 130; women and, 41

Dutch, the, 30, 188, 196

Early man, 1–4. *See also* Archaeology; Stone Age

East Africa, 31–37, 51, 53–58, 139, 193. *See also* specific peoples, places

Economics, 205, 224–25. *See also* specific activities, peoples

Education and schools, 21, 98, 214, 216 (*see also* Universities); in Egypt, 80; Koranic, 139–40

Egypt, 6, 15, 24, 71–87, 144–50, 171, 190, 193

Elaeis gunieensis. See Oil palm

Electoral system, 133

Elegba society, 120

Elephants, 91, 100, 134

Eleusine, 103

Embalming, 83

Endogamy, 222, 223

English, the. *See* British, the

English language, 196, 197

Environment, xii, 2ff., 15–16, 50, 70. *See also* specific places

Epicanthic eyefold, xii

Ethiopia, 15, 139

Europeans, 54, 109ff., 139, 187–88, 189. *See also*

Colonial powers; Slavery; specific countries

Ewe, the, quotation from, 167

"Executioner, the," 181, 182

Exogamy, 38, 222, 223

Eyefold, epicanthic, xii

Facies neolithique, 92

Falcon, 81

Families, 12, 13, 39, 60, 114–15, 172, 196, 203, 205, 214, 219 (*see also* Ancestors; Children; Descent; Inheritance; Kinship; Marriage; Totemism; specific peoples); serfs and slaves adopted into, 191–92

Famine, 134, 212–13

Farming. See Cultivation

Fashoda, 61

Fathers (*see also* Families): paternity, 224

Fauresmith industries, 4

Feather headdress, 48

Female principle, 186

Females, 173, 178. See also Descent; Inheritance; Women

Fertility, 39, 40–41, 80; fish associated with, 108

Fertilizer, 103

Fetishes, 113ff.

Fetus, magic protection against malformation of, 113

Feuding, 152–53

Fighting. See Feuding; Raiding; War

Fire, 4, 97

Firearms, 172, 195

Fish and fishing, xiv, 4, 11, 101, 105–8, 134, 154, 199 (*see also* Masks; Totemism); in Egypt, 75; and rhythm, 128

Fishhooks, 134

Flakes, flake-tool industries, 4, 6, 22

Flax, 74

Florisbad Man, 4

Foggara, 146, 152

Fonio, 94, 157

Food (*see also* Cooking; specific foods, groups): famine, 134, 212–13; rations by Egyptian government to workers, 76; surpluses, 71, 74, 89, 107, 167

Force, belief in spiritual, 112–20, 228

Forest, 88–130. See also Savanna

Forging. See Iron and ironworking

Fortresses, 29–30. See also Citadels

French, the, 143, 157, 188

Fruits, water in, 160

Fulani, the, 12, 63, 140, 176

Funerals, 77, 83. See also Burial

Furniture, Pygmy, 98

Gall, 160

Game, children's cattle, 67

Ganda, the, 30

Gandhi, Mohandas K., 216

Gao, 177, 178

Gathering. See Hunting/gathering

Gedi, 31

Georgia, 197

Ghana, 63, 92, 168, 171, 176, 177, 227

Gift-giving: Bushman, 164, to wives, 38

Gikuyu, 65

Gio, the, 182

Giraffe, 134

Girls. *See* Children; Women

Glass beads, 30

Goats, 132

God (Creator), 97, 118ff., 155. *See also* Kingship; Religion

Gola, 178

Gold, 28, 29, 63, 168–69, 170, 173–74, 176, 177, 193, 194; Ashanti weights for, 184–86

Gold Coast, 188, 192

Gong, 130

Gossip, 114

Gouges, 92

Government, 50–53. *See also* Democracry; Kingship; State, the; specific peoples

Grain (cereal crops), 94, 143, 153–54. *See also* Cultivation; specific crops

Grass, 51, 65, 66, 160, 161

Grassland, 18–67, 92. *See also* Cultivation; Herding

Graves. *See* Burial; Tombs

Great Rift Valley, 32

Guilds, 184

Guinea coast, 92

Guinea pepper, 170

Guinea yams, 94

Hand piano, 127

Hapy, 75

Haratin, the, 137–38, 143

Harlem, 200

Harpoons, 107, 108, 134

Hart, David M., 137

Hausa, the, 63, 140

Headdresses, 121, 158, 187; age sets and, 48; antelope, 156

Health. *See* Medicine; Sickness

Heb-sed festival, 81

Height, differences in, xii

Herbal remedies, 113

Herding (herders), xv, 8, 10–11, 13, 18–19, 31, 32, 34–35, 39, 47, 51, 54, 64–67, 132ff., 142, 208ff., 220. *See also* Cattle; specific peoples

Hieroglyphics, 80

Hippopotamus, 108

History of Egypt, A, 68

Hoes, 28, 30, 92, 93

Hogon, 155

Holy wars, 63, 140

Homo erectus, 3–4

Homo habilis, 3

Homo sapiens, 3ff.

Honey, 11, 24, 98, 208

Honey guide, 11

Hornbills, 179, 185

Horus, 81

Houses and housing (shelter), 24, 51, 98, 225. *See also* Caves

"Houses of Light," 80

Hughes, Langston, 195n

Human relationships, 7, 70, 169. *See also* specific peoples

Humoi society, 178–79

Hunting/gathering, xiv, 4, 8–11ff., 22, 24, 34, 71, 89ff., 95–99, 206–11 (*see also* specific peoples);

desert, 131–32, 134–35, 158–66
Hybridization, 5
Hygiene, 218

Ibis, 80
Ibo, 187
Idiophones, 127
Ife, 169ff., 174, 175
Ihaggaren Tuareg, 141–42ff.
Ik, the, 22, 206–14, 217
Ikhnaton, King, 68
Ijaw, the, 108
Illness. See Sickness
Impurity, 61, 79, 117
Incest, 38, 116, 179, 191, 222
Identured labor, 190
India, 193, 216
Individualism, 225
Indonesia, 171
Infants. See Babies
Ingombe Ilede, 29
Inheritance, 38, 54, 224 (see also Descent; Women; specific peoples); slaves and, 192
Initiation, 112, 123, 124–25, 127. See also Age and age grouping; Sacred societies; Secret societies
Injured persons in desert, 132
In-laws, 179, 223
Intestines, witchcraft in, 117
Intoxicants (see also Beers): for fishing, 107
Iron Age, 29, 30, 93. See also Iron and ironworking
Iron and ironworking (smithing), 16, 22, 24–29ff., 93, 98, 102, 104,

154, 155, 170, 208; and music, 128
Irrigation, 32ff., 71, 77, 84ff., 144–52. See also Shaduf
Islam (Muslims), 87, 112, 136, 138–43, 169, 170, 194, 205 (see also Arabs); Black Muslims and, 200; prayer facing Mecca, 132
Isolation, genetics and, 5
Ituri Forest, 89ff., 111, 122–24, 135, 214–16
Ivory, 30, 31, 104, 110, 122, 170, 193, 194

Jazz, 200
Jbil Saghru Mountains, 138
Jehads (djihads), 63, 140
Jenne, 171, 177, 178
Jewelry (see also specific metals): Egyptian, 85; gifts to wives, 38
Jie, the, 48, 208
Joking relationship, 223
Judaism, 82
Justice (judges, jural system), 16, 63, 90, 115–17, 226; leopard-man society and, 122–24; masks and, 180–82; music and, 128; Muslim courts, 141

Kabaka, 62
Kalahari Desert, xii, 131, 135, 136, 158–66, 204. See also Bushmen
Kalamo culture, 29
Kanembu, the, 154
Kangaba, 176
Karimojong, the, 11, 67, 208ff., 213, 215, 217
Kasai district, 93

Kasai River, 109
Katanga, 93
Katonga River, 30
Kavirondo, the, 54, 55, 59
Kel Rela, 142
Kenya, 11, 22, 32–37, 55–58, 206, 208, 209. *See also* specific peoples
Kete, the, 109
Khami, 30
Kharga, 151
Kidepo Valley, 208ff., 213
Kigezi, 25
Kikuyu, the, 55, 58, 64ff.
Kiln for wire making, 26–27
Kingship (chiefs, kings), 16, 59–60ff., 170, 172–79, 190, 222; sacred societies and, 120ff.; slaves in royal courts, 192; and sneezing, 227
Kinship, 41, 51ff., 109, 203–4, 219ff. *See also* Families; specific peoples
Klu ge, 182
Knives, knife blades, 6, 8, 22, 51, 92, 93, 98, 208
Kola nuts, 170
Kola palm, 94
Kongo Empire, 109, 110, 170
Koran, 193
Koranic schools, 139–40
Korok, 33ff.
Kota, the, 119
Kromdraii, 3
Ksar, 138
Kuba, the, 109, 110, 170
Kumasi, the, 172, 175
Kumbi, 176, 178
!Kung, the, 160, 161, 162
Kush, 29
Kwele, the, 101–3, 104

Labor (work), 16, 190–92 (*see also* Slavery; specific countries, groups, kinds of labor); division of, 101 (*see also* Age and age grouping); music during, 127; women and, 39–40
Lagos, 200
Lake Rudolph, 208
Lake Tchad, 103, 153
Lake Victoria, 54
Land, 64ff., 150, 204 (*see also* Fertility; Irrigation; specific peoples); women and, 37–41
Language, 183; Arabic, 139; early man and, 4; English, 196, 197
Law and order. *See* Justice
Leadership. *See* Authority; Government; Social organization
Leaves, 9
Lebu, the, 157
Left-handedness, 186
Lele, the, 101
Leopard-man society, 122–24
Leopards, 122, 123, 124, 179
Leopard Skin Priest, 52–53
Liberia, 181, 182
Libya, 135
Life span, xv, xvi
Light and lighting: resin for, 98; torchlight fishing, 108
Lineages, 12, 39, 51, 54ff., 60, 65, 219. *See also* specific peoples
Lion, 179
Lip plug, 48
Lo, the, 119
Logone River, 154

Lost-wax casting, 171, 184–85
Lovedu, the, 40
Lozi, the, 30, 40
Luba, the, 93, 109, 110, 170
Lunda, the, 109, 110, 170
Lupemban culture, 92
Luxor, 151
Luxuries, xv

Machetes, 98
MacLean, George, 192
Madagascar, 110, 111
Maghreb, the, 134, 135
Magic, 14, 112 (see also Medicine; Sorcery, Witchcraft); Egyptian, 82, 83, 86; Islam and, 141
Magosian culture, 22
Maize, 94, 101. See also Corn
Makapansgat, 3
Makata, 123
Male principle, 186
Males. See Descent; Inheritance
Mali, 63, 168, 176, 177; modern, 156, 169
Malindi, 31
Mammals, evolvement of, 2
Mandingo, the, 169
Mandinka, the, 176
Mangbetu, the, 103–4, 105, 116
Mangetti, 161
Manihot manihot. See Manioc
Manioc, 94, 100, 101, 103, 157
Mano, 182
Mansa Musa, 176
Markets and marketing,
85–86, 110–12. See also Trade
Marriage, 24, 33, 36–38ff., 77, 157, 220, 222–23 (see also Bridewealth; Families; Wives; specific peoples); Christian weddings, 199; exchange of iron at, 28; Kikuyu-Masai, 65; music, dance, and, 127
"Marriage money." See Bridewealth
Masai, 64–66, 215; and age sets, 45, 46, 48
Masks, 119, 121, 122, 123, 180–82
Masons, Egyptian, 75, 85
Master of the Fishing Spear, 52–53
Mathematics, Egyptian artisans and, 75
Matrilineal families. See Descent
Matting, 51
Mbuti. See Pygmies
Meat, 3, 51, 65 (see also Hunting/gathering); sharing of, by Bushmen, 164
Mecca, 87, 132
Medicine, xv, 8, 40, 99, 112–13, 124, 125, 179. See also Sickness
Mediterranean, the, 74–75
Melons, water in, 160
Membranophones, 127
Memphis, 80
Mende, the, 178–79
Menes, 148
Mental illness, 114, 178
Merimdeh, 71, 73, 74
Meroë, 24, 29, 171

Metals (metalworking), 6, 8, 51, 74, 85, 199. *See also* specific metals, objects

Middle Ages, 139

Midwives, 77

Military (army), 63, 177. *See also* War; specific peoples

Milk (milking), 11, 13, 35, 51, 65

Millet, 154

Minstrels, 128

Mirrors in fetishes, 117

Mobutu, 227

Mogya, 221

Mombasa, 31

Monkeys, 2, 2, 97, 186

Monogamy, 225

Monomatapa confederacy, 29

Moon, the, 174, 184, 186

Moors, 177

Morality, 89, 121, 169 (*see also* Religion); in Egypt, 82, 83, 87

Moran, 47–49, 64

Morocco, 137

Mortars and pestles, 128, 199

Morungole range, 208ff.

Mosques, 87

Mossi, the, 63

Mothers, 173. *See also* Babies; Births

Mothers-in-law, 223

Mountain People, The, 210

Mourners, professional, 77, 83

Mud, 51

Multiple births, fish associated with, 108

Mum, the, 62

Mummification, 80. *See also* Embalming

Murder, 191

Musa sapientum, 94, 103

Music, 127–130, 183, 200; Bushman, 165; Egyptian, 77, 79; Pygmy, 99, 130; slaves and singing, 197; Tuareg, 142; women and, 41, 77

Muslims. *See* Arabs; Islam

Mutation, 5

Mwina, 32

Myths, 175. *See also* Belief; Religion; specific peoples

Nail fetishes, 116, 117

Names: and age sets, 42, 46; Bushmen and, 163–64

Namuso, 40

Naron, the, 161

Nattalak, 150

Ndaka, the, 105, 125

Ndorobo, the, 11, 35, 208

Nefernefruaton, Queen, 68

Nehru, Jawaharlal, 216

Neolithic cultures, 135

Nets, 105, 107ff., 160, 199; hunting, 96, 97

Nguni, the, 63

Niani, 176, 178

Nigeria(ns), 49–60, 108, 140, 143, 177, 200, 225–26 (*see also* Yoruba, the); and aging, 49–50

Niger River, 70, 142, 167ff., 176, 177

Nile River and Valley (Nilotes, Nilotics), 5, 47, 51–53, 56ff., 63, 68, 71–87, 139, 144–52, 153, 171

Njayei society, 178–79

Nkrumah, Kwame, 216, 220, 227
Nobility, Egyptian, 76–77
Nok, the, 171
Nomads. See Desert; Hunting/gathering; specific groups
Nomarch, 78
Nomes, 78
North Africa, 132–33ff., 193. See also Arabs; specific areas, peoples
North America. See America
Nsuta, 171
Ntoro, 221
Nubia, 24, 139
Nudity, 215
Nuer, the, 51–52, 56, 220, 222
Nupe, the, 63
Nyame, 186
Nyankopon, 186
Nyerere, Julius, 215
Nyikang, 61
Nyoro, the, 30

Oases, 134, 137, 142–43, 151–52
Oba, the, 174–75
Occupations, 16. See also Crafts; Professions; specific occupations
Ogboni society, 120–21
Oil palm, 94, 103
Old age, 162, 211 (see also Age and age grouping); slaves and, 193
Olduvai Gorge, 3
Olive trees, 151
Omda, 86–87
Orange trees, 151
Oryza glaberrima, 94, 157
Oryza sativa, 94, 157

Oshogbo, 175
Oshun society, 120
Osiris, 80, 82
Ostrich eggshells, 160ff.
Oxen, 11, 152 (see also Cattle); for irrigation implements, 85
Oyo, 170

Painting(s): body, 24; rock and cave, 24, 134; tomb, 72, 83, 84
Palms, 94, 103, 151, 153
Papyrus, 51
Parallel-cousin marriage, 223
Paranthropus, 3
Paternity, 224
Patrilineal families. See Descent
Peace, grass symbol of, 65
Peanuts, 100, 101, 103
Peasants, Egyptian, 76, 77, 82, 84, 190
Pebble tools, 6, 22
Pende, the, 109
Penduline tit, 160
Pepper(s), 101, 170
Persia, 193
Persian wheel, 84, 147, 148
Pestilence, 116
Pharaohs, 77, 79ff., 190
Phoenicians, 134
Physical differences, range of, xii–xiii, xiv, 5
Picnics, xvi
Planes, 92
Plantains, 100, 101
Plants, 93, 94 (see also Cultivation; Vegeculture); and water storage, 160
Pleistocene, the, 3
Poetry, 183; Tuareg, 142

Points, 22, 92. *See also*
   Arrowheads; Spears
Poison for arrows, 9
Police, 143; Egyptian, 86
Political authority, 12 (*see
   also* Government;
   Kingship; Social
   organization; specific
   peoples); women and, 40
Polygyny, 38, 225
Pokot, 16, 31–37, 56, 208
Population, xvi. *See also*
   specific areas
Portuguese, the 30, 31, 109,
   111, 170, 174, 188, 194,
   196; and introduction of
   plants, 94
Potatoes, 103, 157
Pottery, 16, 22, 29, 93, 104,
   199; Egyptian, 74, 85;
   terra-cottas from Ife, 171
Poverty, material, xv
Prayer, 132
Pregnant women (*see also*
   Fetus): and fish, 108
Priests, 54, 115 (*see also*
   Age and age grouping;
   Religion); Egyptian, 77ff.;
   Leopard Skin, 52–53
Prisoners (captives): in
   Egyptian army, 78; and
   serfdom, 190–91, 192
Professions (*see also* Crafts;
   Occupations; specific
   professions): of women in
   Egypt, 77
Projectile points, 92. *See also*
   Arrowheads; Spears
Prophets, 54
Proto-Stillbay industries, 4
Proverbs, 122, 185–86, 189
Ptah, 80
Puberty. *See* Youth

Purity/impurity, 61, 79, 117
Pygmies (Mbuti), xii–xiii,
   xiv, 5, 8–9, 88–89, 90–92,
   93, 95–99, 100, 103, 135,
   227; and music, 99, 130;
   quotation, 88; Zaïre
   government and, 214–18

Ra, 81
Raffia palm (*Raffia ruffia*),
   94
Raiding, 13, 35, 38, 53, 64,
   136, 142, 143, 209, 210,
   213, 220; captives and
   serfdom, 190
Rain (*see also*
   Transhumance; specific
   areas): and sympathetic
   magic, 14; women and
   rituals, 40–41
Ram, 80
Rattles, 116, 160; women
   and, 41
Red ocher, 24
Red Sea, 74
Reed: boats, 74; for
   weapons, 9
Rega, the, 105, 122
Religion, 10, 14–15ff., 24,
   41, 62ff., 114–26, 155,
   156, 184ff., 205 (*see also*
   Ancestors; Belief;
   Kingship; Magic;
   Medicine; Priests; specific
   peoples, rituals);
   Bushman, 165; Egyptian
   (priests), 73, 75ff.,
   78–82ff., 87; holy wars,
   63, 140; Islamic (*see*
   Islam); Pygmy, 99; sacred
   societies, 120–27, 178,
   182; sacred state, 171–79,

194; slaves and, 197, 198ff.
Resin, 98
Revue de l'Institut de sociologie, 137
Rhinoceros, 134
Rhodesia, 29–30; Khami, 30; Sawmills, 22
Rhodesian Man, 4
Rice, 85, 94, 100, 157, 182
Ridicule, 97, 128, 163
Rites de passage. See Initiation
Ritual. *See* Age and age grouping; Initiation; Magic; Religion; specific rituals
Rivers (riverbeds, valleys), 68–87, 167ff., 174 (*see also* Fish and fishing; specific rivers); archaeologists and, 24ff.
Rivus, 149
Rock paintings (cave paintings), 24, 134
Roman Catholics, 216
Romans, and Egypt, 73
Root crops, 93, 157. *See also* Digging sticks
Root fibers, 160
Rubber, 110
Rwanda, Tussi in, xii
Rwozi, the, 30

Sacred societies, 120–27, 178, 182
Sacred state, 171–79, 194
Sahara Desert, 134ff., 159, 169, 176, 193. *See also* specific peoples
Sakya, 84, 147, 148
Salaries, 224
Salt, 142–43, 170, 177

Sanza, 127
Saplings, bent for fishing, 106
Sara, the, 154
Saran peoples, 153
Saudi Arabia, 193
Savanna, 152–58
Sawmills (Rhodesia), 22
Scarification, 36
Schools. *See* Education and schools
Science, 112–20
Scrapers, 4, 21, 22
Scribes, Egyptian, 79, 80
Secret societies, 175
Segmentary systems, 12. *See also* specific groups
Senegal, 178, 194
Senegal River, 176
Senegambians, 157–58
Senghor, Leopold Sadar, 194
Senufo, the, 119, 121, 179
Serer, the, 157
Serfs, 157, 189–92
Sesame, 103
Seti II, 82
Sewing, in Egypt, 85
Sexual behavior: adultery, 37, 191; fishing and intercourse, 108; sacred society regulating, 178, 179
Shaduf, 75, 84, 145ff.
Shango society, 120
Sheep, 132
Sherbo, 178
Shilluk, the, 61, 172, 227
Shona people, 30
Shrines, 115
Sickness (disease, illness), xv, 91, 104, 115ff., 179, 218 (*see also* Medicine); and antisocial behavior,

191; desert nomads and, 132, 162; slaves and, 193

Sierra Leone, 178

Signaling, 194. See also Drums and drumming

Silica, 26

Silver, 174

Sinai, 74

Singing. See Music

Siroto, Leon, 103

Sisters, 38, 40, 173, 221, 223, 225

Sisters-in-law, 223

Skins. See Clothing

Skulls, ancestral, 119

Slavery, 31, 63, 75 109ff., 170, 177, 187–88, 189–202

Slippers, Ashanti King's feet in, 173

Smelting. See Iron and ironworking

Smithfield tools, 21

Smithing. See Iron and ironworking

Smoke, 97

Snakes, 179, 185

Snares (snaring), 9, 160

Sneezing, King and, 227

Social organization (order), 4, 5–17, 89ff., 144, 203–30. See also Democracy; Government; State, the; specific peoples

Soldiers. See Army

Somali quote, 18

Songe, the, 109

Songhai (people and place), 63, 140, 168, 177

Songs. See Music

Sorcery, 91, 100, 117

Sorghum, 143, 151, 154, 157

South Africa, 198, 204. See also specific peoples

South America. See America

Spain, 139

Spears, 8, 9, 24, 34, 51, 93, 134, 160, 208; fishing, 107–8

Spirits. See Death; Religion

Squash, 103

Standard of living, xv–xvi

Stanley, Henry Morton, 110

Stanley Pool, 109, 111

Stanleyville, 110

Stars, Masai and, 65

State, the, 60–63 (see also Government; Kingship; Social organization): sacred, 171–79, 194

Status, 103, 158. See also Classes

Steatopygial buttocks, xii

Sterkfontein, 3

Sterkfontein Extension, 3

Stomach, witchcraft in, 117

Stone(s), 4, 6, 8, 9, 21ff., 75, 92, 171 (see also specific objects); for cattle game, 67; fortresses, 29–30

Stone Age, xiii, 8, 21ff., 92ff., 135

Stools. See Chairs

Strangers, villages and, 58

Strikes, 76, 190

Sudan, 22, 29, 74, 154, 171; Ik and, 206, 208, 210, 213

Suffocation, death of Kings by, 61

Sugar, 143, 188

Suicide, Kings commanded to commit, 121

Sun, 173–74, 184, 186

Sun god, Pharaoh as, 81

Sunni Ali, 177
Surinam, 196–97
Surpluses, 71, 74, 76, 89, 167 (see also Trade); of fish, 107
Survival, 6–7, 70. See also specific areas
Swartkrans, 3
Swastika, 184, 186
Symbiotic relationships, 11
"Sympathetic magic" (remedies), 14, 113

Taboos, 38, 80, 179, 184, 191
"Talking drum," 130
Tambur, 84, 145, 146
Tamesna, 143
Tanzania, 209; honey guide in, 11; Olduvai Gorge, 3
Taung, 3
Taxes and taxation, 76, 78, 80, 176, 177, 190
Tea, making, 132
Teda, the, 153
Teke, the, 109
Temne, 178
Temples, 76ff., 149
Terra-cotta, 171
Teuso. See Ik, the
Textiles, Egyptian women and manufacture of, 77
Thebes, 80, 83
Theft, protective medicine against, 113
Thoth, 80
Thought, abstract, 4
Thrones. See Chairs
Timbuctu, 140, 169, 177, 178
Tin, 29
Tippu Tib, 110

Tobacco, 103, 208; pouches, 160
To la ge, 181, 182
Tombs, 72, 75, 80, 82–84
Tools, 3, 4, 6, 8–9, 21ff., 34, 92, 134, 171. See also Crafts; specific materials, objects
Toposa, the, 208
Torchlight fishing, 107
Tortoise shell, 160
Totemism, 124, 179–80, 182
Tourism, 214
Towles, Joseph A., 125
Toys, 67, 99
Trade, 29ff., 33, 51, 63, 73, 74, 107, 109–12, 136, 139, 140ff., 167, 169, 170–71, 175ff. See also Markets and marketing; Slavery
Tradition, 219–30
Traitors, 186
Transhumance, 12, 56–59, 133, 137. See also specific groups
Traps and trapping, 9, 105ff.
Trees, 34 (see also Forest; Woodlands); resin, 98; and water storage, 160
Tribes, 12, 39, 54, 59, 108, 219 (see also specific peoples); and exogamy/endogamy, 222–23; and lives of slaves in America, 196ff.
Tribute, 190
Trickiness, 163
Trumpets, for signaling, 104
Tsetse fly, 31
Tsi, 161
Tswana, the, 41
Tuareg, the, 140, 141–43
Tunnels, water, 146, 152

Turkana, the, 208, 213
Turkey, 193
Turkish rule, in Egypt, 73
Turnbull, Colin M., 210
Tussi, the, xii
Tuyeres, 25

Uganda, 11, 22, 62; Bigo, 30; Ciga, 25–28; Ik and, 206–14
Universities, 140, 169, 216
Urine, use in desert, 159
Usuman dan Fodio, 140

Vaal River, 22ff.
Vegeculture, xiv, 85, 92, 135, 161
Venda, the, 62
Vizier, Egyptian office of, 77
Vocal symbols, early man and, 4

Wagenya, the, 107
Walking, rhythm of, 128
War, 13, 64, 133 (*see also* Army; specific peoples); captives and serfdom, 190; holy, 63, 140
Water, 12, 13, 144–52 (*see also* Irrigation; Rain; Rivers); holes, xiv, 11, 51, 132, 142, 161; transhumance, 12, 56–59, 133, 137 (*see also* specific groups)
Water buffalo, for irrigation, 85
Water yam, 94
Wealth, 103, 133, 224. *See also* Bridewealth
Weapons, 8, 29 (*see also* Tools; specific weapons); firearms, 172, 195
Weddings. *See* Marriage
Weights, 184–86; digging stick, 22, 93, 135
Wells, 148ff.
West Africa, 15, 58–60, 63–65, 92ff., 189, 193, 195. *See also* specific areas, peoples
West Indies, 188, 200
Wheat, 85, 151
Wheel, the, 69
Widowhood, 157
Widow inheritance, 224
Wigs, 157–58
Wild plants, cultivation of, xiv, 8. *See also* Vegeculture
Wire making, 25–28
Witchcraft, 91, 100, 117–18, 191; and Egyptian kings, 82
Wives, 62, 77 (*see also* Marriage; Women); of slaves, 193
Wolof, the, 157, 158
Women, 36–41, 51, 102, 107, 108, 115, 163, 201 (*see also* Families; Females; Marriage; Mothers; Sisters; Wives); Aït'Atta, 137; Egyptian, 77, 83; and Mangbetu crafts, 104; and music, 41, 77; new Muslims and, 140; pregnant, 108 (*see also* Births; Fetus); Pygmy, 96–98; and rhythm of mortar and pestle, 128; Tuareg, 142; Wolof headdresses denote status, 157–58

Wood and woodworking, 8, 21–22, 34, 74, 93, 104, 160, 167 (see also Carpenters; specific objects); ash for fertilizer, 103
Woodlands, 167–68
Work. See Labor
Writing, 69; Egyptian scribes and, 79, 80; of Koranic texts, 141

Xylophone, 123

Yaka, the, 109, 110
Yams, 94, 157

Yoruba, the, 63, 120–22, 170, 171, 191, 200, 207
Youth (puberty), 36, 89, 178. See also Age and age grouping; Children; Initiation; specific groups

Zaïre, xii, 89, 214–18, 227. See also Ituri Forest
Zambezi River, 29, 70–71, 167
Zambia, 29
Zea mays. See Maize
Zimbabwe, 29
Zinzanthropus boisei, 3
Zulu, the, 41, 63